**2**
edition

# CONDUCTING
# ONLINE SURVEYS

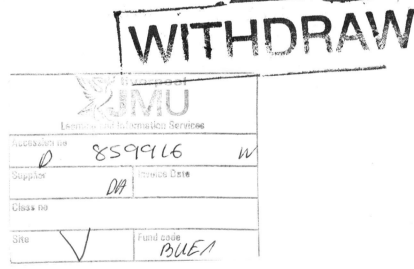

*In loving memory of Jack. —vs*
*For Don, because quitting is too easy. —lr*

**2** edition

# CONDUCTING ONLINE SURVEYS

## Valerie M. Sue
*California State University, East Bay*

## Lois A. Ritter
*California State University, East Bay*

Los Angeles | London | New Delhi
Singapore | Washington DC

Los Angeles | London | New Delhi
Singapore | Washington DC

FOR INFORMATION:

SAGE Publications, Inc.

2455 Teller Road

Thousand Oaks, California 91320

E-mail: order@sagepub.com

SAGE Publications Ltd.

1 Oliver's Yard

55 City Road

London EC1Y 1SP

United Kingdom

SAGE Publications India Pvt. Ltd.

B 1/I 1 Mohan Cooperative Industrial Area

Mathura Road, New Delhi 110 044

India

SAGE Publications Asia-Pacific Pte. Ltd.

33 Pekin Street #02-01

Far East Square

Singapore 048763

Acquisitions Editor:   Vicki Knight

Associate Editor:   Lauren Habib

Editorial Assistant:   Kalie Koscielak

Production Editor:   Eric Garner

Copy Editor:   Megan Granger

Typesetter:   C&M Digitals (P) Ltd.

Proofreader:   Jennifer Gritt

Indexer:   Rick Hurd

Cover Designer:   Candice Harman

Permissions Editor:   Adele Hutchinson

Copyright © 2012 by SAGE Publications, Inc.

Printed in the United States of America

Library of Congress Cataloging-in-Publication Data

Sue, Valerie M.

Conducting online surveys / Valerie M. Sue, Lois A. Ritter. — 2nd ed.

p. cm.
Includes bibliographical references and index.

ISBN 978-1-4129-9225-1 (pbk. : alk. paper)

1.  Social surveys—Methodology. 2.  Internet surveys. I. Ritter, Lois A. II. Title.

HM538.S84 2012
001.4'33—dc23          2011039868

# Brief Contents

# Detailed Contents

# About the Authors

**Valerie M. Sue** is a senior consultant in the Internet Services Group at Kaiser Permanente (KP). She manages online survey projects for KP and is one of the lead developers of KP's online member research panel. Prior to working at KP, Sue was an associate professor of communication at California State University, East Bay, where she taught communication theory, research methods, and survey research courses and was director of the Communication Department's graduate program. She also has authored numerous journal articles and delivered presentations at the conferences of the International Communication Association, American Evaluation Association, and American Public Health Association. Sue is a graduate of Stanford University, where she earned a PhD in communication.

**Lois A. Ritter** is an assistant professor in the Nursing and Health Sciences Department at California State University, East Bay, and a consultant in public health and education. She teaches courses in community health and research methods and has extensive experience in program planning and evaluation. She earned a doctorate in education from the University of San Francisco and three master's degrees in health science, anthropology, and healthcare administration. Her research interests are in health information technology and community and multicultural health.

# List of Tables

# List of Figures

# Preface

The pace of modern life and the rapid development of technology have had a significant impact on survey methodology. The pervasive use of mobile phones, fewer land phone lines, and do-not-call lists make phone-interview surveys increasingly difficult to administer. The abundance of sales appeals and other "junk" mail render postal mail surveys ineffective for many purposes. And for many researchers, the cost of face-to-face survey administration is prohibitive. Online surveys hold the promise of overcoming many of these obstacles; however, as some problems are solved, others are revealed.

Ubiquitous computing, the widespread adoption and sophistication of mobile devices, and the increase in the availability of software and web hosts for developing and disseminating surveys have created many opportunities and challenges for survey researchers. These technological opportunities and challenges necessitate up-to-date instruction in digital survey research methodology.

## Purpose

This book is designed to address the needs of researchers who would like to use the Internet and other digital devices to conduct survey research. The types of surveys we cover are reliant on software for their creation and computer or mobile technology for delivery and data collection. Some of the issues we discuss, such as sampling from online populations, developing online and mobile questionnaires, and administering electronic surveys, are unique to online surveys. Others, such as creating reliable and valid survey questions, data analysis strategies, and writing the survey report, are common to all survey environments. While excellent book-length treatments of some of these topics exist elsewhere, our aim is to provide a single resource that captures the particulars of conducting digital surveys from end to end.

# New in the Second Edition

In the 5 years since the publication of the first edition of *Conducting Online Surveys,* the field of online survey research has changed significantly. A multitude of low-cost software options has opened the area to a broad range of researchers, and the need for a comprehensive text aimed at guiding the development, implementation, and reporting of digital surveys is greater than ever. To keep pace with the development of technology and the methodological literature surrounding survey research, we have made significant additions and changes to this second edition.

First, readers will notice a slight change in the language we use to describe the surveys under consideration. In the previous edition of this text, we used the term *online surveys* to discuss electronic surveys delivered to potential respondents by e-mail or on a website. We continue to use the term *online* in this edition but also use the synonyms *electronic* and *digital* to include surveys delivered to mobile phones; tablet computers, such as iPads; and public kiosks.

The foundational material in Chapter 1 is largely unchanged. We retained our discussion of the common characteristics shared by all survey projects and explanation of the steps involved in creating a survey.

We updated Chapter 2 substantially. The selection of digital surveys from which to choose now centers on three options: e-mail surveys, website surveys, and mobile surveys. In the first edition, we discussed sending questionnaires in the body of an e-mail message or as an e-mail attachment. That option is obviously still available; however, the advent of free and easy-to-use survey software has rendered e-mail questionnaires an unappealing choice for most purposes. We have, therefore, eliminated that material and now refer to e-mail surveys as those that are accessed from a link in an e-mail invitation.

A successful digital survey project is highly dependent on choosing suitable software; we have, therefore, expanded our discussion of factors one should consider when purchasing software and signing up for a web survey host. Information about data security and a list of security-related questions to ask when evaluating software vendors will be especially useful for researchers who wish to collect sensitive or confidential data from respondents. Additionally, market researchers will appreciate the new material at the end of Chapter 2 concerning anti-spam compliance.

Chapter 3 remains focused on sampling techniques for online surveys. We have increased our coverage of prerecruited panels with expanded information about the benefits and limitations of building online panels.

In Chapter 4, you will find expanded treatment of closed-ended survey questions. We have added greater depth to the discussion of survey scales, covering topics such as number of points to include on scales, the positioning of scale labels, and more. To assist beginning researchers, we also have included a list of commonly used survey scales. We retained the section on demographic questions and added a library (Appendix B) of frequently asked survey questions that includes demographic and other items.

The examples throughout Chapter 5 have been refreshed, and we have updated and expanded the discussion of questionnaire matrices. Our goal was to provide ample illustrations of how digital survey questions may be presented so that survey creators can make informed decisions when designing their questionnaires.

Chapter 6 has been overhauled. Coverage of survey deployment methods was enhanced by including information about the use of mobile phones and social media websites. Readers will also find greater detail surrounding best practices for writing e-mail invitations, a new discussion of message deliverability, and more on techniques to increase survey response rate.

Information pertaining to manual tracking and coding of e-mail survey responses has been eliminated from Chapter 7. In its place, we have inserted the review of basic summary statistics, formerly contained in an appendix. This material is intended to aid researchers who are in need of a brief refresher as they review survey reports produced by digital survey hosts.

Chapter 8 contains detailed information about survey data reporting. In addition to the description of academic research reports, you will find new material about dashboard reports and expanded coverage of best practices for creating PowerPoint slide shows and delivering presentations in person and in virtual settings.

Finally, instructors using this text will notice the addition of class exercises accompanying each chapter. We hope that the expanded and updated information included in this edition has improved the text and that online survey researchers will find it to be a useful resource.

## Audience

The first edition of *Conducting Online Surveys* was written primarily with the academic audience in mind. It was designed to be a supplemental text in research methods courses. We now broaden our scope to include business professionals and other individuals who may need to conduct electronic surveys for nonprofit, community, or social organizations. This shift in audience orientation was accomplished by augmenting the content to include a wider range of examples and by expanding the topics covered. The additional examples will appeal to new audiences, and the greater depth on many of the topics from the first edition will be useful for those involved in academic survey research. Although introductory courses in statistics or research methods are helpful, they are not necessary to grasp the concepts presented herein. We have tried to ensure that the material is accessible to general audiences.

This book may be successfully used as a supplemental text in undergraduate research methods courses in business, science, and the social sciences; by graduate students writing theses or dissertations; and for self-study by professionals in marketing research, opinion polling, scientific consulting, and other areas of business and government.

## Organization

The organization of this text follows the general progression of the survey research process. We begin with a discussion of survey research and compare the various methods of collecting survey data. We also point out the situations for which online surveys are most effective. In Chapter 2, we examine the benefits and limitations of various types of surveys. We also present factors to consider when purchasing software and deciding on a web survey host.

Chapter 3 covers sampling strategies appropriate to online surveys, and Chapter 4 discusses best practices for writing good survey questions. Chapters 5 and 6 offer details for designing and conducting the survey, and Chapters 7 and 8 focus on data analysis and presentation. Finally, in Chapter 9, we offer concluding thoughts about the opportunities and challenges that lie ahead for online survey researchers.

As anyone who has ever conducted a research project knows, the process is seldom neat and linear. We have written these chapters so that readers can direct their attention to particular areas that meet their immediate needs. While a novice researcher may find it helpful to begin at Chapter 1 and progress chapter by chapter, an intermediate-level investigator might begin with Chapters 2 and 3 and then jump to Chapters 5 and 6 without loss of continuity.

## Acknowledgments

Two names appear on the cover of this book; however, many individuals have contributed to its completion. We are grateful to the staff at Sage Publications, particularly Vicki Knight, for her support and assistance in moving this project from idea to finished product. We also are thankful to the reviewers, who provided numerous thoughtful comments and helpful suggestions:

Justin A. Tucker, California State University, Fullerton

James Lindner, Texas A&M University

Brian Vargus, Indiana University–Purdue University Indianapolis

Margaret S. Kelley, University of Illinois at Urbana-Champaign

Terri Shapiro, Hofstra University

Ronald McGivern, Thompson Rivers University

Terry Richardson, George Washington University

Lisa Chiapetta, Dominican University of California

Jon Lester, Old Dominion University

Michaela Hayes, Dominican University of California

Linda Gallant, Emerson College

Finally, we are indebted to our families for their encouragement and patience.

.

# CHAPTER 1

# Introduction

Low-cost computing and the rapid development of technology have created new environments for conducting survey research. Like all research methods, online survey research has benefits and drawbacks; the method works well for some research projects but is by no means appropriate for all research objectives. This book provides practical information for researchers who are considering using the Internet, mobile devices, and other technologies to conduct surveys. We will evaluate the advantages and disadvantages of using digital surveys and offer guidelines for the creation and implementation of these surveys. The topics covered herein will be of interest to survey researchers in a wide variety of academic and professional settings who wish to evaluate their options for data collection and analysis.

In this chapter, we begin by setting the context within which digital surveys are conducted. We review the research process generally, discuss concepts common to all surveys, and evaluate the conditions under which online surveys are optimal.

## The Research Process

The research process typically begins with a question that needs an answer or a problem that must be solved. In the case of commissioned research, the questions will be provided to you at the start of the project. Researcher-initiated studies allow investigators more discretion in terms of the specification of the research goals and objectives. Before framing the goals and objectives of a particular project, it is useful to identify the purpose of the research. Social research projects can be classified into three categories: exploratory, descriptive, and explanatory research. An individual study can have multiple purposes or may be part of a program of research that spans two or all three purposes.

## Exploratory Research

The goal of exploratory research is to formulate problems, clarify concepts, and form hypotheses. Exploration can begin with a literature search, a focus group discussion, or case studies. If a survey is conducted for exploratory purposes, no attempt is made to examine a random sample of a population; rather, researchers conducting exploratory research usually look for individuals who are knowledgeable about a topic or process. Exploratory research typically seeks to create hypotheses rather than test them. Data from exploratory studies tends to be qualitative. Examples include brainstorming sessions, interviews with experts, and posting a short survey to a social networking website.

## Descriptive Research

Descriptive studies have more guidelines. They describe people, products, and situations. Descriptive studies usually have one or more guiding research questions but generally are not driven by structured research hypotheses. Because this type of research frequently aims to describe characteristics of populations based on data collected from samples, it often requires the use of a probability sampling technique, such as simple random sampling. Data from descriptive research may be qualitative or quantitative, and quantitative data presentations are normally limited to frequency distributions and summary statistics, such as averages. Customer satisfaction surveys, presidential approval polls, and class evaluation surveys are examples of descriptive projects.

## Explanatory Research

The primary purpose of explanatory research is to explain why phenomena occur and to predict future occurrences. Explanatory studies are characterized by research hypotheses that specify the nature and direction of the relationships between or among variables being studied. Probability sampling is normally a requirement in explanatory research because the goal is often to generalize the results to the population from which the sample is selected. The data are quantitative and almost always require the use of a statistical test to establish the validity of the relationships. For example, explanatory survey research may investigate the factors that contribute to customer satisfaction and determine the relative weight of each factor, or seek to model the variables that lead to shopping cart abandonment.

An exploratory survey posted to a social networking website may uncover the fact that an organization's customers are unhappy. A descriptive study consisting of an e-mail survey sent to a random selection of customers who made a purchase in the past year might report the type and degree of dissatisfaction. The explanatory research would attempt to understand how different factors are contributing to customer dissatisfaction.

## What Is a Survey?

A survey is a system for collecting information. Often, in discussions about conducting surveys, emphasis is incorrectly placed on questionnaires. To employ surveys most effectively, it is important to understand that a questionnaire is one element of a process that begins with defining objectives and ends with data analysis and reporting of results (Dillman, 2000). In explicating total survey design, Fowler (2002) emphasized that taking a view of the entire survey process is critical to the success of a research project. Total survey design requires that researchers take a holistic approach by considering all aspects of the survey process. In doing so, one increases the likelihood of collecting data that adequately address the study's objectives while balancing time and cost constraints.

The basic steps in the survey process (see Figure 1.1) are the same for all types of surveys. The process begins with defining the study's goals and objectives and continues with a literature review and consultation with experts. Many researchers also choose to conduct preliminary research, such as focus group discussions or personal interviews with members of a target audience. Results of this type of investigation are used as a basis for deciding on the survey type to employ (or if a survey is even appropriate). Focus group transcripts also can be a useful starting point for developing the survey questionnaire. Selecting a sample of participants can be challenging and sometimes represents the point in the process when the survey project is abandoned in favor of a different research method. If a sample cannot be identified or reached, a survey will not be possible. The period between the launch of a survey and the downloading of data is typically spent monitoring the survey responses and preparing for data analysis. Finally, all survey studies, like most research projects, culminate with some sort of report and/or presentation of findings.

The methods for administering surveys include telephone interviewing, self-administered mail questionnaires, and face-to-face interviewing. Added to these methods are a host of new techniques made available by the development of technology—notably e-mail, web-based, and mobile surveys. In e-mail surveys, the questionnaire is accessed by a link in a survey invitation. In most cases, the **respondent** completes the questionnaire by clicking on the link, responding to the questions, and submitting the completed questionnaire by using a submit button on the final page of

**Figure 1.1    Survey Research Process Flow**

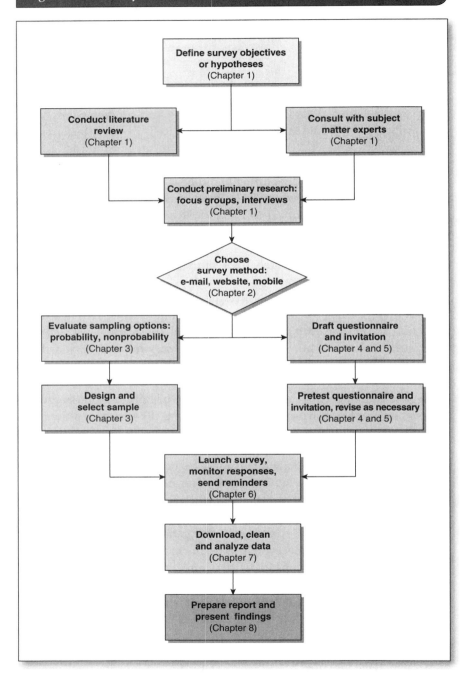

the questionnaire. In web-based surveys, the questionnaire resides on a website. Respondents visit the site and access the survey either by clicking on a **hyperlink** located somewhere on the page or by responding to a pop-up invitation to complete the questionnaire. Mobile surveys take advantage of the pervasiveness of cell phones by inviting respondents to participate in SMS (short message service) surveys or those designed to be answered using **smartphone** applications.

Online surveys provide a wealth of opportunities and challenges for researchers. It is important that researchers recognize these opportunities and limitations so that they may make informed decisions when selecting a data collection method (see Table 1.1). It is doubtful that digital surveys will replace other modes of data collection; rather, these methods most likely will be used to complement existing techniques.

**Table 1.1   Comparison of Survey Methods**

| Survey Type | Advantages | Disadvantages |
|---|---|---|
| Postal mail | • Low cost<br>• Wide geographic reach<br>• No interviewer bias<br>• Anonymity allows for sensitive questions | • Low response rate<br>• Lengthy response period<br>• Contingency questions not effective<br>• Don't know who is responding to the survey |
| Telephone interview | • Limited coverage bias<br>• Fast response<br>• Can ask complex questions<br>• Wide geographic reach | • Fewer land phone lines<br>• Confusion with sales calls<br>• Intrusive<br>• Call screening |
| Face-to-face interview | • Good response rates<br>• Can ask complex questions<br>• Longer interviews may be tolerated | • Limited geographic reach<br>• Time-consuming<br>• Expensive<br>• Susceptible to interviewer bias<br>• Sensitive topics difficult to explore |
| Online | • Can be low cost<br>• Fast<br>• Efficient<br>• Contingency questions effective<br>• Direct data entry<br>• Wide geographic reach | • Coverage bias<br>• Reliance on software<br>• Too many digital surveys, causing overload |

## Research Goals and Objectives

After identifying the purpose of the research project and deciding that an online survey is an appropriate mode of data collection, it is next necessary to define the study's goals and objectives. What are you trying to find out by conducting a survey? The objectives of the project determine whom you will survey and what you will ask them. If your objectives are unclear, the results probably will be unclear. Commit to these objectives in writing to help keep the survey focused. Make sure that you can tie in every questionnaire item to one or more of the survey's objectives.

A research goal is more broadly defined than the objectives. Goals are distinguished from objectives in that they are not necessarily measurable. For example,

Goals:

(A) Establish a solid foundation for Acme's economic future.
(B) Investigate the need for local networking between our industrial and service sectors.

Objectives: To conduct a needs assessment survey of our suppliers to determine

(A) current use of resources,
(B) resource gaps, and the
(C) need for outsourcing.

Goals:

(A) Determine the current state of breast cancer screening among Asian-American women.
(B) Understand the psychological, economic, and cultural barriers to breast cancer screening among Asian-American women.
(C) Create culturally appropriate, persuasive messages encouraging breast cancer screening among Asian-American women.

Objectives:

(A) to describe the incidence of breast cancer screening among Asian-American women in the Tri-Valley area;
(B) to identify the psychological, economic, and cultural barriers preventing Asian-American women from getting screened for breast cancer; and
(C) to test three messages designed to persuade Asian-American women to get screened for breast cancer.

## Guidelines for Writing Survey Objectives

1. *Make objectives specific.* To write specific objectives, it is useful to start with a general goal statement that begins with the word *to* followed by an action verb, such as *describe, explain, explore, identify, investigate, gauge,*

*measure, assess,* or *test*—for example, "To investigate customer satisfaction levels." A list of specific objectives can then be generated from this goal statement. Example 1.1 shows a general research goal followed by a list of objectives. The level of specificity in the objectives will guide the researcher when writing questionnaire items.

---

*Example 1.1*

*Goal:* To assess credit union members' satisfaction with the current services

*Objectives:* To assess credit union members' satisfaction regarding the following:

A. The waiting time to speak to a customer service representative
B. The loan application process
C. Membership fees
D. Telephone banking services
E. Checking account services
F. Savings account services
G. Bilingual services

---

Be sure that the survey objectives are in alignment with the format you choose to administer the survey; e-mail, website, and mobile surveys have innate coverage biases. For example, if your objective is to determine the satisfaction level of residents of the XYZ Retirement Village, then placing that survey on the village's website may not target the correct set of respondents. Evidence indicates that people aged 65 and older access the Internet less often than younger people. The website of a retirement village may be viewed more often by family members of the residents than by the residents themselves.

2. *Write measurable objectives.* Whether an objective is measurable should be evaluated in light of the proposed survey format. Some objectives, such as those involving physiological variables, may very well be measurable but not in an e-mail or mobile survey. Example 1.2 presents some measurable digital survey objectives.

---

*Example 1.2*

A. To assess students' opinions about the proposed mascot
B. To determine the percentage of citizens who are likely to vote for Candidate A
C. To determine employees' attitudes about the new delivery system
D. To collect members' ratings of the workshop

---

3. *Have your objectives reviewed by experts.* There are two types of experts to consider: (a) subject-matter experts and (b) methodologists. Subject-matter experts have in-depth knowledge in specific areas. For example, if you are conducting an election study, you might seek out political scientists or sociologists with expertise in voting behavior. These individuals can offer advice about the topic of the survey and provide a context for the research. Methodologists, on the other hand, are experts in the survey process. They can help you create specific and measurable objectives and offer advice about the feasibility of achieving your objectives with an online survey.

4. *Review the literature related to your topic.* A literature review is a basic component of most academic and many applied research papers. Even if your project does not require a formal literature review, it is valuable to conduct one anyway. In doing so, you can learn from the work of others; specifically, you will see how others have formulated their research objectives and approached specific problems in the research process. In addition, you may find that the data you are seeking to collect already exist. Numerous research consortiums and institutes routinely collect a host of social data (e.g., the General Social Survey conducted by researchers at the University of Chicago) and make it available to member institutions and their constituents.

## Survey Timelines

Timelines need not be complicated. They can be as simple as listing what you plan to accomplish each week. If there is an external project deadline, you will need to start from that deadline and work backward to the present. In this scenario, researchers often find that they need more time than is available. There are two options for this situation: (a) limit the research objectives to only those that can be adequately addressed in the available time or (b) decrease the acceptable sample size, thereby reducing the amount of time the survey stays in the field. Note that by decreasing the sample size, you will increase the error associated with the statistical estimates obtained from the sample data.

Figure 1.2 is a timeline organized by week showing the major steps in conducting a digital survey research project. We have not included the review and selection of survey software in this timeline. The vendor selection and procurement process can be lengthy and subject to many legal and organizational obstacles. We assume that as the researcher begins the process of

**Figure 1.2   Research Timeline**

| Week 1 | • Define survey objectives<br>• Begin literature review |
|---|---|
| Week 2 | • Continue literature review<br>• Have objectives reviewed by experts |
| Week 3 | • Revise objectives<br>• Conduct preliminary research<br>• Choose survey method |
| Week 4 | • Choose sampling strategy<br>• Locate or compile sampling frame<br>• Select sample |
| Week 5 | • Draft questionnaire and invitation |
| Week 6 | • Pretest questionnaire and invitation<br>• Revise questionnaire and invitation |
| Week 7 | • Launch survey<br>• Send reminders |
| Week 8 | • Send additional reminders |
| Week 9 | • Download and clean data<br>• Analyze data |
| Week 10 | • Continue data analysis<br>• Write first draft of report |
| Week 11 | • Write second draft of report |
| Week 12 | • Finalize report<br>• Prepare presentation |
| Week 13 | • Present survey results |

developing a particular digital survey project, appropriate software has been procured and staff has been adequately trained on its use.

Obviously, timelines for research vary greatly depending on the nature of the project, the hours per week devoted to the research, the number of researchers involved, and the complexity of the data analysis required. Figure 1.2 is intended to outline the major tasks to be accomplished and not to suggest time limits for the completion of each task.

# When Should an Online Survey Be Used?

Digital surveys are not appropriate for every research project. What follows are some questions for researchers who are considering using technology for survey data collection.

1. *What is the desired sample size, and how is the sample distributed geographically?* If the sample size is fairly large and widely distributed geographically, digital administration is a good option. E-mail and web-based surveys typically involve higher start-up costs than other methods but become cost-effective as the number of completed questionnaires increases. It is, therefore, most efficient to conduct an Internet survey when a large number of participants are to be contacted. Additionally, if the respondents are concentrated in a narrow geographic region, telephone or face-to-face interviews are feasible—albeit more expensive—options, which may result in a higher response rate, thereby reducing nonresponse error.

2. *What are the time constraints?* Digital surveys have the potential for fast turnaround. E-mail communication is fast, and text messages delivered to mobile phones are instantaneous, whereas postal mail must be physically delivered, obviously taking more time. Researchers should be cautioned, however, about making the general conclusion that digital surveys are always faster than other methods. It is important to consider the total time required to administer the survey; this may include an advance letter or e-mail message plus one or more follow-up reminders. Moreover, to achieve a sufficiently high response rate, a researcher may choose to keep a digital survey in the field for an extended period of time.

3. *Does the questionnaire contain sensitive information?* If so, anonymity might be a concern. Participants who are asked to respond to an e-mail questionnaire may lose their anonymity. If, however, participants are directed to a website to complete the questionnaire, some measure of anonymity can be promised. With regard to socially desirable responses, e-mail and website surveys are similar to self-administered postal mail questionnaires. Because there is no interviewer on the phone or in person, respondents tend to feel safer providing honest answers in an online environment.

4. *Who is your target?* Clearly, digital surveys require that target respondents have access to the appropriate technology, either Internet access or a mobile phone. Physical, psychological, or financial limitations to technology may prohibit the use of digital surveys for certain populations. Digital surveys work well in closed populations where the potential respondents are known

to have e-mail or Internet access—for example, a group of employees at a company, students at a university, or members of a professional association. They are less ideal when attempting to collect general public opinion data.

5. *Is there a sampling frame?* Responses to digital surveys are greatest when respondents are prenotified of the upcoming survey request. If you do not have an e-mail list, can one be created or obtained? Government agencies, businesses, and educational institutions maintain e-mail lists of their constituencies. Access to the appropriate list makes an e-mail or mobile survey a reasonable choice. Alternatives to using an organization's list include (a) advertising the survey, perhaps on websites (such as Craig's List), in promotional literature, or in an online community bulletin board; and (b) purchasing a list from a vendor. Using these alternatives deprives the researcher of the benefits of speed and efficiency that an existing list provides and introduces validity concerns related to the integrity of the sample.

6. *Is a convenience sample sufficient, or is a probability sample necessary?* To make inferences about underlying populations based on sample statistics, selecting a **probability sample** of respondents is necessary. Because there is no general population e-mail list and currently no Internet equivalent to telephone random digit dialing, researchers requiring data gathered from probability samples are best advised to consider other types of surveys. The **nonprobability samples** that can be selected quickly for Internet or mobile surveys work well for exploratory research or as part of a multimethod approach.

7. *Would multimedia or interactive features enhance the questionnaire?* Unlike paper questionnaires, electronic surveys may include streaming audio or video. Additionally, online questionnaires are arguably the most effective self-administered format for asking contingency questions. Web questionnaires can be programmed to avoid logical inconsistencies in follow-up questions. While programming errors may still exist, the automation of skip patterns eliminates the possibility of respondents answering the wrong questions—for example, participants who were not registered to vote responding that they had selected Candidate A in a recent election.

8. *Does the researcher have the technical ability to create an online survey, or are funds available to hire someone?* If the researcher does not have the technological knowledge or skills to create the digital survey, then either a consultant must be included in the budget or another method should be employed. There are presently hundreds of commercial services available to aid researchers in the creation, distribution, and analysis of digital surveys. These businesses vary greatly in the quality of customer service and data they provide as well as in their pricing structures.

## Summary

The field of online survey research is rapidly developing. Electronic methods of survey data collection have been touted as the wave of the future, with supporters citing speedy response, low cost, and easy fielding as major benefits, while detractors lob harsh criticism about the low response rates and claims that samples do not adequately represent populations. Although the particulars of the technology may be new, the controversy surrounding the research methodology is not. In fact, much of the current debate about digital surveys is reminiscent of a previous era when mail and telephone surveys were met with suspicion. More than 30 years ago, survey authority Don Dillman (1978) noted,

> Neither mail nor telephone has been considered anything more than a poor substitute for the much heralded face-to-face interview. Perhaps this view is justified, because the two methods had many deficiencies and problems. Surveys by mail typically elicited extremely low response rates, even with short questionnaires. . . . Further, it is not possible to reach many people with mail questionnaires; among those to whom questionnaires could be delivered, the best educated were far more likely to respond. Even completed questionnaires left much to be desired. . . . It is not surprising, then, that users of the mail questionnaire treated response rates well below 50 percent as "acceptable" and explained away problems of data quality with disclaimers such as, "this is the best we can expect from a mail questionnaire." (pp. 1–2)

Substitute the word *online* in place of *mail* in the above quotation, and you will have a good indication of the contemporary discussion surrounding the use of online surveys. In the decades since Dillman wrote these words, a plethora of methodological research has resulted in techniques for mitigating the deficiencies inherent in the mail and telephone survey methods. In the decades to come, researchers will likely develop procedures to similarly compensate for the limitations of online surveys. Although there is still a great deal to learn about electronic surveys, the research to date provides valuable guidance to digital survey developers and forms the basis for our recommendations throughout this text.

All surveys, whether conducted in person, by mail, e-mail, or mobile phone, have common features. All require clear objectives, well-crafted questionnaires, a sampling strategy, and so on. However, the idiosyncrasies of the technology associated with electronic surveys, with respect to planning, development, distribution, and analysis of the results, warrant detailed attention.

Internet and mobile surveys are effective for gathering information quickly and relatively inexpensively from geographically dispersed participants. E-mail and web-based surveys are useful in many situations, and mobile surveys can be effective for many exploratory research projects. However, it is important to emphasize that these methods are not appropriate for all types of survey research. Researchers should carefully assess the target audience, research objectives, and data reporting needs when selecting a survey format.

## Exercises

1. Identify and describe the three main purposes for conducting social research. Describe how an online survey may serve each purpose.

2. Imagine you were assigned to conduct a customer satisfaction survey for a local credit union.

   a. What sort of preliminary research would you conduct in preparation for designing the survey?
   b. Whom would you contact for information and advice on your survey questionnaire?
   c. Would you recommend an online survey for this project? Why or why not?
   d. Write one goal and one objective for this survey project.
   e. Create a timeline for the project outlining the major activities that would need to be completed.

# CHAPTER 2

# Planning the Online Survey

A sound plan is essential to the success of any research endeavor. Survey research is a process, and each element impacts the others. Research objectives guide questionnaire format; questionnaire format determines the types of questions that may be used; the types of questions used determine data analysis; data analysis reflects research objectives; and all this is bound by time, budget, and ethical considerations.

The first step in the planning process is to articulate a plan for the survey. This plan will be a handy map to which you can continually return as you address the individual components of the survey planning process. These outlines are also particularly useful when the survey is part of a team research project.

In this chapter, we consider the major elements of a survey plan—namely, choosing the type of digital survey you will use, selecting survey software, writing clear project objectives, preparing timelines, and addressing ethical considerations important in the online survey environment.

## E-Mail Surveys

E-mail surveys can be economical and fast to create and deploy. When we refer to e-mail surveys, we mean surveys created using survey software and accessed by respondents through a link in an e-mail invitation. These are among the most common online surveys because anyone who has access to online survey software, such as SurveyMonkey, Zoomerang, or InstantSurvey, can create an e-mail survey.

According to an August 2010 report on the Pew Internet and American Life Project website, 79% of Americans use e-mail daily (Smith, 2010). This is a substantial proportion of the overall population and renders surveys delivered by e-mail a viable option for many projects. However, percentages of e-mail users vary by age, racial/ethnic group, income, and educational attainment (see Table 2.1). It is, therefore, important to consult current data regarding the demographic makeup of individuals who use Internet and e-mail to make sure this distribution method is appropriate for the population you are considering surveying.

**Table 2.1  Internet Use in the United States by Demographic Characteristic**

| Characteristic | Percentage |
|---|---|
| Men | 79 |
| Women | 79 |
| *Race/Ethnicity* | |
| White, non-Hispanic | 80 |
| Black, non-Hispanic | 71 |
| Hispanic | 82 |
| *Age* | |
| 18–29 | 95 |
| 30–49 | 87 |
| 50–64 | 78 |
| 65+ | 42 |
| *Household Income* | |
| Less than $30,000/year | 63 |
| $30,000–$49,000 | 84 |
| $50,000–$74,999 | 89 |
| $75,000+ | 95 |
| *Educational Attainment* | |
| Less than high school | 52 |
| High school | 67 |
| Some college | 90 |
| College+ | 96 |

*(Continued)*

## Table 2.1  (Continued)

| Characteristic | Percentage |
|---|---|
| *Community Type* | |
| Urban | 81 |
| Suburban | 82 |
| Rural | 67 |

SOURCE: Based on data from the Pew Internet and American Life Project, http://www.pewinternet.org/Static-Pages/Trend-Data/Whos-Online.aspx.

NOTE: Data are based on telephone interviews with 2,258 adults living in the continental United States. Interviews were in English and Spanish.

The following are specific advantages and disadvantages of e-mail surveys.

## Advantages

- *Speed.* An e-mail questionnaire can be sent to hundreds or thousands of people by entering or importing a distribution list and hitting the *send* button. Responses typically are received quickly, and data can be described and distributed via the software tool in real time.
- *Economy.* Most e-mail software vendors (such as those mentioned earlier) offer free versions of their services. The free software often limits the number and types of questions and responses allowed. If these limitations pose a problem, a low-cost, monthly contract may be purchased that will expand the options and offer the survey creator the vendor's full suite of tools.
- *Convenience.* Online survey software allows researchers to create the questionnaire, write the e-mail invitation, upload a distribution list, and send reminders directly from the software. In most cases, it is a seamless approach that automatically inserts such elements as the survey link and a link for respondents to opt out of the survey if they so choose.
- *Simplicity.* Online survey software of the type we have been referencing does not require technical expertise on the part of the survey developer. Tools such as SurveyMonkey and Zoomerang are user-friendly, offer a selection of survey templates to jump-start the questionnaire creation process, and contain help features that include step-by-step instructions, tutorials, and online chats with support staff.

## Disadvantages

- *Availability of a sampling frame.* You must have access to an e-mail list for the population you wish to survey. If you do not have such a list, you must be able to purchase or compile one.
- *Unsolicited e-mail (i.e., spam).* Most e-mail programs use filters to flag unsolicited messages as junk mail. Some filters will not accept bulk e-mails. With the proliferation of e-mail surveys, e-mail marketing messages, online newsletters, and more, spam filters have become sophisticated and can permit users to block any message not from a preapproved sender. This often results in a large number of e-mail invitations bouncing back to the sender.
- *Gray- and Blacklisting.* Along with the ability to block unsolicited messages, many e-mail service providers use programs that search for patterns of bulk e-mails coming from one source and perform other functions, such as searching subject headings for certain key words or identifying the domain from which the e-mail messages originate. When potential spam is detected, the sender (in this case, the software vendor) may be placed on a gray- or black-list. With **graylisting**, every time the e-mail service provider receives a message from an unknown sender, it rejects the mail with a "try again later" message. Spam software will *not* try again later, and legitimate messages will eventually make it to the intended recipient. However, messages may be delayed as much as 72 hours before finally arriving at their destination, undermining the advantage of collecting survey results quickly. In the extreme case, a sender's server may be **blacklisted** and messages from that server will not be delivered at all. Surveyors can inquire about a vendor's history with gray- and blacklisting and should ask about the mechanisms in place to combat this issue. This will help but will not guarantee success, because e-mail providers regularly upgrade their protocols for identifying potential spam.
- *Too many e-mail surveys.* Because online survey software is free or inexpensive, convenient, and easy to use, many people who otherwise would not have chosen to conduct a survey are opting to collect data via e-mail surveys. The large volume of e-mail surveys appearing in recipients' inboxes has created a problem for the industry, as potential respondents experiencing e-mail survey overload are ignoring invitations.

## Internet/Intranet (Website) Surveys

Surveys posted on websites can be created using the same software applications used to create e-mail surveys. The difference is that, instead of e-mailing a link to a sample of respondents, these surveys appear on a webpage, either as a link posted somewhere on the page or as a pop-up or crawl-in link. They have many of the speed and convenience advantages of e-mail surveys and offer all the same questionnaire features, plus the ability to collect data from individuals for whom you may not have a sampling frame.

## Advantages

- *Speed.* If posted on a popular website, a questionnaire can potentially gather thousands of responses within hours.
- *Audience.* You can post the link on numerous websites with the permission and cooperation of the sites' owners. This might broaden your audience, as the link could appear on sites whose users consist of researchers, teachers, children, students, employees, and so on.
- *Economy.* Compared with other modes of survey data collection, website surveys are the most economical means by which to collect data from large numbers of respondents who may be geographically dispersed. After the initial set-up expenses (software, web hosting, etc.), it costs no more to target large samples than small ones.
- *The ability to ask sensitive questions.* Website surveys are similar to other forms of self-administered surveys in that no researcher is present and participants complete the questionnaire at their own pace. This also is true of e-mail surveys; however, the survey that appears on a webpage is not linked to respondents' e-mail addresses and, therefore, affords participants an added measure of anonymity, allowing them to more freely and honestly answer the questions.
- *Ability to evaluate websites.* There is perhaps no better way to ask users to evaluate a website than to do so while they are navigating the site. If your research objectives include testing the usability of a webpage, for example, you could include a survey link on the page you wish to evaluate. Visitors can provide feedback about their experience while still on the site.

## Disadvantages

- *Limited populations.* Internet use is quickly becoming the norm in America, and the number of people using computers and accessing the Internet continues to increase each year. There is some disagreement about the exact number of households online; however, one fact is clear: The online population does not reflect the general population of the United States (see Table 2.1). An upward bias in socioeconomic status is evident among Internet users, and they are not evenly represented across racial/ethnic groups. This precludes the use of website surveys for projects focused on populations not well represented online.
- *Abandonment of the survey.* Respondents can easily quit in the middle of a questionnaire. To minimize the likelihood of respondents quitting, questionnaires should be as short as possible—that is, ask only questions related to

the project objectives. Avoid the temptation to add a few more questions because "you're conducting the survey anyway." It also helps if the questionnaire is easy to navigate and fun to complete. Pretesting the questionnaire will provide feedback about ease of navigation, and an understanding of the **target population** will aid in the inclusion of items that are interesting and relevant to the respondents. Offering incentives may help prevent abandonment of the survey.

- *Limited information about respondents.* Unlike an e-mail survey, for which you may have existing information about the respondents—for example, demographic characteristics, the department in which they work, their purchasing habits—this information will not be available for respondents to website surveys. Surveyors can, of course, collect this information on the website questionnaire, but the added questions will lengthen the survey and the validity of the data cannot be verified.

- *Limited sampling options.* The majority of surveys that appear on websites are of the volunteer opt-in variety. That is, any site visitor who happens across the link or clicks on the survey icon may participate. There are some opportunities to randomly present the survey to a subset of site visitors; however, for the most part, sampling for these surveys is limited to nonprobability sampling options. The most serious consequence of this limitation is the inability to generalize findings based on the survey results.

## Mobile Surveys

Several years ago, the term *mobile survey* referred primarily to a series of text messages sent to respondents' mobile phones. Participants responded to these surveys by selecting from among a series of options. Open-ended questions were not used, and the ability to route respondents to different sets of questions based on previous answers was limited. The widespread adoption of easy-to-use **smartphones**—most notably the Apple iPhone—and other mobile devices, such as tablet computers, has resulted in a shift in the concept of mobile surveys. Obviously, researchers still conduct text-based mobile surveys, but this format is quickly being relegated to the realm of event-satisfaction and live-audience feedback polls.

The range of capabilities available on most smartphones and tablet PCs, combined with high-resolution displays and usable keyboards, has greatly expanded the options for mobile surveys. Software vendors have been quick to recognize the potential, and many now offer the ability to optimize just about any fully functioning online survey for smartphones and tablet PCs. As with the other two classes of online surveys, this opportunity to reach new audiences comes with some challenges.

## Advantages

- *Potential to reach new audience.* Survey participants who are not likely to respond to an e-mail or website survey may be more inclined to acknowledge and participate in a mobile survey.
- *Speed.* Because many individuals keep their mobile phones with them most of the time, in-the-moment surveys (e.g., during an event) are possible.
- *Questionnaires can be feature rich.* Surveys created for smartphones and tablet PCs can include images, multimedia features, and skip logic.
- *Use of device features.* Surveys can take advantage of the native features of mobile devices, such as cameras, sound recorders, and Global Positioning Satellite (GPS) locators.

## Disadvantages

- *Audience reach.* Smartphone adoption in the United States is projected to reach 50% by the end of 2011. Although an impressive proportion, it clearly does not include everyone in some target audiences. The socioeconomic factors associated with smartphone adoption and use limit the types of individuals who can be surveyed.
- *Number and types of questions.* Surveys designed for smartphones and tablet PCs are not limited to text. Technically, they can include many of the features you might include in any other online survey. However, the nature of the devices (i.e., they are mobile, and so are their users) dictates that surveys be short and question types be limited to those that can be answered quickly.
- *May be viewed as intrusive.* Mobile phone users consider many factors when selecting a particular device, but the ability to respond to surveys is probably not among those considerations. Annoying an organization's members or customers with survey requests to their mobile phones could result in participants permanently opting out of all surveys sent from the organization.

## Purchasing Survey Software and Selecting a Web Survey Host

To conduct an e-mail, website, or mobile survey, you will need software and the services of a web-based survey host. Hundreds of commercial software programs and web-based survey hosts are on the market. Web-based survey hosts (also known as application service providers, or ASPs) typically offer customers a full range of services, including the ability to create questionnaires, conduct surveys, analyze data, and produce and share reports, all via the company's website. Some **web survey** companies offer the option of purchasing software that can be used locally on the researcher's computer or local network; questionnaires can be uploaded to websites or sent to respondents as a link in an e-mail invitation the same way that software is used on a vendor's hosted site. This option leaves researchers responsible for installing the software and providing their own technical support for the system. Many of the ASPs offer free or trial versions of their services, and most software vendors provide pared-down versions of their full packages for customers to try.

The multitude of commercial survey software packages and web-based survey hosts available, at many levels of complexity, greatly reduces the need for individuals or organizations to develop proprietary software applications for conducting surveys. Although in some situations a company may need specialized features or perhaps heightened security, most requirements can be addressed by working with the software vendor to customize existing software to meet the organization's needs. The challenge comes in selecting an appropriate software and online survey host for your needs and level of technical expertise. Although we will not evaluate specific vendors here, we will address some important considerations for choosing software and a survey host.

- *Expense.* Survey software and ASPs vary greatly in price. The range starts at $0. As mentioned previously, the free software available online is typically limited; questionnaires can contain only a few questions (usually about 10), not all question types are available, and the number of completed surveys allowed in a given period of time is also limited. Providers such as SurveyMonkey and Zoomerang offer a variety of "premium" or "professional" subscriptions that range in price from about $200 to $800 annually. With this type of account, users generally have access to all available question types; the number of questions that can be included on a questionnaire and the number of responses that can be collected are unlimited; and semicustom features, such as the ability to manipulate questionnaire templates and redirect respondents to your website at the end of the survey, become available.

There is no upper limit when it comes to the price of survey software. The annual license fees can be as much as $25,000 for highly complex software packages. This option allows for unlimited customization of the software, for which there is often additional expense. Although costly, the surveys created with semicustom or custom software will have the precise look and feel required, and custom programming will make available any question types and response options desired. Moreover, security concerns associated with the transfer of data can be addressed during the development process, and additional features, such as the ability to automatically update database tables with respondent information, can be added.

The issue of cost is usually one of finding a product that contains the features you will actually use for the lowest price. Custom software packages may be appropriate if your needs are specific and you have a lot of lead time and a large budget; however, you may find that an off-the-shelf product is adequate if your survey requires only basic features. Clearly, the more you pay, the more you get, but if you do not make use of those added features, they will slow down the questionnaire development process, as you will have to navigate around them.

• *Ease of use.* Look for survey software that has an easy-to-use design interface with drag-and-drop capabilities for questions and scales, notes, and other text. **Wizards** that walk users through the survey creation process and questionnaire templates can be useful if you are new to using survey software. You also should be able to save a survey you create as a template so that you may use it again in the future. Question libraries also can be valuable for new survey researchers. These libraries typically include standard demographic and opinion items and can speed up the creation of the questionnaire. A valuable feature is the ability to create your own question library that includes your commonly used questions and response sets. Using the free- or limited-trial version of the software will provide an opportunity to test the usability of the product. The full version will offer more features, but the user interface will be the same as that of the limited version.

• *Question number, formats, and response options.* Check for the capacity to ask a wide variety of questions using different **response options**. Question formats that should be included are single response, multiple response, scale response (i.e., agree–disagree; 1–5 points, etc.), and matrix response. Radio buttons, check boxes, and open-text boxes are basic and should be included in any online survey software package. Another useful feature allows surveyors to randomize the order in which response options and questions are presented to respondents; this is essential if you believe order effects may be associated with the way responses are selected. Also desirable is the ability to choose whether respondents will be allowed to skip questions or whether answers will be mandatory for continuation of the questionnaire. Forcing responses can lead to abandonment of the survey. The software should not limit the number of questions you place on a questionnaire; this choice should be guided by the survey objectives and a concern with respondent fatigue.

Visual questions (e.g., those that allow researchers to add photos or other images) and options such as response scale sliders, date pickers, card sorting, click maps, page turners, and highlighter tools can greatly enhance the look and interactivity of a questionnaire. For example, you might present a design for a new advertisement and ask respondents to highlight the areas of the image that interest them the most. These features will add expense and development time and, therefore, are necessary only for surveyors who conduct complicated surveys on a regular basis.

- *Contingency questions.* Contingency questions (also called skip-logic questions) direct your respondents to a new set of questions based on their responses to previous questions. With online surveys, this means that participants are not forced to read and answer unnecessary questions. This is an important feature that will greatly contribute to the validity of the survey responses. Contingency questions vary in levels of complexity and are usually not available in free software. Purchasing a professional subscription will offer the user basic skip-logic questions (e.g., if "Male," respondents are directed to question 3; if "Female," they are sent to question 4). Multilevel contingency questions and related features such as piping (including responses from one question in the text of a subsequent question) and hiding or masking (presenting limited response options for a question based on responses to previous questions) are usually available only in higher-priced software.

- *Questionnaire options.* Less expensive software packages and ASPs sometimes limit the number of questions you can place on the questionnaire and the number of responses you can collect with any one survey. Other typical limitations include the inability to use tables, images, audio, video, and **ALT tags** on the survey. If you know you will be conducting simple surveys with small samples, these limitations may not pose a problem. If, however, you wish to expand to longer questionnaires or survey large samples of respondents, you will need to look for software without these limits.

- *Questionnaire appearance.* Evaluate the options for customizing questionnaires. Ask if the software allows you to include logos; also, investigate the ability to manipulate fonts and colors. If you will be surveying special populations, such as children or the elderly, this is especially important, as you will want to ensure that large font sizes are available. Most inexpensive software will offer the option of including logos and selecting from a limited number of color schemes and fonts. For specialized branding of questionnaire templates, however, you will need to select custom or semicustom software. Also, inquire about the configuration of navigation, progress bars, and automatic question numbering.

Similar consideration should be given to the appearance of e-mail invitations. That is, to what extent will you be able to customize the invitation? Can you add images such as a logo; change the font types, sizes, and colors; include links to an FAQ list or your website?

• *Sampling features.* If you do not have an e-mail distribution list, some web survey hosts will generate a sample for you, for a fee. Look for the ability to select random, stratified, systematic, and cluster samples. If you plan to place your survey on a website, you might be interested in sampling the site's visitors. Many vendors will offer the option of sampling every *n*th visitor, the first 500, or the first 100 every hour, and so on. Another common feature that some researchers find useful is the ability to automatically close the survey after a predetermined quota has been reached.

• *Distribution options.* Look for survey software that allows for different modes of survey delivery. Even if you are interested only in conducting e-mail surveys, you may want the option of placing your survey on a website, mobile device, or kiosk, or perhaps printing a paper copy as an alternative for respondents who have disabilities or prefer a hard copy.

• *Respondent lists.* Your survey software should allow you to import a respondent list from another software program or your e-mail address book. At a minimum, you should be able to upload a **comma-separated values** file with your respondents' e-mail addresses and first and last names. The ability to upload a few more fields of data, such as a membership number, customer or student identification, or respondents' geographic region or state, can be particularly helpful and will allow you to further customize your invitation and questionnaire.

• *Respondent mailings.* In addition to the e-mail invitations, software that allows you to send prenotification e-mail messages, a series of reminders, and thank-you messages is convenient and will greatly facilitate the survey process.

• *Tracking respondents.* In e-mail surveys, you will want to track who has responded and limit replies to one per recipient. A higher response rate means less error; effective survey software offers the option of follow-up reminders to **nonrespondents**. The software should give you the option of automatically filtering nonrespondents and respondents who have partially completed the questionnaire for reminders. Tracking these nonrespondents in the software application provides quick access for follow-up correspondence. In addition to tracking who replied, you also should be able to limit replies to one respondent. This is especially important for website surveys because multiple replies from one user can skew the data. The use of **cookies**, Internet protocol addresses, and randomly generated codes should be potential options for limiting responses to prevent multiple replies from a single user.

• *Reporting and analysis options.* It is important to choose software that allows you to analyze your data and provides user-driven views of the results. How much data analysis you want to conduct online will vary according to your research purpose. Most survey software applications allow users to conduct descriptive analysis online and produce basic reports. For more complex analyses, look for software that provides the option of exporting data directly to a data analysis package such as **IBM SPSS Statistics\***; at the very least, data should be easy to export to Excel for later importing to the statistical software package of your choice. For individuals and businesses involved in frequent online data collection and intricate data analysis, an all-inclusive package may be the appropriate solution; STATPAC, for example, offers a reasonably priced product that includes software to create e-mail and web-based surveys and conduct basic and advanced statistical analysis (including analysis of open-ended survey questions) and provides free web hosting of surveys.

• *Sharing results.* You may want to post your results on a website or share them with the respondents or the study's sponsor. Many web hosts give researchers the option to share results with others by providing a **URL** for a webpage containing the results. These programs allow survey developers to post the URL on a website so that viewers can see the real-time or final responses, depending on when you post the URL. The developer also has the option to allow respondents to see the results immediately after they have completed the survey. Note that posting real-time poll results on a website will have implications for subsequent respondents who have not yet participated in the poll.

• *Accessibility.* You may require a web host that can create questionnaires in an accessible format for those with visual impairments. WebSurveyor, for example, can create surveys for respondents who use screen readers. Some web hosts, such as Zoomerang, will translate a survey into different languages and, if necessary, translate the responses. This service is provided for an additional fee.

• *Accounts and roles.* Some web-based survey hosts provide only one password and username for each account. Therefore, a company with 100 people and one account can have only one person at a time logged onto the web-based host. Other web-based hosts will provide more than one password and username for the price of one account. If multiple members of the research team will need access to the web host at the same time, it is important to investigate the vendor's account restrictions.

Further, if your organization will have different levels of survey creators—for example, administrators, authors, editors, and so on—you will need a system that allows you to assign roles to individuals who will be involved in

\*IBM SPSS® Statistics was formerly called PASW® Statistics.

the research process. System administrators maintain rights to all elements of the software program and can assign rights to others. Survey authors program questionnaires and usually have permission to upload lists and deploy surveys. Editors have the ability to make changes to a questionnaire but may not be able to send surveys to the potential respondents. These designations vary from one software vendor to another. Some include an "observer" role, someone who cannot make changes to a survey but can review the work of other team members; others have an "approver" role, someone whose responsibility is to approve surveys before they are deployed. The labels are less important than the ability to assign individuals to different roles with varying levels of privileges depending on their function in the survey process.

• *Survey security.* Password protection of questionnaires inhibits unauthorized users from responding to a survey. Depending on the nature of the survey you will be creating, you may need to add a password to prevent anyone other than the intended respondent from responding.

• *Data security.* If you will be collecting sensitive information, such as financial or personal health information, the security of your survey data files is of paramount importance. To ensure that the vendor you choose maintains the appropriate level of data security, review their information security policy; if the vendor does not have an information security policy, eliminate them from consideration. Additionally, it is advantageous to ask the following questions, most of which concern the confidentiality and integrity of your data that will be stored on the vendor's server. Reputable software vendors will have ready answers to these questions and will be willing to provide you with documentation to support their assertions. Researchers who will be routinely collecting sensitive, confidential information may need to go further and have the software evaluated by a network security consultant who can run vulnerability scans to determine where potential security threats exist.

### Questions to Ask Survey Software Vendors

1. What is the date of the last revision of the information security policy?

2. What is the process by which third parties are granted access to the data stored on your servers?

3. What security controls are in place to keep individual customer data separate from other customer data?

4. What is your screening process for employees, contractors, and third parties who will have access to the data stored on your servers?

5. Describe the location and physical space in which data is stored. What security mechanisms exist to prevent unauthorized access to your offices and data storage facilities?

6. How do you protect your systems from environmental hazards such as fire, smoke, water damage, and dust?

7. Who manages and maintains your data center?

8. How do you prevent end users from installing potentially malicious software?

9. Do you scan traffic coming into your network for viruses?

10. How are your systems backed up? What is the schedule for system backups?

11. How are software malfunctions handled?

12. What is your process for handling security breaches?

13. What is your protocol for encrypting data, both in transit and storage?

Secure Sockets Layer uses a cryptographic system to create a secure connection between the respondent's browser and the server to ensure all survey responses are sent securely and cannot be accessed or viewed during transmission. This system is supported in all modern browsers. Cryptography protects information by transforming it (i.e., *encrypting* it) into an unreadable format. Encryption refers to algorithmic schemes that encode plain text into nonreadable form, or cyphertext, providing privacy. The receiver of the encrypted text uses a "key" to decrypt the message, returning it to its original plain-text form. The key is the trigger mechanism to the algorithm. You may want to use this feature to obtain confidential information from your respondents, such as their Social Security numbers or residential addresses.

• *Customer support and training.* Be sure to evaluate the online help and customer support features of the survey software provider. Most applications come with help menus, and some are more helpful than others; it is advisable to test the software's help menus during the trial period. Also, look for toll-free customer service phone numbers, live online support, and on-site training options. Complex software systems should include training and ongoing support, at least during the first months or year of the contract. The exact number of hours of training and any limitations on the type or volume of support requests should be negotiated when making the decision to purchase the software.

## Ethics and Legal Issues

Sometimes, all the daily activities involved in conducting a research project cause us to forget about the "big-picture" issues related to surveys. Survey researchers frequently encounter situations that are open to a variety of interpretations. Situations requiring an ethical interpretation are no different.

Two individuals faced with an identical situation will likely perceive that situation in their own way and consider two different courses of action to be equally acceptable. As a result, organizations concerned with research (e.g., the American Psychological Association), and survey research in particular (e.g., the Council of American Survey Research Organizations and the American Association for Public Opinion Research, or AAPOR), have developed guidelines outlining researchers' ethical responsibilities. The AAPOR code of ethics is reprinted in Appendix A. We will discuss three of the major issues covered in most ethical guidelines: (a) informed consent, (b) ensuring respondent confidentiality and anonymity, and (c) ethical interpretation and reporting of results.

## Informed Consent

In almost all cases, respondents to online surveys will be volunteers. To make an informed decision about participating in the research, volunteers should be briefed on (a) the general nature of the survey, especially if sensitive or potentially embarrassing information will be addressed; (b) the identity of the sponsor of the research; (c) how the data will be used; (d) the average length of time to complete the survey, and if they will be contacted in the future with additional surveys; and (e) whether any risks are involved in participating in the survey, such as being asked to disclose uncomfortable or embarrassing information.

This information can be provided in the e-mail survey invitation or as part of the introduction to the questionnaire. Institutional review boards generally do not require signed consent forms for participants in surveys. If you are in doubt about requirements surrounding consent, you should consult with the appropriate review board representative at your institution. If gaining explicit consent is necessary, the task is normally accomplished by providing respondents the information about the survey, its sponsor, threats and benefits, and so on, either in the invitation or on the first page of the questionnaire, and asking them to check a box indicating their agreement to participate in the research. Those who choose the "do not agree" box are thanked and disqualified from participating in the study.

## Confidentiality and Anonymity

Perhaps one of the most stringent requirements in all social research is maintaining the confidentiality of participants. Frequently, the respondents to your survey will expect that the information they provide will be confidential—that is, neither the fact of their participation nor the information they provide will be disclosed to third parties. If you have promised confidentiality, you have an ethical responsibility to ensure that participants' identification and information is protected. If you cannot (or will not) prevent the disclosure of respondent information, you must make this fact abundantly clear in the invitation to participate in the online survey so that respondents have the opportunity to refuse participation.

Often, the promise of anonymity is included in the same sentence that guarantees confidentiality, almost as if the two concepts were the same. The statement typically reads, "All your responses will remain strictly confidential and anonymous." Unfortunately, many people forget that anonymity extends beyond not requiring names and addresses on a questionnaire. Technically, responses to e-mail surveys are never truly anonymous because researchers know the respondents' e-mail addresses. Even without this information, it is easy to attach identifying code numbers to questionnaires or to link survey numbers to databases containing respondent information. As a result, many potential respondents are skeptical of electronic surveys offering anonymity. The important fact here is not that researchers *must* promise anonymity; rather, what is essential is that if the promise is made, the researcher is obligated to take the necessary steps to ensure that identifying information about survey respondents is kept separate from their responses.

Additionally, even if survey respondents know their anonymity is not guaranteed (e.g., so follow-up information can be gathered or so you can contact the respondent again in the future), you have a responsibility to the respondent to guarantee that subsequent contact is appropriate. For example, do not tell a potential respondent that he or she may be contacted to gather more information when you are really selling the name to a marketing company.

## Survey Reporting and Data Interpretation

The process of reporting survey results is fraught with situations that can jeopardize respondent confidentiality and the accurate interpretation and presentation of research results. When gathering demographic information that can identify respondents, the survey researcher is obligated to produce reports that cannot lead to the identification of individuals. For example, in an employee survey, it is reasonable to ask about gender and ethnic background to ensure that the needs of all employees are being met. If this information is gathered, be careful not to provide a report that can lead to the identification of individual employees. For example, when providing information at the department level, do not present the data so the only male, Hispanic employee can be identified. A rule of thumb to avoid this problem is to produce results only for groups containing at least 10 individuals. This way, no individual can be singled out.

Data interpretation can present another set of problematic issues for survey researchers. Efforts should be made to fully and accurately represent the results gathered by the survey. Too often, people do not present enough information about the procedures used for gathering the data, the sampling strategy, the error and confidence levels, the response rates, or how the data were analyzed. Without this information, it is easy to misinterpret the results or over-interpret some findings, which will lead to erroneous conclusions.

Another situation arises when researchers are asked not to report data that present the host organization in an unfavorable manner. As mentioned previously, every effort should be made to present the results of the survey completely and accurately. This may mean presenting some information that suggests areas of discord or opportunities for improvement. These results should not be hidden or simply forgotten. Doing so would be a disservice to the organization and the people who responded to the survey, not to mention questionable ethics.

## Anti-Spam Compliance

The CAN-SPAM (Controlling the Assault of Non-Solicited Pornography and Marketing) Act was enacted in the United States in 2003. To comply with the Act, surveyors who wish to contact individuals with whom they have no established relationship must do three things:

1. Accurately explain the nature of the message in the e-mail subject line. The subject must relate to the body of the message, and the body must contain a valid physical address for the sender. Surveys about sexual topics must be labeled in the subject header as containing sexually explicit content.

2. Provide an "unsubscribe" link. All e-mail messages must contain a visible, working method for recipients to unsubscribe from your list. All opt-out requests must be processed within 10 days, and individuals who have opted out should not be contacted in the future.

3. Do not send messages through an open relay or with false headers. When sending messages from within the online survey software, this will not be an issue, as almost all hosted applications comply with this requirement. Moreover, messages cannot be sent to e-mail addresses harvested from webpages.

The penalty for failing to comply with the CAN-SPAM Act ranges from a misdemeanor charge to an aggravated offense. Keep in mind that this regulation is applicable to *unsolicited* messages sent to recipients with whom you have no prior relationship. Research surveys (as opposed to marketing surveys) are exempt, and contacting current or former members, customers, or employees is acceptable.

## Summary

In this chapter, we have addressed some foundational issues relevant to many online survey situations. We reviewed the advantages and disadvantages of the three major classes of online surveys: e-mail, website, and mobile surveys. We will return to this discussion when we evaluate online survey deployment options in Chapter 6. For now, this introduction should have provided you with enough information to make a decision about the type of survey you wish to conduct.

The list of factors to consider when purchasing software and signing up with a web survey host is lengthy, and some of the considerations can be complex. If you're in the enviable position of having a large budget with which to conduct your online surveys, you will most likely take your time evaluating multiple software vendors and choosing the one that best serves your needs. If, however, you're in the more common predicament of having a limited budget and a short timeline, your task will be to find as many relevant features as you can at the lowest price.

The practice of conducting online surveys is governed by many of the same ethical principles that guide other social research activities. The principles of informed consent, maintaining respondents' confidentiality and anonymity, and reporting survey results with integrity are just a few of the ethical considerations relevant to survey research. The AAPOR code of ethics provides greater detail on these and other ethical responsibilities and should be reviewed completely before undertaking your survey project.

## Exercises

The commissioner of Parks and Recreation in your city notices a decline in the number of residents using many of the city's parks. She suspects that lack of awareness of the parks might be the underlying issue. The commissioner has asked you to conduct an online survey of the city's residents.

1. What type of online survey would you recommend? Explain to the commissioner the advantages and disadvantages of the choice you recommend.

2. The Parks and Recreation Department has never conducted an online survey before; therefore, they have no software with which to create and deploy the survey. As the survey consultant, it will be your responsibility to evaluate software vendors and make a recommendation to the commissioner. Describe the criteria you would use to evaluate the vendors.

3. The survey you create will be sent to the city's residents. Assume that the potential respondents have not requested communication or surveys from the Parks and Recreation Department. What will you do to be ethically responsible and legally compliant as you design the survey and associated materials?

# CHAPTER 3

# Sampling

In this chapter, we examine the methods of selecting participants for online surveys. The decisions surrounding sample selection are critically important and should be considered in light of the survey objectives. For exploratory studies, convenience samples may be sufficient; when aiming to make statistical inferences about populations, however, it is necessary to employ a probability sampling technique. Before beginning our discussion of specific sampling procedures for online surveys, we will review some fundamental concepts related to sampling. Next, we will discuss the probability and nonprobability approaches that may be used in online surveys. Finally, we will consider the sources of error in online surveys.

## Populations and Samples

In much of social research, investigators are interested in the opinions or attributes of the group of people who participate in the research because of what those individuals can tell researchers about the population from which they are selected. When a researcher writes objectives for a survey project, he or she already has a specific population in mind. A **population** is the entire assembly of individuals, groups, or objects to which you would like to generalize your research results—for example, citizens of a country, students at a university, or employees of a company. When you collect data on every member of a population, you are conducting a **census**. For many research projects, collecting census data is neither feasible nor practical. For example, say you are interested in determining the career plans of all college seniors in the United States. It would be impossible to conduct a census of this group. By the time you finish questioning each student, some might be nearing retirement age. As we will see shortly, however, online surveys may provide one of the few opportunities for conducting censuses in a reasonably timely manner.

Once the population has been identified, the next task is to find or generate a list of the population members. This list is called the **sampling frame**. Readily available sampling frames include e-mail distribution lists of employees of an organization, members of an association, or subscribers to a service.

With a sampling frame in hand, you are ready to draw your sample. A **sample** is a subset of the population. It consists of the group of people selected to participate in the research. Data are collected from sample participants to reach conclusions about population characteristics. When we ask a group of 1,000 citizens about their opinions of a government policy, our real purpose is to make inferences about the population's opinions based on the data provided by the sample. A good sample is representative of the population from which it is drawn.

Some web survey hosts will, for a fee, generate a list of potential respondents that match your sampling frame. For example, Zoomerang will allow the researcher to select a variety of potential respondent attributes. These attributes include characteristics such as demographics (e.g., ethnicity, marital status, language spoken at home), geographic region, occupation, interests, and consumption (e.g., shopping, home and pet ownership, restaurant dining frequency). Typically, the more sampling criteria you specify, the more expensive the sample will be. Likewise, specialized samples, such as orthopedic surgeons, opera singers, and beekeepers, can be particularly expensive to obtain.

The sample selected from the population is not necessarily the group that completes the research. For every sample selected, there will be individuals who are unreachable, as well as nonrespondents—individuals who choose not to participate in the study. Even among the individuals who initially agree to participate, there will be **dropouts**—respondents who do not finish the questionnaire. We will address nonresponse error later in this chapter.

A final issue to consider before deciding on a sampling strategy is the **eligibility criteria** for participants in your research. Consider two elements of eligibility: (a) inclusion criteria—the characteristics that allow a potential respondent to participate, such as being an adult, a nonsmoker, or a registered voter—and (b) exclusion criteria—characteristics that prohibit an individual's participation, such as a language barrier or men in a study on women's health issues.

# Sampling Techniques for Internet and Mobile Surveys

## Saturation Sampling

Saturation sampling is not a sampling technique per se but an attempt to conduct a population census. Recall from our earlier discussion that conducting a census, or collecting data on every member of a population, is an alternative—albeit an infrequently used one—to traditional survey sampling. The factors that usually render population censuses impossible—expense, timeliness, large population sizes, and inaccessibility—can largely be overcome in online surveys.

In an online or mobile survey, as opposed to telephone or face-to-face interviewing, there is no difference in the expense or effort involved in sending an e-mail or text message invitation to 10 or 10,000 members of an organization. Because online survey data have the benefit of automatically posting to a database, there will be no added staff costs for data entry if thousands of questionnaires are returned. Moreover, the distribution of the questionnaires, as well as the data analysis, can be completed relatively quickly. Finally, the researcher opting for a digital survey does so only if the population of interest is accessible in an online environment or via mobile phone.

This approach begins with a sampling frame containing e-mail addresses or cell phone numbers of every member of the target population. All members of the population are sent an e-mail or text message invitation to participate, with appropriate measures taken to ensure that participants respond only once. (Commercial software programs send cookies to the respondents' computers to prevent them from responding more than once.) The questionnaire is accessed through a link in the survey invitation or presented as one or a series of text messages.

Saturation sampling is commonly used in settings such as universities, corporations, government agencies, and professional associations. Using this technique eliminates coverage error because every member of the population is invited to participate in the survey. Although coverage error is not an issue when using saturation sampling, nonresponse error remains a concern. Researchers can, however, compute response rate (because the number of potential respondents receiving invitations is known) and take steps to increase participation. Some scenarios for the use of saturation sampling can be found in Example 3.1.

---

*Example 3.1*

- A university sends out an e-mail invitation to all students, faculty, and staff to participate in an opinion survey about a proposed name change.
- A health management organization e-mails all participating physicians to collect data about the new patient referral system.
- The human resources department of a corporation e-mails all managers asking them to participate in a web survey about improving employee performance reviews.
- The telecommunications firm sends a text message to all customers who have a cell phone number to ask about customer satisfaction.

---

## Probability Sampling

The traditional classification of survey sampling methods into probability and nonprobability techniques is useful for Internet and mobile surveys. Probability samples are those for which the probability of each participant's inclusion can be computed. These samples depend on random selection of participants from a defined sampling frame and afford the researcher the opportunity to reach conclusions about population characteristics based on sample statistics. Table 3.1 shows the probability and nonprobability samples that may be used in online surveys.

**Table 3.1   Types of Probability and Nonprobability Samples for Online Surveys**

| Probability Samples | Nonprobability Samples |
|---|---|
| *For closed populations* | |
| Simple random | Convenience |
| Systematic | Volunteer opt in |
| Stratified | Snowball |
| Cluster | |
| *For open populations* | |
| Intercept | |
| Prerecruited panel | |

### Random Sampling From a Closed Population

With a comprehensive sampling frame, such as an employee or membership list, it is possible to employ a random sampling technique to select potential survey respondents. Even if the list does not contain e-mail addresses or cell phone numbers, it may still be possible to select a random sample of potential respondents, invite them by postal mail, and then direct them to a website containing the survey. To select a random sample of participants from a closed population, first obtain (or create) the sampling frame, then select a simple random sample, a systematic sample, a stratified sample, or a cluster sample.

*Simple Random Sampling.* To select someone "at random" from a given population means that everyone in the population has a chance of being selected. A simple random sample is one in which every subset of the population of the same size as the sample has an equal chance of being selected. The first step in selecting a random sample is to secure (or create) a sampling frame. Sampling frames such as rosters, membership lists, and directories are usually ordered in some way—for example, alphabetically, by department, or by serial number. First, randomize the sampling frame. For example, in Microsoft Excel, this is simply a matter of assigning a random number to each entry on the list using Excel's random number function. Once each element is assigned a random number, the list can be sorted by number and a subset of units selected.

---

*Example 3.2*

To select a simple random sample from a population of 12,000 students at a university, begin with the registrar's list of all students. Randomize the list by assigning each student a random number in the range 00001 to 12,000. Sort the list by the random numbers. Select the first 200 names from the list.

---

*Systematic Sampling.* A systematic sample is a variation on the simple random sample in which every $n$th element of a population is selected. As in the simple random sample, this procedure begins with a sampling frame. In this case, however, instead of simply choosing the first 200 names from a randomized list, you would choose every $n$th person on the list. If $n = 2$, then every second person would be selected; if $n = 3$, every third person would be selected; and so on. The distance between each element selected for participation is called the skip interval. The first element selected from the list should be selected randomly; this is easily accomplished using Microsoft Excel or some other spreadsheet software on which the list is stored. This procedure ensures that elements from all sectors of the sampling frame are selected.

---

*Example 3.3*

Suppose you wanted to select a sample of 100 from a list of the 2,000 employees at a company. You would first obtain the list of all employees, identify a random starting row on the list, and then choose every 20th name on the list for the sample.

---

*Stratified Sampling.* Selecting a stratified sample is a two-stage procedure. First, divide the population into subgroups (strata); second, select either a simple random sample or a systematic sample for each subgroup. Common stratification variables include gender, age, membership status, and job category. This procedure is useful if there is a chance that a simple random sample will yield disproportionately large numbers of participants in one or more categories. For example, when surveying department managers at a corporation, simple random sampling might, purely by chance, yield a result containing all men and no women—a sample not representative of the population. To correct for this sampling error, the population could be stratified by gender before selecting percentages of respondents that reflect the population percentages.

---

*Example 3.4*

To select a stratified sample of 400 faculty members from four colleges at a university, you could first stratify the sampling frame by college. Then, using each stratum as a separate sampling frame, select a simple random sample of 100 respondents from within each college.

---

*Cluster Sampling.* When the target population is especially large, cluster sampling is a useful approach. A cluster is a preexisting group in a population. Obvious clusters include classes in a school, schools in a district, local chapters of a national organization, and so on. Any of the procedures mentioned above—simple random sampling, systematic sampling, or stratified sampling—may be used to select clusters from a population. Each individual in the selected cluster is invited to participate in the survey. Cluster sampling also can be used as the first step in a multistage sampling procedure. First, a sample of clusters is drawn from the population, and then, individuals from each cluster are randomly selected.

---

*Example 3.5*

Say you are interested in surveying nurses employed by a healthcare provider. You could begin by obtaining a master list of all member hospitals in the United States and then stratify them by region of the country: Northeast, Southeast, Southwest, and Northwest. Then, randomly select five hospitals from each region and obtain the lists of all nurses at those hospitals. Finally, draw a simple random sample of nurses from each hospital and e-mail each one an invitation to participate in the survey.

---

## Probability Sampling From an Open Population

Open populations are those for which no sampling frame is readily available—for example, residents of a city. Selecting a probability sample of these individuals is considerably more challenging than in a closed population. Currently, the only way to achieve a truly random sample of an open population is to employ a multimethod approach, such as contacting respondents by phone (using a random digit dialing protocol) and inviting them to log on to a website to participate in the survey. Although the benefit of speed associated with Internet surveys will be lost, the researcher can take advantage of other online survey features such as direct data entry and the ability to present still images and video.

Two methods currently used to select probability samples from open populations are the multimethod approach that creates prerecruited panels of respondents and a technique that restricts the population of interest to visitors of particular websites.

*Prerecruited Panels.* A prerecruited panel is a group of survey respondents who are recruited by a variety of methods (e.g., e-mail solicitation, telephone random digit dialing, mail invitations, and face-to-face interviews) and who agree to be available for repeated research participation. Once empaneled, participants for particular research projects are selected randomly and are sent invitations to participate in surveys and other research.

The California-based company Knowledge Networks (www.knowledge networks.com) claims to have the only probability-selected, statistically valid online panel that is nationally representative. All participants are randomly selected from households with telephones. Individuals may not volunteer to join the panel; they must be invited to participate. Households that do not have Internet access are provided with hardware and free web access.

Knowledge Networks will sell access to their panelists for research projects, or they will create and manage specific panels for clients.

Proprietary online panels are a growing phenomenon in consumer research. They are commonly found in businesses, nonprofit organizations, and media companies. Two types of panels can be developed: branded or blind. A branded panel relies on an organization's existing databases to randomly select participants. Constituents are invited to join the XYZ Company's panel and are typically offered incentives (e.g., cash, coupons, loyalty points, or sweepstakes entry) for participating in the surveys. Familiarity with the company facilitates recruitment but can result in a panel that expresses overly favorable opinions toward the company. For this reason, some organizations choose to create a blind panel—one in which the sponsor's identity is concealed. Recruitment for a blind panel is considerably more difficult and costly than for a branded panel, but the blind panel has a greater likelihood of providing unbiased research results because panelists don't know who is sponsoring the research. These panels are especially useful for investigating market trends and evaluating a company's position relative to its competition. Panel sizes range from a few hundred members to hundreds of thousands; the larger the organization and the more subgroups needed for analyses, the larger the panels tend to be. Building a survey research panel is a weighty, long-term endeavor and requires a commitment to the continued health and maintenance of the panel. Panels do, however, provide a host of benefits, such as the following:

- They can be used for many research purposes, such as creating customer profiles, gauging satisfaction, message testing, website usability analyses, brand research, and new product feedback.
- Panels permit researchers to employ a variety of methods and conduct surveys that may be considered too lengthy or complicated for nonpanel participants. Moreover, longitudinal studies can be effectively conducted because the same participants will be available for sampling over a period of time.
- Panelists' data are maintained in a database, making it unnecessary to replicate questions across surveys. For example, once demographic data is collected, it can be accessed and appended to any panel survey without burdening respondents to repeat this information.
- Nonresponse, while still an issue, is generally lower in prerecruited panels than in other samples because the members have previously agreed to participate. The nonresponse rate can be computed and nonrespondents evaluated. In other words, because researchers have demographic information for all panel participants, it is possible to test for systematic biases among nonrespondents that may limit the study's generalizability.
- Research turnaround time is greatly reduced when sampling from a panel. A typical e-mail survey that may be in the field for one or two weeks can be

completed in a few days. Panelists expect to be contacted with research requests and tend to respond more quickly than nonpanelists.

- Survey research panels can be cost effective. Cost-effectiveness, however, is realized in the long run. Building a panel and the support staff required to maintain it necessitate substantial upfront costs. Over time, however, respondent recruitment costs for individual studies can be virtually eliminated, and existing data can be leveraged for multiple projects.

Although the benefits are numerous, relying on prerecruited panels has drawbacks. Ongoing survey participation may create "professional survey respondents"—individuals who become proficient at answering questionnaires based on familiarity with surveys or who choose to participate to receive the incentive. Panel administrators manage this by limiting the number of surveys panelists may complete in a given period of time, as well as panelists' overall tenure. When participants have reached their limit, say one or two years on the panel, they are thanked and removed from the panel. This leads to another challenge associated with panels: to remain representative of the underlying population, panels must be continually refreshed. For example, as a subscriber population changes, so must the panel composition.

Finally, participation on the panel has the potential to create brand loyalists. Many would consider this occurrence a benefit; however, when seeking to collect valid data about an organization or industry, it can be a detriment. Increasing the rate at which the panel is refreshed can help control the issue, although it will limit the opportunities for longitudinal research. The impact of this threat to validity can be measured by periodically conducting parallel surveys with nonpanel samples and comparing results.

*Intercept Sampling.* This procedure uses pop-up windows to invite respondents to participate in the survey. Web survey software can be programmed to issue pop-up invitations randomly or systematically—say, for every *n*th visitor to the website. This is an intrusive approach and is often accompanied by an incentive for participation. The sampling frame is limited to visitors to a particular website; therefore, generalizations to broader populations must be made with caution. Nonresponse is also a concern, hence the accompanying incentives. Intercept sampling can be effective in certain situations—for example, customer satisfaction surveys for an online merchant.

## Margin of Error and Confidence Level for Surveys Conducted With Probability Samples

When we say the results of a survey are precise, we mean our estimates are correct to within a small margin of variability. To illustrate, we will consider an example of estimating a population proportion based on a sample statistic when the sample is selected using a probability method. For most opinion polls, we can usually tolerate a **margin of error** of a few percentage points around the estimated percentage of the population who have a certain opinion, provided we have a high level of confidence in this estimate. For example, say you are conducting a survey aimed at determining citizens' opinions about a new zoning ordinance. If you come within 5 percentage points of the true percentage of those who feel a certain way (favor or oppose) and are 95% confident of this result, you will probably be satisfied. On the other hand, if you were conducting a survey just before a major election, you would want to be more precise, perhaps getting within 3% of the true proportion of the population who favor a particular candidate. This concept is called the margin of error.

How well a sample represents a population is gauged by both the margin of error and the level of confidence. For example, a public opinion survey question may have a margin of error of 3% at a 95% confidence level. This means that if the survey were conducted 100 times, the true percentage would be within 3 percentage points of the sample percentage in about 95 of the 100 surveys. If you find in a random sample that 50% of the residents of a city favor a bond measure and your confidence level is 95% with a margin of error of 3%, you're saying that you're 95% confident that the true percentage of the population who favor the bond measure is between 47% and 53%. The margin of error is related to sample size (the number of respondents) and is commonly reported at one of two levels of confidence: the 99% level is the most conservative, while the 95% level is the most frequently used.

Keep in mind that the margin of error tells you only about sampling error and is meaningful only if you are using a probability sample. It does not take into account other potential sources of error, such as coverage error, nonresponse error, and bias in the question wording.

## Sample Size

As sample size increases, margin of error decreases for a particular level of confidence. Table 3.2 provides the sample sizes necessary to guarantee a particular margin of error for a given degree of confidence when using data from a simple random sample to estimate a population proportion (or percentage). At the 95% confidence level, a sample size of 384 will guarantee a maximum 5% margin of error when estimating a proportion; when the sample size is increased to 600, the margin of error will be no greater than 4%, and when it is increased to 1,067, the margin of error will be no greater than 3%.

**Table 3.2 Sample Sizes for Estimating a Population Proportion With Various Levels of Confidence and Margins of Error**

| Margin of Error | 90% Confidence Level | 95% Confidence Level | 99% Confidence Level |
|---|---|---|---|
| ± 5% | 272 | 384 | 666 |
| ± 4% | 425 | 600 | 1,040 |
| ± 3% | 756 | 1,067 | 1,849 |
| ± 2% | 1,702 | 2,401 | 4,160 |
| ± 1% | 6,806 | 9,604 | 16,641 |

NOTE: Assumes a simple random sample.

Although continuing to increase the sample size yields lower margins of error, there are diminishing returns. You would have to select a sample of more than 9,000 individuals to report findings at the 95% confidence level with 1% margin of error.

Table 3.2 serves as a guideline for determining the sample size you will need for the particular amount of sampling error you are willing to tolerate when estimating a population proportion with the sample statistic obtained from a simple random sample. It is important to note that if your analysis plan includes evaluating subgroups of the sample (e.g., different age groups or ethnicities), a larger sample may be necessary because the margin of error for each subgroup is determined by the number of respondents in that group.

## Nonprobability Sampling

Nonprobability samples do not employ random selection procedures and, thus, may or may not represent the population well. This is why most statistical texts advise against using nonprobability techniques or suggest they be reserved for exploratory research. While this advice is theoretically sound, in online and mobile survey research, it is often impractical. Hence, we present three nonprobability strategies that can be used for online and mobile surveys: convenience sampling, volunteer opt-in panels, and snowball sampling. The appropriateness of the chosen sampling method should be evaluated in light of the research objectives.

In all cases, researchers using nonprobability sampling should refrain from making inferences about population characteristics based on sample data.

## Convenience Sampling

Convenience sampling is a nonsystematic approach to recruiting respondents that allows potential participants to self-select into the sample. There are neither restrictions to participation nor controls over multiple submissions by a single respondent. The questionnaire is posted on the website for anyone to fill out. Examples of this sampling strategy can be found on news websites that conduct "question of the day" polls. Also, a growing number of websites are dedicated to hosting web polls (e.g., www.survey .net, www.misterpoll.com). Another convenience sampling strategy involves posting survey invitations on online community bulletin boards, discussion forums, chat rooms, and social networking websites. It should be noted that many members of online communities find this practice inappropriate, offensive, and a violation of their privacy.

Convenience sampling requires less time and effort than generating probability samples; however, statistical inference is problematic. Respondents who self-select into web polls are not representative of any underlying population; they tend to be individuals who have a particular interest in the survey topic. Online polls employing convenience samples should not be presented as legitimate scientific research.

## Volunteer Opt-In Panels

The volunteer panel relies on assembling a group of individuals who have volunteered to participate in future surveys. Individuals are recruited via some form of advertising (usually web based), and demographic information is collected when participants register. Panel members are selected (by convenience or quota sampling) to receive a questionnaire, and steps are taken to ensure that participants respond only once. Two well-known examples of organizations using volunteer opt-in panels are the Harris Poll Online (www.harrispollonline.com) and Greenfield Online (www.greenfield.com). Both organizations point to their large and geographically dispersed panels as major benefits and claim that with the proper statistical corrections, their samples accurately represent various populations of interest.

The volunteer opt-in panel should not be confused with the prerecruited panel. Members of the volunteer opt-in panel respond to advertisements and sign up to participate in the panel. Participants in prerecruited panels are randomly selected from the online and offline populations and invited to join the panel; individuals who were not randomly selected are not permitted to volunteer for the panel.

To use a volunteer opt-in panel, researchers may post an ad on a website inviting volunteers to participate or use a commercial service that "sells" samples of volunteer respondents.

## Snowball Sampling

The snowball sample begins by identifying one participant who meets your inclusion criteria. This first individual is asked to refer someone else for the survey; then, you ask this second individual to refer someone else, and so on. This method is commonly used when dealing with hard-to-reach populations, such as citizens who may be reluctant to participate in surveys. Snowball sampling works best with small populations in which the members know one another. While hardly representative of any general population, snowball sampling can be a good way to select members of specifically defined, highly targeted populations.

## Sample Size for Nonprobability Samples

One of the most common questions associated with any type of survey sampling is how many elements of the population should be sampled. Statistical theory provides us with specific procedures for estimating the number of respondents necessary to make population inferences with various levels of confidence when we employ probability samples. As we have seen, these formulas are based on the particular probability sampling procedure used and the amount of sampling error we're willing to tolerate (Table 3.2 is the result of employing such a formula for simple random samples). No formulas for statistical inference exist for estimating sample size when using nonprobability samples. This is because, in a nonprobability sample, it is impossible to know the likelihood of any particular participant selected for the sample; therefore, there is no estimate of the variability in the underlying population—essential information for the calculation of a suitable sample size.

Some of the answers that have been proffered in response to the question of how large a nonprobability sample should be include "large enough," "as big as your budget will allow," and "as large as it can be given your time frame." These answers are unsatisfying and offer little guidance to investigators involved in applied research. In an attempt to offer more concrete guidelines, survey methodologists grappling with this issue have suggested the following rules of thumb, which may be useful for researchers engaged in online research with nonprobability samples (Alreck & Settle, 1995; Hill, 1998):

- Sample sizes of fewer than 30 or more than 500 can seldom be justified.
- Within the limits of 30 to 500, select a sample of about 10% of the parent population.
- When samples are to be broken into subsamples, the rules of thumb for sample sizes should apply to the subsamples.
- In multivariate research, sample size should be at least 10 times larger than the number of variables being studied.
- Generally, larger samples are better than smaller ones; select the largest sample you can afford.

Although it is not specifically related to online survey research, Martin and Bateson (1986) suggested a method for checking the adequacy of one's sample that may be useful for Internet surveys: the split-half analysis for consistency. The procedure involves randomly dividing the sample into two halves and analyzing them separately. If the two sets of data are consistent, then you've collected enough data; if the conclusions differ, more data are needed.

Survey results based on data collected from nonprobability samples do not contain estimates of margins of error. Because convenience or volunteer samples have no known mathematical properties that would allow for the computation of sampling error, including statements about the margin of error would be misleading. Readers may infer that margin of error can be interpreted as in a probability sample survey. The American Association for Public Opinion Research suggests the following wording in reports when respondents are selected using a nonprobability method:

> Respondents for this survey were selected from among those who volunteered/ opted in/registered to participate, etc. The data have been/have not been weighted to represent the demographic composition of the target population. Because the sample is based on those who self-selected for participation rather than a probability sample, no estimates of sampling error can be calculated.

Sampling for online and mobile surveys can be a thorny task. Time and budget constraints typically lead researchers to settle for smaller samples than originally desired, and technical restrictions often prohibit the selection of the preferred simple random sample. This limits the generalizability of the research findings and may call the **reliability** of the data into question. Should survey researchers limited to the use of nonprobability samples just give up? In response to this query, Hill (1998) noted that it is better to have collected some data and gained some insight than to have collected no data and gained no information. We agree but hasten to add that researchers should exercise caution when making inferences about populations when results are based on nonprobability samples of any size.

## Sources of Error in Online Surveys

### Coverage Error

Coverage error occurs when the sampling frame does not completely represent the population of interest. It is a function of the proportion of the population not covered by the sampling frame and the difference between the characteristics of those individuals included and not included in the sampling frame.

Estimates of household access to the Internet vary greatly. Household Internet penetration is growing rapidly, but the online population still differs from the general population in many ways, and subgroups in the population vary widely in Internet access (see Chapter 2 for a breakdown of Internet use in the United States). However, in some segments of the population, connectivity is almost universal. Many universities, for example, routinely assign all students and faculty e-mail addresses, and employees in many sectors of the workforce have constant Internet access and can be found listed in company directories. In these situations, coverage error poses less of a problem than when attempting to employ novel or emerging technology to collect data.

Conducting surveys via short message service (SMS) or applications designed for smart mobile phones is fast becoming a preferred method for reaching potential respondents to collect immediate feedback (a discussion of deploying mobile phone surveys can be found in Chapter 6). The technique has many benefits and some limitations. One of the notable drawbacks concerns coverage error. Effective mobile surveys require high mobile phone coverage among the target respondents. This statement may seem obvious; however, many researchers contemplating cell phone surveys fail to consider that owning a mobile device is a necessary but not sufficient condition for survey participation. In addition to owning a mobile phone, potential respondents must use the phone on a regular basis, be familiar with the functions of their phones, and have the technical expertise to respond to a survey on their phones. When evaluating the coverage error associated with a cell phone target population, it is important to consider regular *use*, not ownership of cell phones.

## Nonresponse Error

Whereas coverage error exists when members of the population have no chance of being included in the sample, nonresponse error is a function of selected respondents choosing not to participate in the survey. The error can take two forms: unit nonresponse, when the respondent does not participate in the survey at all, and item nonresponse, when the respondent skips particular questions on the questionnaire. Unit nonresponse is calculated by dividing the number of individuals who fail to respond by the total number of potential participants invited to complete the survey. To determine nonresponse (or response rate), the denominator (those eligible to participate) must be known. Note that potential participants are those who actually received the research invitation. Bounced e-mails and bad mobile phone numbers should be subtracted from the total before response rate is computed.

Item nonresponse can be evaluated by conducting item analyses of all survey questions. The descriptive statistics associated with each question should be analyzed, with particular attention paid to the number of missing cases on each item. If you find that a large number of respondents skipped a particular question, then that question should be reviewed for clarity and proper functioning (i.e., a possible software error).

Nonresponse is a problem to the extent that those who choose not to participate are systematically different from those who choose to complete the survey. If the decision to participate (or not) were random, then nonresponse would not be an issue. The research literature surrounding nonresponse in Internet surveys is not as well developed as for mail and telephone surveys. In telephone surveys, for example, the literature tells us that socioeconomic status, suspicion about telemarketing calls, and interviewer skill are important factors influencing participation. Knowing this, we can employ strategies to compensate for nonresponse in those settings.

The emerging body of knowledge about nonresponse in Internet surveys is currently centered on response rates in e-mail surveys. Couper (2000) outlined three sets of explanations for the low response rates in Internet surveys: (a) the motivation tools used in mail or phone surveys cannot be used the same way in online surveys, and analogous instruments have not yet been developed; (b) technical difficulties may prevent some respondents from starting to answer questionnaires or cause them to abandon the survey halfway; and (c) concerns about the confidentiality of e-mail responses discourage some prospective participants.

While the field of research surrounding nonresponse in online surveys matures, we can use the existing literature as a basis for suggesting some techniques for improving the response rate in online surveys (see Chapter 6 for more on this topic):

- Include appeals to respondents' self-interest in survey invitations. Point out how they can "make a difference" by taking part in the survey. If appropriate, you also might note that important decisions will be made based on the survey data.
- Keep questionnaires as simple as possible so they load quickly and without error on web browsers.
- Remind respondents that their answers will be kept confidential. This is especially important in e-mail surveys, where anonymity may be lost.

## Sampling Error

Sampling error occurs when statistical estimates are made based on sample data rather than population data. The particular sample selected for a survey is only one of a number of possible samples that could have been selected. The estimates (e.g., **means** or proportions) from each sample can, therefore, vary from sample to sample just due to chance. When using a probability sample, chance variability in sample estimates can be measured by standard errors of estimates associated with a particular survey.

So why sample from populations? As we noted earlier in this chapter, the effort required to invite all members of a closed population to participate in an online survey is minimal. For example, if you invited all 12,000 students at a university to take part in a survey, then you would have no sampling error—assuming you were not using these data to make inferences about students at other universities. Of course, you would still have to contend with nonresponse error. A problem is that if you plan to conduct multiple surveys with the same population, you will quickly burn out your respondents. Sampling allows you to repeatedly survey the same population without continually contacting the same individuals.

## Summary

In this chapter, we have reviewed some of the basic concepts relevant to online survey sampling, discussed a variety of probability and nonprobability techniques for selecting a sample, and presented the sources of error associated with sampling. The preferred probability sampling methods afford researchers the ability to estimate population parameters, assign margins of error, and employ standard statistical techniques. The less ideal, but more commonly used, nonprobability sampling methods available to online survey researchers provide no such luxuries. Prerecruited panels offer researchers statistical power and flexibility but are practical only for large organizations that engage in ongoing survey research.

Survey sampling is complex, and we presented an admittedly superficial treatment of the topic with the goal of addressing the main concerns so online survey researchers will have enough information to start their projects. Readers interested in a more complete treatment should consult one of the many excellent books on sampling—for example, Scheaffer, Mendenhall, and Ott (2006); Levy and Lemeshow (1999); or the classic text by Kish (reprinted in 1995).

## Exercises

1. For the following situations, describe the inclusion and exclusion criteria you would use to target potential respondents:

   a. an e-mail survey of Medicare beneficiaries covered by a large health maintenance organization.
   b. a mobile (SMS) survey of college freshmen at the end of orientation week.
   c. a website satisfaction survey presented at the conclusion of every 10th successful purchase at an online lamp store.

2. Describe the differences among coverage error, nonresponse error, and sampling error.

3. A mayoral candidate wants to conduct a public opinion poll to determine how many of the city's residents intend to vote for her. She wants to be 95% confident in the estimate with a margin of error of ±5%. Assume that selecting a simple random sample of registered voters for the poll will be possible. How many responses are necessary to meet the requirements of the estimate?

4. Imagine that you wish to survey physicians about the impact electronic medical records have had on how they care for their patients. Assume that the American Medical Association has given you a list of 600,000 physicians in your region of the country. The list contains the physicians' names, specialties, e-mail addresses, and cell phone numbers. Suggest an online survey technique for this project and describe how you would select a stratified random sample based on physician specialty.

# CHAPTER 4

# Writing Survey Questions

A survey question is a measurement tool, a way for researchers to discover a respondent's opinion, knowledge, and behavior. Properly constructed questions are essential to any survey, and all good survey questions share some common characteristics. The best questionnaire items are short, unambiguous, and meaningful to the respondent. Poorly written questions—those that are lengthy or **double-barreled**, for instance—confuse and frustrate participants, often resulting in increased nonresponse and survey abandonment. In this chapter, we cover the basics of writing effective survey questions. We start with some general considerations and a discussion about creating valid questions. We then discuss the distinction between **open-ended** and **closed-ended questions**; the types of closed-ended questions; the level of measurement; and the writing of questions to collect factual, demographic, and attitude data.

## General Considerations

Every question you ask should be related to the survey's objectives. As you write each question, refer to your survey plan to confirm that the question does indeed address one or more of your research objectives. If you find you have written a question that is not obviously related to one of your objectives, ask yourself what you intend to do with the data collected from the question. This is the time to revisit your survey plan and either revise your objectives or delete the question. Resist the urge to add questions simply because you are conducting the survey anyway. Not only will this needlessly lengthen the questionnaire, but you also risk confusing respondents because your questionnaire will lack coherence.

Questions written for online surveys share features with those created for self-administered paper-and-pencil questionnaires. In both formats, respondents complete the survey in their environment, at their own pace, and without the help (or hindrance) of the researcher. If you have written questions for other self-administered questionnaires, many of the guidelines for online survey questions will be familiar to you. For example, questions must be self-explanatory, easy to understand and answer, free of jargon, and visually appealing. Digital surveys have the added capacity to include graphics and audio and video content, greatly increasing the type and format of data that can be collected. The most important distinction between online surveys and other self-administered questionnaires is the ability to effectively ask contingency questions—that is, to automatically skip questions that are irrelevant to some respondents. Electronic surveys can easily be programmed so that, for example, men and women are asked different sets of questions. We will discuss contingency questions shortly, but first, we address some foundational issues surrounding measurement.

## Validity of Measurement

Survey questions are valid to the extent that they measure the underlying concepts being investigated. A questionnaire item is not valid or invalid per se; the **validity** of a measure can be evaluated only by examining the connection between the question and the attitude, behavior, or fact it purports to measure. Put simply, valid questions measure what they are supposed to measure. For example, if you wanted to know about respondents' magazine-reading habits, asking how many magazine subscriptions they have would not make sense. Purchasing a magazine subscription is not a valid indicator of magazine *reading*. Many people purchase magazines and never read them, while others read magazines without ever paying for them. It would be more valid to ask directly about the amount of time spent reading magazines. Validity refers to the link between individual questions and the concepts they seek to measure, as well as to how groups of questions combine to measure multidimensional concepts.

### Respondent-Centered Threats to Validity

Research participants may provide inaccurate information on a survey for several reasons. They may deliberately report misinformation to avoid embarrassment or to fit in with what they believe is the social norm for the situation. They may not have access to the information—for example, when asked about details, which may be difficult to recall. And, finally, respondents may offer opinions on surveys simply because someone is asking them for an opinion, not because they really have one.

### Social Desirability

Social desirability and political correctness can often lead respondents to give the "right" answer rather than the real or valid answer to a survey question. The desire to conform to social norms can be powerful. This is why more people say they vote, go to museums, exercise regularly, do volunteer work, and give money to charities than is actually the case. Social desirability bias is more of a problem in interview surveys than in self-administered formats. People generally give more honest answers when faced with a computer screen than when faced with an interviewer (even if the interview is over the telephone). This is not to suggest, however, that electronic surveys are immune from the problems created by individuals' desire to be viewed in a positive light. It is, therefore, useful to review some techniques for reducing social desirability bias.

### Ways to Reduce Social Desirability Bias

- Repeat the promise of anonymity and confidentiality (that is, if it was promised in the first place).

---

*Example 4.1*

"Remember, all your responses are anonymous and will be kept confidential."

---

- Employ face-saving strategies, such as giving respondents permission to behave in socially unacceptable ways.

---

*Example 4.2*

"Everyone gets angry now and then. How many times last week did you find yourself getting angry?"

---

- State that the behavior you are asking about is not unusual.

---

*Example 4.3*

"A recent study found that 80% of college students have cheated on an exam. Have you ever cheated on an exam?"

---

### Inaccurate Estimates

When survey respondents provide information about past behavior or events, they are almost always reporting an estimate rather than a precise value. For example, if asked how many hours of television they watch per day, most people would have to guess. The key to valid measurement of factual information is to ask respondents focused questions covering a limited range of time and situations. Participants may provide inaccurate estimates for several reasons: for example, they may not understand the parameters of the question, they may not be qualified to answer the question, or the question may ask about distant behaviors or events that are no longer salient.

### Ways to Improve Accuracy of Estimates

- Ask about specific behavior within a limited, recent time period.

---

**Example 4.4**

*Poor:* "How many miles have you driven since you received your driver's license?"

*Better:* "How many miles did you drive last week?"

---

- Ask respondents about their own behavior, not the behavior of others.

---

**Example 4.5**

*Poor:* "What is your wife's favorite sport to watch on TV?"

*Better:* "What is your favorite sport to watch on TV?"

---

**Example 4.6**

*Poor:* "What is your annual household income?"

*Better:* "To the nearest $1,000, what is your annual income?"

---

- Ask respondents to think about a specific event rather than a category of events.

---

**Example 4.7**

*Poor:* "In an average week, how much do you spend on groceries?"

*Better:* "How much did you spend on groceries last week?"

---

### Nonattitudes

Not every issue that is important to you will be important to the participants in your survey. You should ask yourself, "Is this topic one about which respondents have genuine opinions?" Several factors may account for why respondents sometimes answer opinion questions when, in fact, they have no opinion about the issue. First, few people want to admit to being uninformed; second, they would like to be viewed positively (i.e., social desirability bias); and finally, respondents may feel the need to "help" the researcher by completing all the questionnaire items.

- Make it socially acceptable for respondents to say they are unfamiliar with the topic.

---

**Example 4.8**

"Some people are interested in politics and some are not . . . would you say you are interested in national politics?"

---

- Use screening or filter questions.

---

**Example 4.9**

"Are you familiar with Proposition 101?"

"Do you have an opinion about Proposition 101?"

"Have you thought much about Proposition 101?"

---

- Provide an explicit "no opinion" choice as a response option.

---

**Example 4.10**

"Should slot machines be allowed in card rooms?"

O Strongly agree   O Agree   O No opinion   O Disagree   O Strongly disagree

---

## Question Format and Wording

We have seen that the validity of a questionnaire response may be compromised in three ways: (a) if respondents feel pressure to respond in socially desirable ways, (b) if respondents do not know or cannot accurately estimate the information requested, and (c) if respondents do not have opinions on topics about which they are asked. Validity, and the related concept of reliability or consistency of measurement, also can be threatened when the wording of survey questions is faulty or when questions contain inadequate or inappropriate response options. We will now proceed with a discussion of the two main categories of survey questions, open-ended and closed-ended, paying particular attention to techniques for writing questions that will elicit valid and reliable responses.

## Question Formats

### Open-Ended Questions

Open-ended questions are those for which response options are not provided. These questions allow participants to answer in their own words by typing their response in an empty text box (see Figure 4.1). They are particularly useful when investigating new topics and offer an opportunity to learn unexpected information. Conventional wisdom dictates that open-ended questions should be used sparingly in interview surveys and not at all on self-administered questionnaires. The reasoning is that respondents are turned off by the difficulty of recalling and articulating information and will usually skip open-ended items when they can.

It is reasonable to assume that the same advice would hold for online surveys; after all, it is easier to click with a mouse than to type in a response. Research on Internet and mobile surveys provides important insight into respondent behavior with respect to open-ended questions. In a comparison of surveys distributed by e-mail and postal mail, results regarding the answers to open-ended questions in web and e-mail surveys are mixed. Denscombe (2007) found that, although the online answers to three of the four questions in the study tended to be slightly longer than those from the paper version, the differences were not statistically significant. Aoki and Elasmar (2000), on the other hand, showed that a web survey resulted in significantly fewer answers to open-ended questions compared with a mail survey.

**Figure 4.1   Open-Ended Question Example**

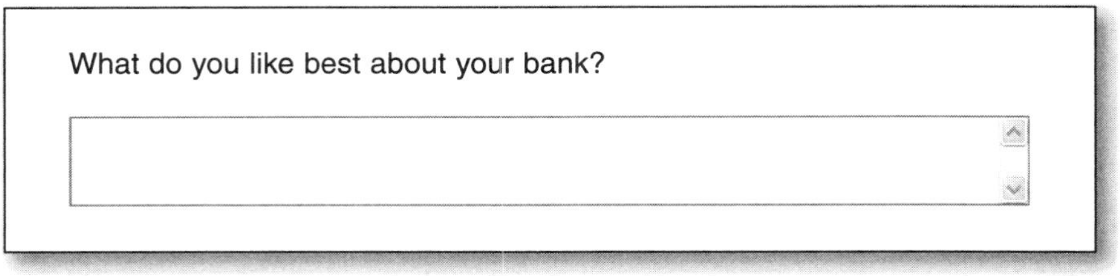

What do you like best about your bank?

Small keyboards on mobile devices lessen the likelihood that respondents will provide lengthy open-ended feedback. Peytchev and Hill (2010) found that, because text input can be difficult, some respondents in mobile surveys select options specifically to avoid typing. Couper, Traugott, and Lamias (2001) found that, although item nonresponse was indeed higher for questions with open text boxes than for those with a list of options, the responses provided for open-ended questions tended to have a high degree of validity. Reja, Lozar Manfreda, Hlebec, and Vehovar (2003) also discovered that open-ended questions yielded less data than the same questions asked in a closed-ended format; however, the open-ended questions produced a more diverse set of answers.

Greater length and variety of answers to open-ended questions do not necessarily indicate that the answers are better than those collected via closed-ended questions. These findings do suggest, however, that the information obtained from open-ended questions on Internet surveys is similar in terms of validity to that yielded by other survey methods. Open-ended questions tend to result in more valid responses than closed-ended questions because respondents are not forced to select from a list of response options created by the researcher.

Although information about the usefulness of open-ended questions on electronic surveys is still emerging, we can make some general recommendations. Use open-ended questions when

1. exploring new or unfamiliar topics;

2. the list of response options is lengthy—that is, if it would take longer to read the list than to type in a response; and

3. the question elicits short answers—that is, a few words, a phrase, or a brief sentence.

---

*Example 4.11: Open-Ended Questions*

- "What is the one bit of advice you would give to new members joining our organization?"
- "What would you say is the main reason you voted for Brown?"
- "If you could change one thing about your job, what would it be?"
- "Please list three words that you think describe our company."

---

Despite the potential to collect valid and detailed information with open-ended questions, researchers are sometimes reticent to include them on surveys because they require additional data handling before analysis can commence.

The process is essentially a content analysis of the open-ended responses. Example 4.12 displays a portion of output showing responses to an open-ended question from an online voting survey.

---

*Example 4.12*

**Why did you vote for Pam Jones?**

1. Because she's a woman.

2. I like her positions on the issues and think she'll do the best job for our city; I especially like that she's an outsider and doesn't have ties to the corrupt members of the current council.

3. Don't know . . . she just seems like a nice lady.

4. I met her at a community open house and liked the way she presented herself. She answered questions honestly and wasn't afraid to say that she didn't know the answers to some of the questions people asked her. She stands for the values I stand for, and I think she'll be a good city council member.

5. Best of the bunch.

6. Because of her position on the development of the Lakeview area.

7. She's a working mom, and I can relate to that.

8. Her position on the issues, plus her personal qualities—such as that she's smart and honest.

9. Her campaign platform.

10. She has good plans for our city, including her ideas about the Lakeview district; her positions on the other issues that are important in my neighborhood; her integrity and family values.

---

The researcher would look at a sample of the responses and perhaps devise coding categories for the reasons for voting: (a) issue positions, (b) personal qualities, (c) plans for the city, and so on. Coders would then read through each of the open-ended responses and decide into which category to place the individual responses. The procedure typically involves two coders so that a measure of intercoder reliability (i.e., agreement between the two coders) can be computed. Clearly, this additional work requires time and resources and does not lend itself to fast turnaround of survey results. The benefit is that the coding categories are created based on participants' responses rather than being created a priori based on the researcher's decisions, thus increasing the validity of the data.

For large data sets, hand coding of open-ended responses is prohibitively expensive and time-consuming. Text-mining software applications can hasten the process. The procedure is similar for most of the programs: Raw data from the web survey tool must be downloaded and then imported into the text-mining software. The software searches the survey responses and counts unique words and/or phrases that appear in the text. Variations of the same word (e.g., plurals, different tenses, prefixes, and suffixes) are combined into a single root word. The result is a list of root words and the number of respondents who used each one. The researcher then reviews the list and makes decisions about which words are "important." Those key terms are then carried forward into the second stage of the analysis, where the actual open-ended responses are reviewed by the researcher; he or she can choose to accept the code category suggested by the software, select another category from a list, or create a new category. Some text-mining software offers sentiment coding, which helps researchers categorize open-ended responses into positive, neutral, and negative categories.

Verbastat is one program that is fully compatible with some web survey development tools, such as SurveyCrafter and mrInterview. It is used by market research companies that routinely analyze a large volume of open-ended survey questions. Verbatim Blaster is an option included with STATPAC's basic statistics package and is a natural choice for researchers who are already using STATPAC's online survey development software. Clarabridge is a stand-alone package that can be used for coding survey comments as well as blog and social media content. Some web survey hosts, such as SurveyMonkey, offer a premium package that includes coding of verbatim text. The result of text mining is usually displayed in a word cloud; the size of each word indicates its relative rank in terms of how many times it appeared in the responses. Figure 4.2 shows the responses to the open-ended question, "What

Figure 4.2   Word Cloud Example

Showing **19** Most Important Words and Phrases

Able Advertising Aspects Classmates Communication Doing Everyday Life Giving Goals Internship Learning Oral Presentations Peers Pioneer Portfolio Public Speaking Relationships with Professors Rewarding Variety Writing experiences in your education were most rewarding?" From this illustration, it is clear that *communication* was the most frequently mentioned term.

Although programs such as these, and other text-mining software, reduce the time it takes to process open-ended responses by initially searching text and creating coding categories, a substantial amount of human labor is still involved in verifying the coding categories and reviewing the individual responses.

## Closed-Ended Questions

Closed-ended questions provide respondents with a list of response options from which to choose. These questions typically make up the bulk of online questionnaires because they are easy to answer, are familiar to most respondents, and provide reliable measurement. The list of response options for closed-ended questions must be exhaustive—that is, cover all possible response options. Additionally, the items on the list should be mutually exclusive; a respondent should not be able to select more than one category at a time. Formats for closed-ended questions include dichotomous, multiple choice, rankings, and rating scales.

### Dichotomous Questions

Dichotomous questions are those that present two possible response options—for example, yes/no, male/female, or true/false.

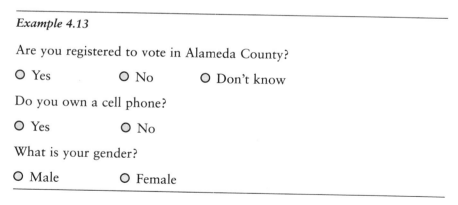

*Example 4.13*

Are you registered to vote in Alameda County?

O Yes          O No          O Don't know

Do you own a cell phone?

O Yes          O No

What is your gender?

O Male          O Female

Even though the first question in Example 4.13 contains the "don't know" option, it is considered a dichotomous question. Note that the second and third questions in the example do not offer "don't know" as a choice. There are different schools of thought with respect to providing the "don't know" option on survey questionnaires. Some researchers choose not to include it, as they believe it offers some respondents an easy way to avoid thinking about and answering the question. Others include the "don't know" option, claiming that it provides valid data because some respondents really may not know the answer.

As a rule of thumb, if it is reasonable to expect that respondents may not have the answer to a question—for example, on knowledge-based items— then include "don't know" as an option. If it seems, however, that most respondents should know the answer—as in the cell phone question above— then it is generally safe to omit "don't know" as an option.

### Multiple-Choice Questions

Multiple-choice questions are a popular option for many surveys because they are easy to answer and quick to analyze. Pay particular attention to response options to ensure that your list covers all possible answers. A question such as, "Do you use regular or premium gas in your car?" does not cover all possible answers. The question ignores the possibility of diesel or electric-powered cars. A better way of asking this question is shown in Example 4.14.

---

*Example 4.14*

Which type of fuel do you use in your primary vehicle?

- ○ Regular gasoline
- ○ Premium gasoline
- ○ Diesel fuel
- ○ Other [_____]

---

If you want only one answer from each person, be sure that the options are mutually exclusive (see Example 4.15).

---

*Example 4.15*

**What is your current employment status?**

- ○ Employed full-time
- ○ Employed part-time
- ○ Unemployed
- ○ Full-time student

---

This question does not take into account the fact that the respondent currently may be a student and employed part- or full-time. There are two solutions: instruct respondents to "check all that apply," or rewrite the item as two questions (see the following examples).

---

*Example 4.16a*

**What is your current employment status?**

O  Employed full-time

O  Employed part-time

O  Unemployed

*Example 4.16b*

**What is your current student status?**

O  Full-time student

O  Part-time student

O  Not a student

---

Research evidence indicates that forcing respondents to choose one answer from a list is preferable to the "check all that apply" format for online surveys (Dillman, Smyth, Christian, & Stern, 2002; Smyth, Dillman, Christian, & Stern, 2006). In experimental studies, respondents took longer to answer forced-choice questions than check-all questions, suggesting a deeper processing level of the response options. The check-all-that-apply option can be especially problematic when asking respondents to report their preferences for new products or new features for an existing product, for example. Participants tend to select all options that seem interesting, even if only mildly appealing. This creates challenges in data interpretation and can make delivering recommendations difficult, as it might appear that all the suggested new products are of interest to the participants. In this type of situation, using a series of forced-choice or ranking questions is preferable.

As with the "don't know" choice discussed earlier, offering a "no opinion" option for multiple-choice questions is controversial. Krosnick et al. (2002) found that offering the "no opinion" option may actually discourage some respondents who have true opinions from sharing them. In their research, they found the selection of the "no opinion" option to be greatest among respondents lowest in cognitive skills, among respondents answering secretly instead of orally, for questions asked later in the survey, and among respondents who devoted little effort to the reporting process. Moreover, the quality of the attitude reports obtained was not compromised by omitting the "no opinion" option. In general, offer the "no opinion" choice when the question is required (i.e., when an answer must be selected before the respondent is permitted to move to the next item) and if the required question may be difficult to answer—for example, asking for specific details about a past encounter.

## Rankings

The online survey is one of the few venues in which ranking questions can be used effectively. Most software packages include standard response validation for ranking questions that will return an error message or simply not allow the same rankings to be assigned to more than one item in a list. Respondents can easily assign rankings based on most- to least-favorite item, for example. To rank more than two or three items, it is important that respondents be able to view the complete list. The following is an example of a ranking question using a matrix for responses.

---

*Example 4.17*

**Please rank what you look for in order of importance when selecting cleaning products, one is least important and five is most important. Each rank should be used only once.**

|            | 1 | 2 | 3 | 4 | 5 |
|------------|---|---|---|---|---|
| Quality    | O | O | O | O | O |
| Cost       | O | O | O | O | O |
| Quantity   | O | O | O | O | O |
| Brand name | O | O | O | O | O |
| Familiarity| O | O | O | O | O |

---

## Rating Scales

A rating scale offers respondents the opportunity to select a response from among several possibilities arranged in hierarchical order. Selecting a scale for a survey question is not a trivial decision. Methodological research is equivocal when it comes to factors such as how many points and what kinds of labels make the most effective scale questions. Nevertheless, we provide some general guidelines for writing scale questions.

*Even or odd:* Even-numbered scales tend to more effectively discriminate between the positive and negative positions, as there is no neutral option. However, this can sometimes cause respondents who are genuinely neutral to hesitate and perhaps skip the question altogether. The use of this type of scale without a midpoint also has been shown to result in a positive skew in the data. The reasoning is that when forced to choose a side, most people opt to be "nice" and select the positive side of the scale. If a respondent is truly neutral on a topic, then forcing him or her to any one side will yield invalid data and may alienate the participant.

*Unipolar or bipolar:* A unipolar scale allows respondents to think of the presence or absence of a quality or attribute—for example, not at all satisfied, moderately satisfied, very satisfied, or completely satisfied. In analyses, this might be coded 0, 1, 2, and 3. A bipolar scale is balanced between two opposite points—for instance, completely dissatisfied, dissatisfied, somewhat dissatisfied, somewhat satisfied, satisfied, or completely satisfied. This scale would be coded −3, −2, −1, 1, 2, and 3. Which type of scale should you use? It depends. In general, unipolar scales are easier for respondents than bipolar scales because respondents do not have to mentally balance opposite extremes. They also tend to be easier for novice survey researchers, as it is not necessary to ensure that the two ends of the scale are balanced. If, however, the underlying construct being measured is one where attitudes can fall on one side or the other of a midpoint that represents neutrality, then a bipolar scale is required.

*Number of points:* A 3-point scale occupies less visual space on a questionnaire than, say, a 5- or 7-point scale and is less daunting for respondents. For example, you might provide the following options: low, medium, high; or satisfied, neither satisfied nor dissatisfied, dissatisfied. Limiting options on a scale also makes for simplified data reporting. On the other hand, providing only three response options will limit the analysis possibilities and may not discriminate well among respondents' opinions.

Many market researchers use 10- or 11-point scales (e.g., 1 to 10 or 0 to 10) because they feel the greater granularity is necessary for understanding concepts such as customer satisfaction. The rationale is that this type of scale makes intuitive sense to respondents and that the greater range helps avoid the ceiling effect because few participants will select 10. Although 10- or 11-point scales may seem to gather more data than 5-point scales, they do not necessarily discriminate more accurately among respondents. Also, in data analysis, these longer scales are typically collapsed into 3- or 5-point scales.

The debate in the literature is ongoing; however, it is safe to say that 4- or 5-point scales will be serviceable for most attitude or opinion data collection. Choose a 5-point scale if you are measuring a unipolar construct and a 7-point scale for bipolar constructs.

*Scale labels:* Once the number of points on a scale has been decided, you will next need to determine the labels for each scale point or, in some cases, whether or not you will use any labels. Some researchers prefer to anchor the end points—that is, only the first and last scale points are defined with words. Researchers using this approach argue that it prevents respondents from having to make decisions about the differences among word labels for each scale point. Though this may be true, it is also important that each respondent understands the meaning of each scale point. By labeling each scale point, respondents attach the same word or phrase to a particular place on the scale. This helps avoid respondent misinterpretation of scale definitions. Furthermore, fully labeled scales have been shown to be more reliable than numeric scales and easier for respondents with low to moderate education (Krosnick & Fabrigar, 1997). Example 4.18 illustrates the labeling options.

---

*Example 4.18*

How satisfied were you with your last office visit?

| Not at all satisfied | ○ | ○ | ○ | ○ | ○ | Extremely satisfied |

How satisfied were you with your last office visit?

| Not at all satisfied | 1 ○ | 2 ○ | 3 ○ | 4 ○ | 5 ○ | Extremely satisfied |

How satisfied were you with your last office visit?

○ 1      ○ 2      ○ 3      ○ 4      ○ 5

How satisfied were you with your last office visit?

| Not at all satisfied | Slightly satisfied | Moderately satisfied | Very satisfied | Extremely satisfied |
| ○ | ○ | ○ | ○ | ○ |

---

Whether you decide to define all your scale points or only some, the labels attached can affect the validity of your results. Example 4.19 shows a typical product-rating question. The scale ranges from "excellent" to "poor." These words have connotative meanings for respondents—for example, they may associate the labels with grades in school. One individual may regard "good" as a high mark, whereas another might choose "good" to indicate an inadequate product—as in "it was only good." It is important to pretest questions on a small sample of your target population to ensure that respondents understand the scale labels (and the questions) the way you intend them to be understood.

---

*Example 4.19: Product-Rating Scale*

How would you rate this product?

O Excellent     O Very Good     O Good     O Fair     O Poor

---

Because the labeling of scales is an important consideration, it is best to use standard scales when possible rather than creating a custom rating scale.

**Commonly Used Standard Scales**

- Strongly disagree, Disagree, Somewhat disagree, Neither agree nor disagree, Somewhat agree, Agree, Strongly agree
- Not at all aware, Slightly aware, Moderately aware, Very aware, Extremely aware
- Never, Rarely, Sometimes, Often, Always
- Not at all important, Slightly important, Moderately important, Very important, Extremely important
- Not at all likely, Slightly likely, Moderately likely, Very likely, Completely likely
- Very poor, Poor, Fair, Good, Excellent
- Completely dissatisfied, Mostly dissatisfied, Somewhat dissatisfied, Neither satisfied nor dissatisfied, Somewhat satisfied, Mostly satisfied, Completely satisfied (bipolar)
- Not at all satisfied, Slightly satisfied, Moderately satisfied, Very satisfied, Completely satisfied (unipolar)

If a standard scale does not meet your needs and you decide to develop a scale with custom labels, you will need to take care that the labels represent equal intervals on the scale. Additionally, if you opt for a bipolar scale, the zero point will be in the middle and the labels for the end points should represent opposite extremes. For a unipolar scale, a common approach is to use a 5-point scale (0 to 4 or 1 to 5) and assign a label to the low end that signifies the absence of the attribute or opinion and a label to the high end indicating extreme sentiment, such as extremely satisfied or totally satisfied.

## Contingency Questions

It is often necessary to ask one question to determine if the respondent is qualified to answer a subsequent question. This situation requires the use of contingency, or skip-logic, questions. For instance, in election polling, it would be useful to ask if a respondent is a U.S. citizen before asking if he or she is registered to vote. A set of contingency questions might include the following:

---

*Example 4.20*

| | | |
|---|---|---|
| Are you a U.S. citizen? | ○ Yes | ○ No |
| Are you registered to vote? | ○ Yes | ○ No |
| Are you planning to vote in Tuesday's election? | ○ Yes | ○ No |

---

This branching could continue further by asking respondents who marked "Yes" if they had decided on a candidate, who the candidate is, why they have chosen this candidate, and so on. Contingency questions are usually discouraged in paper-and-pencil, self-administered questionnaires because respondents tend to become confused by having to skip questions and often follow the wrong branch of the question. When this happens, the researcher is forced to discard the data for that respondent, as they do not follow a logical pattern. Digital questionnaires, however, can be programmed to activate a different set of follow-up questions based on the options selected in previous questions. In other words, the respondents who click "No," indicating they are not registered to vote, will not see the pages asking about voting intention and candidate choice.

Contingency questions can be multilevel—for example, "Do you use a mobile phone?" If yes, "Do you use a smartphone?" If yes, "Do you download apps for your smartphone?" If yes, "What is the last app you remember downloading for your smartphone?" This can go on indefinitely. Contingencies, or skips, can be tied to single-choice, multiple-response, or open-ended questions. The latter may require custom programming of the questionnaire to ensure that follow-up questions are triggered by the appropriate words or phrases.

# Level of Measurement

There are four levels of measurement to consider when writing questions for your survey. To decide which is the most suitable, you will need to evaluate your data analysis and reporting needs (i.e., the level of statistical analysis required) as well as the appropriateness of the topic for the proposed level of measurement.

## Nominal Data

The values associated with nominal variables fall into unordered categories—for example, race/ethnicity, eye color, or occupation. The response options for the race/ethnicity question—White, Hispanic, African American, Asian, and so on—are not associated with any numerical values and are not ordered in any way. Numbers may be associated with nominal response options, but it is important to realize that the numbers are arbitrary— that is, they do not have any inherent meaning. For example, we might assign the number 1 to blue, 2 to green, 3 to orange, 4 to yellow, and 5 to red. We might just as well label yellow 7, red 8, and so on.

## Ordinal Data

Ordinal data can be rank ordered—for example, the outcome of a race: first place, second place, third place, and so on. There is reasoning behind the numbers: They tell us the order in which the contestants finished. However, the distances between the attributes are not equal; the winner may have finished 2 minutes ahead of the second-place contestant, who might have finished only 2 seconds ahead of the person in third place. On a survey, we might code education as follows: 1 = no high school degree, 2 = high school degree, 3 = some college, 4 = college degree, 5 = postgraduate education. Higher numbers mean more education. Rating scales are a frequently used form of ordinal measurement in survey research.

## Interval Data

The numerical values associated with interval data provide an indication of relative position, and the distances between the values are interpretable. Age is an interval variable. If you have one 20-year-old respondent and one 40-year-old respondent, not only do you know that Respondent 2 is older than Respondent 1, you also know that Respondent 2 is twice as old as Respondent 1. Interval data do not have a meaningful zero point. For example, someone cannot be zero inches tall.

## Ratio Data

Ratio measures have all the features of interval measures plus a zero that is meaningful. Weight, the number of customers, and the amount of money spent on an item are examples of variables that can be studied using ratio measurement.

The levels of measurement are hierarchical—that is, the current level includes all the qualities of the one below it plus a new element. Nominal data represent the most basic level of measurement, discriminating among only categories of responses. Ordinal data introduce the ability to rank responses. Interval measures provide meaningful distances between the values, and ratio measures add an absolute zero.

The decisions surrounding level of measurement should be made in light of the data analysis plan. Consider the income question. You might initially collect this information at the ratio level by asking respondents to record their annual income in an open-ended question, providing a high degree of detail that allows for the greatest discrimination among respondents. If necessary, you could later recode the responses into the following ordinal categories: upper, middle, and low. If that was still more detail than you actually needed, you could further recode the answers to reflect the following nominal categories: income/no income. To provide the greatest options in data analysis, you should always collect data at the highest level of measurement possible, because while you can make a ratio variable nominal, you cannot do the opposite.

# Demographic Questions

Demographic questions ask for background information about respondents such as age, gender, education level, and income. The data are typically used to describe the respondents and sometimes to compare the characteristics of the sample with known population characteristics—from census data, for example. Demographic data also are used to segment and compare groups within the sample.

Much of what we have said up to this point can be applied to the writing of demographic questions; however, we devote a separate section to these questions for two reasons: (a) they are ubiquitous on survey questionnaires, and (b) many people consider these items to be sensitive in nature, and unless they are carefully written, respondents may refuse to answer them. The basic questions are as follows:

1. Are you male or female?

2. What is your age?

3. What is the highest level of education you have completed?

4. What is your annual income?

5. What is your total annual household income?

6. What is your current marital status?

7. What is your religious affiliation?

8. What is your race or ethnicity?

9. What is the highest level of education your mother has completed?

10. What is the highest level of education your father has completed?

11. Are you employed outside the home?

12. How many hours per week do you work outside the home?

13. What is your occupation?

The number and form of the demographic questions used on a questionnaire will vary according to the survey objectives and the researcher's discipline. For many purposes, asking about religious affiliation will suffice; however, some researchers may find that this question by itself is not helpful and will choose to follow it with a question about degree of religiosity. Similarly, we use the categories of "male" and "female" as response options for the question of gender. Researchers occupied with more precise distinctions between biological differences and social categories may want to ask two questions: one addressing sex (male or female) and the other aimed at assessing gender (femininity and masculinity). As a general rule, ask only demographic questions that are relevant to your survey objectives. Asking personal questions that seem unrelated to the rest of the questionnaire may make respondents suspicious and likely to abandon the survey. Furthermore, you would be needlessly lengthening your survey.

Place the demographic items near the end of the questionnaire and include a preface or introduction to the section—something like "We'd now like to gather some personal information about you. Remember, all your answers are confidential." An exception to this is if a demographic question, such as gender, is to be used as a filter question at the beginning of the survey.

Consider using closed-ended questions with ranges as response options for age and income. While it is always useful to collect precise data by leaving these questions open-ended, this benefit must be balanced with the sensitive nature of the questions. Many respondents feel uncomfortable typing in an exact number for their age or income, whereas checking a box provides the relative safety of being included in a category. Unless you absolutely need to know someone's exact age or income, provide the response options as follows.

---

*Example 4.21a*

What is your age?

O 18–24

O 25–44

O 45–64

O 65 or older

*Example 4.21b*

What is your annual income?

O Less than $10,000

O $10,000 to $19,999

O $20,000 to $29,999

O $30,000 to $39,999

O $40,000 to $49,999

O $50,000 to $59,999

O $60,000 to $69,999

O $70,000 or more

---

If you do need to know respondents' specific ages, ask for date of birth. Most people are accustomed to including their date of birth on forms and are less anxious about it than typing in their age.

When considering the range of variation of the response options, knowing something about the sample is necessary. Are you surveying computer programmers, college students, or members of a professional association? For each sample, the ranges of age and income will differ. In addition to adhering to the basic rules of providing an exhaustive and mutually exclusive list of answer choices, think about whether the categories will adequately discriminate among respondents. For example, if you questioned corporate attorneys using the income measure above, most—if not all—of the sample likely would choose the $70,000 or more category. While the data would be valid, they would not be particularly useful.

Questions about ethnicity and religion tend to be especially sensitive. You might need several screens to provide a truly exhaustive list of the categories. One option is to use standardized categories. Useful examples of standard demographic items can be found at the websites for the National Opinion Research Center (www.norc.uchicago.edu/index.asp), the Center for Political Studies (www.isr.umich.edu/cps/), and the U.S. Census Bureau (www.census.gov). An alternative is to leave questions about ethnicity and religion open-ended. Of course, you might get a wide range of answers and then need to spend time tabulating and possibly recoding the responses. Standard demographic questions and answer options are included in the list of commonly asked survey questions in Appendix B.

---

### Guidelines for Asking Survey Questions

1. *Provide instructions:* Let the respondent know what to do on any particular question. The instruction should be simple—for example, "Select one option," "Select all that apply," "Rank the following options: 5 is the most prestigious, 1 is the least."

2. *Use everyday language:* Avoid jargon, slang, and abbreviations unless your sample is narrowly defined and you are certain that the language will be understood by respondents. If it is necessary to use technical language that respondents may be unfamiliar with, include a hyperlink to the definition of the word.

3. *Write in complete sentences:* Instead of asking, "Age," ask, "What is your age?"

4. *Write short, simple questions:* Long questions increase the risk of item nonresponse. A respondent is more likely to skip a question than to read it more than once for clarification. An exception to this rule is if you include a preface to a question to account for social desirability bias.

5. *Ask one question at a time:* Asking more than one question at a time renders data impossible to analyze. Consider this question: "Do you favor increased spending on sports and music programs?" A "yes" response may mean that the respondent favors more spending on sports, more spending on music, or both.

6. *Be consistent with your use of response options:* Constantly switching scales requires more space devoted to instructions and will lengthen the completion time of the survey.

7. *Use consistent wording and phrases throughout the questionnaire:* Questions can be set up with a lead phrase—for example, "How satisfied are you that our staff is . . . [knowledgeable] [responsive] [efficient], etc.?"

8. *Be sure that response options are meaningful to the respondents:* This is an issue of range—that is, making sure the response options cover all possibilities for your respondents—and appropriateness of the question to the respondents, ensuring that the topics you are asking about are relevant to the target respondents.

9. *When comparing products, don't label them "A" and "B":* This brings to mind grades, and respondents are likely to favor the "A" product over the one labeled "B." Use neutral labels, such as "M" and "N."

10. *Watch out for leading questions:* **Leading questions** are those that lead respondents to an answer. Consider this question: "The AIDS epidemic is a national emergency. It already has claimed more than 200,000 lives in the United States alone. More than one and a half million Americans now carry the AIDS virus. Do you favor increased federal spending on AIDS research programs?" The question could be corrected by eliminating the first three sentences.

## Pretesting

Even the most well-crafted questions and carefully constructed response options sometimes fail to collect valid and reliable information. No textbook can cover all the ways respondents may misinterpret your questions. The only way to find out if your questions will work is to **pretest** your questionnaire.

To do this, you will need to select a small sample of your target population to complete the questionnaire and provide feedback about the questions and about the proper functioning of the technical elements of the survey. These individuals will not be able to participate in the actual survey because they have been exposed to the questions. If your population is small and you are reluctant to conduct a pretest for fear of sacrificing potential respondents, consider looking for an analogous population and selecting pretest participants from that group. Do not, however, use your fellow researchers as pretest respondents; they may not catch jargon or leading questions because they are familiar with the survey topic.

Pretesting is an extra step in the survey process and takes away from one of the benefits of online surveys—namely, speed. However, consider this: If you choose not to conduct a pretest and later find that the majority of your respondents skipped key questions because they did not understand them or because the response options were inadequate, you will have to start over. Not only will this delay you, but you will have an additional problem: You will not be able to survey the same respondents about the same topic.

## Summary

Writing valid and reliable survey questions is a skill that is honed over time and with a significant amount of practice. All questions that appear on a study's questionnaire should inform one or more of the project's objectives; this can sometimes be difficult to achieve, especially when the survey is a group project. Clear articulation of the survey's goals and objectives, with each questionnaire item mapped to a particular objective, can help sort out which questions are necessary and which can be omitted.

Many respondent-centered factors may contribute to response invalidity, including the desire to appear informed, conformity with social norms, or the wish to help the researcher by providing an opinion, even if one does not exist. We discussed some techniques that can help mitigate the effects of these threats to validity.

While describing the different types of survey questions available to researchers, we pointed out some potential pitfalls and best practices for dealing with common problems. The attentive reader may have noticed that some popular surveys routinely violate our guidelines for writing valid and reliable survey questions. It is important to underscore that we have provided guidelines, not rules. Our intention is to raise awareness of the important issues surrounding survey question writing and offer alternatives for resolution of those issues. Individual researchers should use their discretion in adopting guidelines that are suitable for their surveys and audiences.

## Exercises

1. Identify the level of measurement for each of the following survey response options:

   a. Types of dogs (spaniels, Labradors, hounds, etc.)
   b. Age (measured by entering date of birth)
   c. Cities in California (San Francisco, Los Angeles, Sacramento, etc.)
   d. Number of apps downloaded from the app store in the past month (open-ended)
   e. Amount spent on last purchase (less than $10.00, $10.00–$19.99, $20.00–$29.99, and so on)
   f. Year in school (freshman, sophomore, junior, senior, graduate student)

2. How can social desirability affect survey responses? Describe some ways to reduce the effects of social desirability when asking respondents how much money they donated to charities last year.

3. Here are some questions collected from a variety of online surveys. Identify what problems (if any) exist in the questions, and rewrite them to correct the errors.

   a. What did you think about the length of today's event? (It was just right, It was too short, It was not long enough)
   b. How much do you agree or disagree with this statement? "Johnson's speech at the summit was informative." (Strongly agree, Agree, Disagree)
   c. Which of the following activities would you like to see more of at the community center? (Community theater productions, Dances, Sporting events, Movies)
   d. How many drinks did you have last week? (Open-ended)
   e. How likely are you to support the president in the upcoming election? (Very unlikely, Unlikely, Likely, Very likely)
   f. Have you ever been diagnosed with depression? (Yes, No) If "Yes," have you been treated for depression? (Yes, No)

# CHAPTER 5

## Developing the Survey Instrument

O bservations of people who try to complete web surveys suggest that two sources of significant frustration are lack of computer knowledge and poor questionnaire design (Dillman & Bowker, 2001). This often leads to premature termination of the survey. This finding, as well as other research, illustrates the need for thoughtful consideration regarding the design of electronic surveys. Digital surveys are more flexible in how they look, the response options, and the types of media that can be used than are paper surveys; therefore, their design requires unique considerations.

In this chapter, we examine survey design techniques in terms of appearance, readability, user-friendliness, and technical compatibility. Topics such as color, font type and size, response option formats, navigational guides, and **download** time are addressed. We also offer suggestions for making the questionnaire appropriate for your sample and accessible to people with dyslexia and visual impairments.

## Questionnaire Design

The best survey questionnaires look professional and motivating, are easy to comprehend, are inviting and not intimidating, make answering the questions a clear and simple process, and are accessible to everyone in the target population. Some of the principles applicable to self-administered paper questionnaires can be effectively applied to digital questionnaires. For example, the first question should be easy to answer, requiring no more than a few seconds of the respondents' time; the questions should progress in a logical order; questions relating to the same topic should be kept together; and bolding or color can be used to direct participants' attention to important words. In addition to these basic principles of good design, online survey designers should evaluate a number of important factors when constructing questionnaires. For example, electronic surveys offer the opportunity to use a variety of graphic and multimedia features, such as colorful images, video, and audio, to enhance questionnaires. When it comes to designing web and mobile questionnaires, however, simplicity is usually best.

## Design Principles for Online Questionnaires

Dillman (2000) identified a set of design principles that can be applied to e-mail and website questionnaires. The principles were developed to account for the task of responding to online surveys, the computer resources required by the finished questionnaires, and the need to ensure compatibility across different computer platforms and **operating systems**. The following discussion is based on Dillman's design principles but modified to reflect recent developments in survey software and the population's increasing familiarity with online surveys.

### Welcome Screen

Introduce the questionnaire with a welcome screen that is motivational, emphasizes the ease of responding, and instructs respondents on the action needed for proceeding to the next page. This will be the first screen the respondent sees (unless there is a language selection screen) when he or she clicks on the link to the survey. The welcome screen provides an opportunity to describe or reiterate the purpose of the survey, explain how the respondent was selected for participation, discuss the conditions of anonymity and confidentiality, and explain how to collect or redeem incentives if applicable. Welcome screens are best when kept brief and are most appropriate for longer questionnaires. If the questionnaire is only one or two screens long, the welcome message can be included at the top of the first screen. (See Figure 5.1 for an example of a welcome screen.)

### Access Control

Provide a password to limit access to only people in the sample. Passwords are primarily necessary when working with probability samples from closed populations. When attempting to generalize survey results to populations, it is important that only those respondents selected for the sample complete the questionnaire; uninvited participants may or may not meet your inclusion

**Figure 5.1    Welcome Page Example**

---

### The Student Experiences Project 2010

---

Help            F.A.Q.            Contact Us

---

**Welcome!**

Thank you for taking the time to participate in this survey. You have been specifically selected to participate in the Student Experiences Project. Taking part in this survey is your opportunity to voice your opinions about your university experience. The data you provide will be used as part of an effort to improve the quality of your education. The questionnaire takes about 10 minutes to complete. If you have any questions about the survey, please feel free to e-mail help@collegestudent.edu or call 555-555-5555.

Click here to begin the survey

---

criteria and could substantially distort the survey results. Passwords can be included on the survey invitation, and the space in which to enter the password should appear on the questionnaire welcome screen. The password should be simple and as short as possible. Figure 5.2 is an example of a password field that may be included on a welcome page. (Note: It is generally not necessary to password protect questionnaires using nonprobability samples from open populations.) Although passwords serve a useful function, they present an additional obstacle for respondents, and their use tends to increase the e-mails and phone calls to survey support staff.

**Figure 5.2    Password Protecting the Questionnaire**

---

### Student Experiences Survey


Please enter your password in the field below

**For example: aaa.aaa**


[                              ]

Continue ⟶

---

# First Question

As respondents work their way through questionnaires, they become more and more invested in the process and are less likely to abandon the survey. It stands to reason, then, that abandonment is most likely to occur early in the questionnaire. It is, therefore, essential that the first question be short, simple, and, if possible, fun for respondents. The first question sets the tone for the rest of the questionnaire; if it is lengthy or complicated or presents unfamiliar response scales, respondents may infer that this is indicative of all the questionnaire items and decide not to complete the survey. For these reasons, it is best to restrict first questions to closed-ended items that present radio buttons or check boxes for responses. Figure 5.3 shows two examples of first questions. Note that the first example requires respondents to indicate their satisfaction level and then rank each option; the second example requires one task and is presented in a familiar format.

**Figure 5.3  Examples of First Questions From a New Employee Survey**

(a) Poor first question: requires ranking of five items

**Please rank the importance to you of each of the following factors when it comes to choosing a place to work.**

*Please select one response for each ranking.*

|  | Least Important 1 | 2 | 3 | 4 | Most Important 5 |
|---|:---:|:---:|:---:|:---:|:---:|
| Your compensation package | O | O | O | O | O |
| The company's health care benefits | O | O | O | O | O |
| The company's training program | O | O | O | O | O |
| The company as a place to work | O | O | O | O | O |
| The company's equality structure | O | O | O | O | O |

(b) Better first question: one question with a standard response scale

**How satisfied are you with the company's training program?**

| Very satisfied | Somewhat satisfied | Satisfied | Dissatisfied | Somewhat dissatisfied | Very dissatisfied |
|:---:|:---:|:---:|:---:|:---:|:---:|
| O | O | O | O | O | O |

## Conventional Format

Present questions in a format that respondents are likely to have seen before. Novel question types, if used at all, should follow conventional radio-button or check-box questions so participants will have time to become familiar with the questionnaire. Specifically, conventional **formatting** includes numbering questions, left justifying text, and presenting response options either to the right of or directly below the questions to which they refer. When employing extensive skip logic in e-mail or website surveys, it is preferable *not* to number the questions. Respondents who notice the survey questions skipping from Number 5 to Number 15, for example, sometimes believe the questionnaire is malfunctioning and will try to use the "back" or "previous" button to look for the missing questions.

## Color

Color can easily be added to online surveys without additional cost, and it can enhance the appearance of the survey, assist with navigation, and motivate the respondent; however, color should be used cautiously. The use of color should be restricted so that figure/ground consistency and readability are maintained, navigational flow is unimpeded, and measurement properties of questions are maintained. Also, colors do not necessarily appear the same on different computer screens. For most purposes, the standard 256-color palette is safest to use.

Colors generally have associated feelings and meanings. Table 5.1 lists some examples of common color associations for adults in the United States.

**Table 5.1    Color Associations for Adults in the United States**

| Color | Positive Associations | Negative Associations |
|---|---|---|
| Red | Power, love, fire, passion, intimacy, courage | Danger, aggression, blood, hot, stop |
| Green | Money, freshness, nature, growth | Inexperience, misfortune, envy |
| Purple | Royalty, luxury | |
| Pink | Female, cute, soft, gentle | |
| Blue | Male, sky, water, peace, truth, calm | Sadness, depression |
| Orange | Autumn, Halloween, creativity | Caution |

| Color | Positive Associations | Negative Associations |
|-------|----------------------|----------------------|
| Yellow | Happiness, sunshine, optimism, summer | Illness, hazard |
| Brown | Earth, nature | Bland |
| Gray | Maturity, dignity | Gloomy, conservative, boring |
| White | Winter, virginity, clean, innocence, truth, peace, snow | Cold, sterility, clinical |
| Black | Formality, style, power, depth | Death, evil, mourning, night, mystery, fear |

Colors do not necessarily have the same meanings on an international level. For example, death and mourning are represented by white in Asia, yellow in the Philippines, and black in the United States. Be conscious of these differences in the meaning of color when you have an international response pool.

*Combining Colors.* Many survey software programs offer developers choices of color palettes that combine two or more colors for individual questionnaires. These combinations are often given labels such as "desert sunset," "midnight ocean," and "orange sherbet," with the resulting design faintly resembling how one might imagine these scenes to be colored. It is tempting to experiment with these options; however, considering readability and mood is important when combining colors.

*Readability.* For maximum readability, the text color and the background color should contrast highly. Dark text on a light background is easy to read. It goes without saying that dark text on a dark background or light text on a light background is difficult to read. Light text on a dark background also is easy to read, but it should be used sparingly as it can be tiring to the eyes to read large amounts of text on a dark background. Some additional guidelines for using colors include the following:

- Saturated colors are easier to see than pastels.
- Using too many colors can create a confused and cluttered effect. Opt for a palette of a few colors used throughout the questionnaire and invitation.
- Consider using multicolored charts, graphs, or maps for maximum accessibility by survey respondents.
- Some people experience color insensitivity. The most common is reduced sensitivity to reds and greens; about 10% of men experience this "colorblindness." If you opt for red letters on a green background, 10% of the men in your audience will not be able to read your questionnaire.

*Mood.* Colors used in combination can create different moods and feelings compared with colors used alone. Basic color theory indicates that the following color combinations are harmonious:

- Two colors opposite each other on the color wheel
- Any three colors equally spaced around the color wheel, forming a triangle
- Any four colors forming a rectangle, opposite one another on the color wheel (see the 12-part color wheel in Figure 5.4)

## Instructions

Instructions for completing the questionnaire should always be included, no matter how obvious the procedure may seem. When writing instructions, avoid jargon and do not use abbreviations without writing out the words first. A link to a glossary of abbreviations and terms can be beneficial if you have doubts about respondents' familiarity with the terms. Directions need not be lengthy, but they should be comprehensive, especially for people who are unfamiliar with electronic surveys (see Figure 5.5). Consider writing

**Figure 5.4   Twelve-Part Color Wheel**

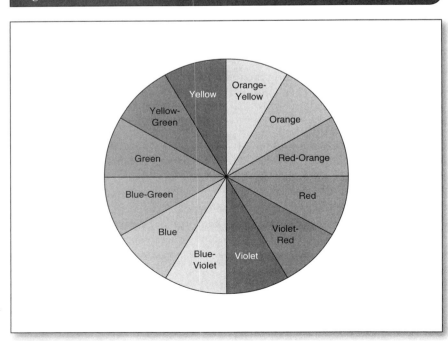

**Figure 5.5    Survey Instructions**

This survey is easy to complete and should take only about 10 minutes or less of your time. If you are unsure about a specific service provided by your organization, you may choose to skip that question and complete it after you have obtained the information needed. Reclicking the link at a later time will return you automatically to uncompleted items.
Please note:

- Only one response per individual please.
- You may move back to a previous page and revise your responses at any time.
- When all answers are completed, simply click the "submit" button and you will be asked to select your gift of appreciation.

**The first 50 respondents will receive a $20 discount coupon to our store!**

**All surveys should be completed by July 14, 2011!**

Please contact us at surveysupport@survey.com or 555-555-5555 if you need assistance. Thank you for your participation.

**Click here to begin the survey.**

brief directions and including a link to more detailed directions for people who may need them. It is best to place the links to the directions for answering specific questions next to the questions instead of placing them all at the beginning of the survey and overwhelming the reader. For example, the first question that uses radio buttons may include a link to an explanation of how to answer the question or change answers.

Instructions might address some or all of the following questions:

- Does the respondent have to answer all the questions?
- Can the respondent select only one answer for the question or more than one?
- How does the respondent move to the next question?
- Is there a time limit for completing the questionnaire?
- Can the respondent skip a question and return to it later?
- How does the respondent change an answer?
- Does the respondent need to single- or double-click on the answer?
- Can the respondent begin the survey and return to it later?
- If the respondent returns to complete the survey later, will he or she have to start all over again?
- What type of computer device should be used to complete the survey?

## Formats for Response Options

When creating online surveys, the developer has a choice of several ways to present the response options, including radio buttons, check boxes, drop-down menus, rank-order matrices, constant sum, and open-ended text boxes. Regardless of the combination of response options you select, it is important to maintain consistency in terms of font type and size, width of response categories, and colors used throughout the questionnaire. Varying any of these elements may cause respondents to interpret some questions as being more important than others.

*Radio Buttons.* A radio button is a small circle with text next to it; when the respondent clicks on the circle, it is filled in with a smaller, solid circle or sometimes with a check mark (see Figure 5.6). Radio buttons are traditionally used when the respondent must select exactly one choice from a list—that is, clicking on a nonselected button will deselect whichever other button was previously selected. Radio buttons are useful for Likert-type and other scale questions. Generally, the response options for multiple-choice questions are listed vertically, while the options for rating-scale questions are displayed horizontally, either next to the item or directly below it.

*Check Boxes.* A check box is a small box with text next to it. As the name implies, clicking on a check box places a check mark in it. They are used when respondents are permitted to select more than one option from a list, such as in the "select all that apply" question type (see Figure 5.7). Check-box responses, like radio-button options, can be programmed to appear randomly or in the order you specify. If you suspect there might be an order effect—for example, respondents might be more likely to select the option at the top of the list—then it will be important to randomize the list of options. Lists that have a logical order, such as an alphabetized list of names, should be presented as ordered lists. Check-box and radio-button lists may contain an exclusive option, such as "not

### Figure 5.6    Radio Button Examples

**How often do you shop in the Lakeview District?**

- O Once a week or more often
- O Once every 2 or 3 weeks
- O Once a month/every 4 weeks
- O Once every 2 or 3 months
- O Once every 4 to 6 months
- O Once or twice a year
- O Less often than once a year

**Figure 5.7    Check Box Example**

**Which of the following sports have you participated in this month (Check all that apply.)**
- ☐ Tennis
- ☐ Golf
- ☐ Running
- ☐ Swimming
- ☐ Bike riding
- ☐ Other [＿＿＿＿＿]

applicable" or "no preference." When this button or box is checked, the other options should be programmed to deselect automatically.

*Drop-Down Menus.* A drop-down menu has a visible title, but the contents (response choices) are shown only when the respondent clicks the title or a small arrow next to the title. The participant selects from the list by dragging the mouse from the menu title to the response option and releasing or by clicking the title and then clicking the response choice (see Figure 5.8). If possible, and practical, it is best to avoid using lists of response categories so long that respondents cannot see all the options. Users may not be aware of how to use them or might not want to take the extra step to scroll down to see all the choices. One common problem among inexperienced users occurs when a default answer appears in the visible window of a drop-down menu (as in the first example in Figure 5.8). The respondent sees that the window is filled in and believes that he or she already has answered the question; or the respondent may not realize that clicking on the arrow will provide more choices. Additionally, if the respondent has not clicked away from the drop-down menu, using the scroll wheel on a mouse will cause the response selection to change, which the participant may not notice.

Drop-down menus are most effective when the list of response options is lengthy and would result in excessive scrolling to see all the options and to get to the next question. It is important not to overuse drop-down menus—for example, for questions that have a few response options that can be displayed easily beneath or next to the question. Moreover, when drop-down menus are used, the visible window should not be left blank or be filled in with a default option; instead, include a "click here" or "select one" instruction.

*Matrices.* A matrix is a convenient way to present several questions that use the same response options. The questions are typically presented in the rows of the matrix and the response options in the columns. Rating questions, such as the "strongly agree to strongly disagree" type, and rank-order questions that allow respondents to rank a list of options in order of preference or

**Figure 5.8    Drop-Down Menu Examples**

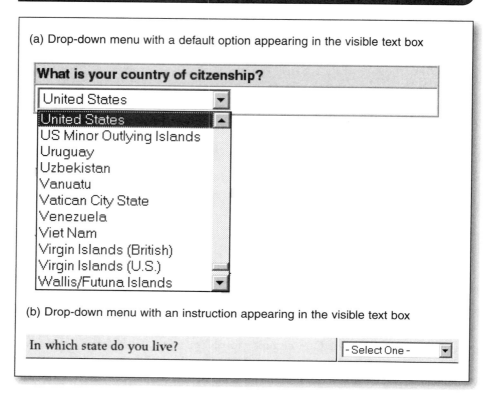

(a) Drop-down menu with a default option appearing in the visible text box

What is your country of citzenship?

United States

United States
US Minor Outlying Islands
Uruguay
Uzbekistan
Vanuatu
Vatican City State
Venezuela
Viet Nam
Virgin Islands (British)
Virgin Islands (U.S.)
Wallis/Futuna Islands

(b) Drop-down menu with an instruction appearing in the visible text box

In which state do you live?    - Select One -

importance are two examples of the use of matrices (see Figure 5.9). In the rank-order example, respondents are not permitted to assign the same rank to more than one option, and all options must be ranked before the respondent is allowed to move on to the next question. Matrices are useful because they save space on the screen, which means less scrolling for respondents. If a matrix is long—say, more than 10 rows—the header row containing the response options is usually repeated somewhere in the middle of the matrix. The exact positioning of the repeating header row will vary depending on the length of the matrix and the other items on the questionnaire page.

Although matrices offer design benefits, some authors caution against them. For example, Dillman, Smyth, and Christian (2009) offer four reasons to avoid matrices: (a) they require respondents to match information in rows with questions in columns (or vice versa); (b) the instructions to fill out the grid are often difficult to understand; (c) the structure of the grid leaves it up to the respondents whether to navigate through the rows first, the columns, or some combination of both; and (d) likelihood of missing items increases.

**Figure 5.9 Matrix Examples**

(a) Matrix of Likert-type questions

How much do you agree or disagree with the following statements about the store you visited?

| | Disagree Completely | Disagree Somewhat | Neither Agree nor Disagree | Agree Somewhat | Agree Completely |
|---|---|---|---|---|---|
| The merchandise displays were attractive | O | O | O | O | O |
| The store had a good selection of products | O | O | O | O | O |
| The store was conveniently located | O | O | O | O | O |
| The store hours were convenient to my shopping needs | O | O | O | O | O |
| The merchandise I wanted was in stock | O | O | O | O | O |

(b) Matrix of scale questions

Using a 1-to-5 point scale where 1 means "not at all" and 5 means "very important," how important are these factors to you when choosing a president? The candidate's...

| | 1 (Not at all important) | 2 | 3 | 4 | 5 (Very important) |
|---|---|---|---|---|---|
| Education | O | O | O | O | O |
| Spouse | O | O | O | O | O |
| Honesty | O | O | O | O | O |
| Religion | O | O | O | O | O |
| Position on issues | O | O | O | O | O |
| Age | O | O | O | O | O |
| Political party | O | O | O | O | O |
| Military experience | O | O | O | O | O |

Experimental studies comparing matrices to single questions have failed to yield compelling findings. Yan (2005) compared a set of six questionnaire items presented in three ways: in one condition, the items were presented on single screens; in another, they were presented as six individual items on one screen; and in the last, the six items were presented as one grid. The items in the matrix condition were found to be more reliable; however, the differences among the groups were only marginally significant.

In another study, Toepel, Das, and van Soest (2009) tested a set of 40 questions where the response options ranged from "totally disagree" to "totally agree" on a 5-point scale laid out horizontally and fully labeled. Respondents were randomly assigned to one of four conditions: 1 item per screen, 2 items per screen in a matrix, 10 items per screen in a matrix, and 40 items per screen in a matrix. The researchers found a modest increase in interitem correlations when the questions were placed in the matrices. They also found that nonresponse increased as more questions were placed on the same screen.

Garland (2009) conducted a similar study with three conditions: a questionnaire with a matrix format, a questionnaire with multiple items per screen, and a questionnaire with a single item per screen. There was no difference in respondents' satisfaction across the three conditions; however, the answers changed significantly across conditions. Contrary to the other research, interitem correlations were higher for the single-item-per-screen questionnaire than for the other two conditions.

In sum, whether placing questionnaire items in matrices increases measurement error remains unclear. Presenting questions one at a time allows respondents to focus more on individual questions and may be preferable when some items in a set are reversed—for example, "I enjoy using the website" and "The website is difficult to navigate." Item nonresponse seems to increase when more questions appear on the screen (in the matrix and individual-item conditions). And, finally, difficulty or satisfaction with the survey does not seem to vary between matrix and nonmatrix questionnaires.

*Constant Sum.* A constant sum question asks respondents to assign values or percentages across options so that the total sums to a predetermined amount. For example, you might want to know the percentage of an employee's workday spent on a variety of tasks, such as inventory control, customer service, and correspondence. The same question could be asked in terms of number of hours per day, assuming an employee works an 8-hour day.

Like the ranking question, constant sum requires a good deal of effort on the part of the respondent, as he or she must consider each of the response options relative to the others and to the total. The potential for error is higher in constant sum than in other types of questions—for example, typing in a set of values that sum to more than 100% will trigger an error message. Likewise, leaving empty boxes will result in error messages (a zero must be entered for activities in which the respondent is not engaged). The likely result of a respondent receiving a series of error messages is abandonment of the survey. When considering using constant sum questions, evaluate the cognitive and technical difficulty of the task you are asking respondents to perform to ensure it is appropriate for your target population. (See Figure 5.10 for an example of a constant sum question.)

**Figure 5.10   Constant Sum**

Please indicate the percentage of your workday you spend on the following activities. (The total must add up to 100%)

Reading e-mail

Answering the phone

Taking orders

Resolving customer complaints

Developing new projects

Other

*Open-Ended Text Boxes.* Open-ended text boxes allow respondents to type in free text. The sizes of text boxes vary; options include short boxes that require one-word answers, single-line boxes for short phrases or sentences, and multiline boxes that span the screen for detailed answers or comments. The length of respondents' answers will be guided by the amount of space you allot for them. Of course, this doesn't mean that respondents will necessarily fill long comment boxes with text or even respond to them at all. However, if you're looking for short answers, providing a single-line box with a character limit on responses is a way to prevent respondents from expounding. Figure 5.11 is an example of an open-ended text box.

**Figure 5.11   Open-Ended Text Box**

What are your future plans?

## Requiring Answers

It is best not to require respondents to provide an answer to each question before they are allowed to answer any subsequent ones. Requiring answers to questions that may be difficult, embarrassing, or not applicable is frustrating to respondents and poses ethical issues. The ethical norm of voluntary participation applies to the survey as a whole and any part of it. In no other survey mode are respondents forced to answer particular questions. In interview questionnaires, respondents can refuse to answer any question and still continue with the survey; in paper questionnaires, they can simply leave questions unmarked. If you find it necessary to receive answers to all questions, it is advisable to include "don't know," "not applicable," or "decline to state" as a possible choice.

## One-Page Versus Multipage Questionnaires

In many situations, whether to place all the survey items on one page or on multiple pages will be at the discretion of the questionnaire developer. Website usability guidelines suggest minimizing the use of vertical scrolling and eliminating horizontal scrolling altogether (U.S. Department of Health and Human Services, 2006). Horizontal scrolling can be eliminated with careful questionnaire programming and pretesting. The appropriate number of questions to place on one page depends on several factors. Some decisions are obvious: if the entire questionnaire is three or four questions long, using multiple pages is not necessary; if the survey contains dozens of questions relating to a variety of topics, multiple pages are in order. Whenever skip logic is used, multiple pages are necessary. Figure 5.12 is an example of a questionnaire with all the questions on one page. The respondent scrolls from one question to the next and clicks the "submit" button when he or she is finished. It is a relatively simple procedure and closely resembles the process of completing a paper questionnaire, which may be useful if data from different survey modes are to be combined.

In many survey software programs, the default is to place each question on its own page (see Figure 5.13). Some researchers prefer this option because respondents focus on one question at a time, perhaps mitigating order effects. Order effects occur if respondents' answers to particular questions are influenced by previously recorded answers. The reasoning is that it is easier to scroll up on a single page than it is to hit the "back" button to review a previous answer.

The research evidence relating to respondent fatigue and premature termination of one-page versus multipage online surveys is ambiguous. Some of the evidence indicates that excessive scrolling is burdensome to respondents,

**Figure 5.12    One-Page Questionnaire**

## Association Membership Survey

**How long have you been a member of the association?**

- ○ Less than 6 months
- ○ 6 months to 1 year
- ○ 2–3 years
- ○ 4–5 years
- ○ More than 5 years

**What kind of membership do you have?**

○ Associate    ○ Emeritus    ○ Student    ○ Regular    ○ Professional

**What was your primary reason for joining the association?**

**Which of the following events have you attended in the past year?**

Check all that apply.

- ☐ National conferences
- ☐ Regional conferences
- ☐ Job fairs
- ☐ Local training events
- ☐ Section meetings
- ☐ Other

**Thank you for completing this survey!**

Finish

NOTE: This entire questionnaire is contained on one webpage. Respondents scroll down the page to see all the questions.

while other research claims that too much clicking ("next," "back," etc.) is annoying. With the caveats regarding skip logic and possible order effects in mind, common sense suggests using one-page formats for short question-naires and multipage formats for longer surveys, with questions grouped by topic or response format.

## Double and Triple Banking

When the number of answer choices exceeds the number that can be dis-played on one screen, consider double (or triple) banking, with appropriate

**Figure 5.13    Multipage Questionnaire**

(a) Page 1

YOUR PROGRESS

Thank you for participating in this survey. Your responses are important to us and will help us improve the service we provide to you.

What was your primary reason for visiting our website today?

[ Next ]

(b) Page 2

YOUR PROGRESS

How easy was it to find the information you were looking for?

O  Very difficult
O  Difficult
O  Neither easy nor difficult
O  Easy
O  Very easy

[ Previous ]  [ Next ]

(c) Page 3

YOUR PROGRESS

How well did these aspects of our website meet your expectations?

|  | Did not meet my expectations | Met my expectations | Exceeded my expectations |
|---|---|---|---|
| Information content | O | O | O |
| Website design | O | O | O |
| Ease of navigation | O | O | O |

[ Previous ]  [ Next ]

(d) Page 4

YOUR PROGRESS

How likely are you to visit our website again?

O  Very unlikely
O  Unlikely
O  Not sure
O  Likely
O  Very Likely

[ Previous ]  [ Next ]

(e) Page 5

YOUR PROGRESS

Thank you very much for completing this survey! You will be entered into a drawing to receive a $10,000 gift certificate and a VitaMix 500.

[ Finish ]

**Figure 5.14   Double and Triple Banking**

(a) Double banking with box enclosure

How old are you?

O  14 years or younger          O  45–54
O  15–19                        O  55–64
O  20–24                        O  65–74
O  25–34                        O  75 years & over
O  35–44

(b) Triple banking with box enclosure

Which of the following services do you use? (Select all that apply.)

☐ Automatic teller     ☐ Checking        ☐ Debit card
☐ Direct deposit       ☐ Insurance       ☐ Education account
☐ Internet services    ☐ Loan services   ☐ Investment account
☐ Retirement account   ☐ Savings account ☐ Travel club

navigational instructions added (see Figure 5.14). If the number of response options exceeds what will fit in two or three columns on one screen, consider other options, such as drop-down menus.

## Navigation Guides

Getting lost when taking a survey is frustrating and can cause respondents to drop out before completing it. People taking the survey will have different levels of computer competency and comfort. Help respondents navigate through the survey within a short time and with limited frustration by providing clear directions and guideposts. Navigational guideposts assist the respondent in completing the survey without getting discouraged or lost. The guideposts are the road map of the survey.

As when looking at a road map, it is helpful for the reader to have an understanding of the location and how far he or she is from the destination point, which is the end of the survey. This can be provided in different ways. One is to identify the screen number the respondent is currently on and the number of screens in total. For example, you could place screen numbers on each page, which would be similar to page numbers in a book—that is, screen 3 of 15. You also could identify the respondents' location by question number—for example, question 4 of 20.

The most common technique is to identify the percentage of the survey that has been completed by using a progress bar (see Figure 5.15). These progress indicators can be placed at the bottom of the screen but are frequently presented at the top because they show how much of the survey has been completed based on the *last* page of questions answered. When placed at the bottom of a new page of questions, respondents can become discouraged, as they may believe the questionnaire is longer than it really is.

Signs also should be posted on your road map. The signs will indicate to the respondent how to go back, move forward, and submit the survey. Road signs usually have a designated color or shape—that is, brown signs indicate a historic site, yellow signs indicate caution, and "yield" signs are triangular. The signs you post on your survey road map also should have consistent colors and shapes and should be placed in a consistent location on each screen. Figure 5.16 shows one common option for the placement of questionnaire navigation buttons.

Web survey developers differ considerably in their opinions regarding the optimal placement of the "next" and "back" or "previous" buttons on questionnaires. Some prefer to place the "next" button on the right side of

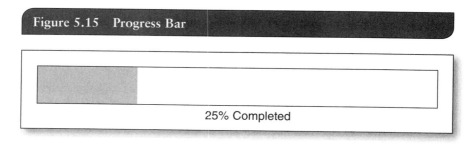

**Figure 5.15    Progress Bar**

25% Completed

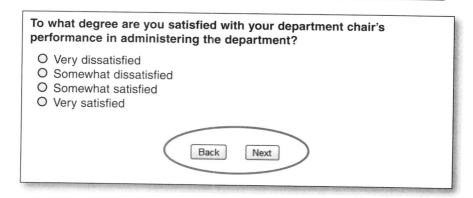

**Figure 5.16    Navigation Aids**

To what degree are you satisfied with your department chair's performance in administering the department?

O  Very dissatisfied
O  Somewhat dissatisfied
O  Somewhat satisfied
O  Very satisfied

Back        Next

the screen and "previous" button on the left. This is consistent with the configuration of many electronic devices and makes intuitive sense; this is how one would navigate through a book. This placement has some drawbacks, however. Placing the buttons apart from each other increases the time it takes to complete the survey and is in conflict with a basic web design principle that dictates placing the most frequently used buttons on the left menu bar.

Couper, Baker, and Mechling (2011) conducted an experiment to test the effects of varying placements of navigation buttons on questionnaires. They concluded that placing the "previous" button below the "next" button was associated with faster questionnaire completion times, but there were no other differences of note as a result of placing the "next" button on the right of the screen or due to the distance between the "next" and "previous" buttons. As Couper et al. point out, experienced survey participants quickly adapt to the design of a particular questionnaire. These variations in the placement of navigation buttons will make a greater difference for respondents who are new to online survey environments. Whatever design and placement you choose, it is important that respondents can easily find the navigation buttons, that their functions are clearly labeled, and that they be placed far enough apart so that respondents will not click "previous" when intending to click "next."

## Font Type and Text Size

There are two main font types: serif and sans serif. Serif fonts, such as Times New Roman, Courier New, and Georgia, have small appendages on the top and bottom of the letters. The appendages help distinguish each letter and make it easier to read strings of text (see Table 5.2). The sans serif

**Table 5.2   Examples of Serif and Sans Serif Fonts**

| Serif Fonts | Sans Serif Fonts |
|---|---|
| Times New Roman | Arial |
| Courier New | Verdana |
| Georgia | Comic Sans MS |
| Century Schoolbook | Century Gothic |
| Goudy Old Style | Tahoma |
| Monotype Corsiva | Bradley Hand ITC |

fonts, such as Arial, Verdana, and Comic Sans MS, are simpler and are generally better for short phrases, such as headings (Morrison & Noyes, 2003). The question of interest to web survey designers is what font type is the easiest and fastest to read and what font size is the most effective. A number of studies have focused on fonts for online reading.

Several studies have been conducted on font types in terms of readability, reading times, and general preference. Bernard and Mills (2000) examined Times New Roman and Arial fonts for readability, reading time, perception of legibility and sharpness, and general preference. Thirty-five adult participants were asked to read passages displayed in 10-point Arial, 12-point Arial, 10-point Times New Roman, and 12-point Times New Roman. The highlights of the study were as follows:

No significant differences were found in detecting errors in the reading passage.

Participants could read the passage fastest with 12-point Times New Roman ($M = 365$ seconds); the 10-point Arial font came second ($M = 368$ seconds).

Participants reported on a 7-point scale that the 12-point Arial font ($M = 5.7$) and 12-point Times New Roman font ($M = 5.6$) were the most legible.

Participants reported on a 7-point scale that the 12-point Arial font ($M = 4.8$) and the 12-point Times New Roman font ($M = 4.7$) were similar in their sharpness.

The researchers determined that the mean preference choice between all font sizes, types, and formats was the 12-point Arial, followed by the 12-point Times New Roman font. The 12-point Arial was selected as the preferred choice approximately 33 times, and the 12-point Times New Roman was selected as the first choice approximately 27 times.

In another study that assessed font types in terms of mood and the readers' general preference, similar results were found (Bernard, Mills, Peterson, & Storrer, 2001). Twenty-two adult participants were asked to read passages presented in the following 12-point fonts: Agency FB, Arial, Comic Sans MS, Tahoma, Verdana, Courier New, Georgia, Goudy Old Style, Century Schoolbook, Times New Roman, Bradley Hand ITC, and Monotype Corsiva.

The researchers first computed a reading score based on font legibility and its associated reading time. Participants were then asked to rate the fonts for readability and aesthetic appeal. No significant differences between font legibility were found. The three top-rated fonts in each of the categories and their scores can be found in Table 5.3. It is important to note that the differences between the top-rated fonts were minimal.

No significant differences were found in terms of legibility. Courier and Times were perceived as being the most businesslike, and Comic was

**Table 5.3   Top Three Fonts in Each Category**

| Reading Time | Perceived Legibility | Perceived as Businesslike | Perceived as Youthful and Fun | Font Preference |
|---|---|---|---|---|
| 1. Tahoma (270 seconds) | 1. Courier | 1. Times New Roman | 1. Comic | 1. Arial |
| 2. Times New Roman (273 seconds) | 2. Comic and Verdana | 2. Courier | 2. Bradley | 2. Verdana and Georgia |
| 3. Verdana (280 seconds) | 3. Times New Roman | 3. Schoolbook | 3. Verdana | 3. Comic |

SOURCE: Data based on Bernard, Mills, et al. (2001).

perceived as being the most fun and youthful font. Bradley and Corsiva were perceived as having the most personality and being the most elegant; they also were seen as being low in legibility and in businesslike appearance, and they obtained the lowest rating in font preference.

Other studies have found somewhat different results. For example, Bernard, Lida, Riley, Hackler, and Janzen (2002) found the most legible fonts were Arial, Courier, and Verdana. Comic Sans was found to be the most illegible of eight fonts evaluated. Georgia and Times New Roman were reported as the most attractive fonts, and Times and Arial were read faster than Courier, Schoolbook, and Georgia.

Bernard and Mills (2000) studied children's font preferences when reading online. Thirty-seven participants between 9 and 11 years of age participated in a study that compared preferences of 12- and 14-point fonts. Four font types were evaluated: Arial, Times New Roman, Courier New, and Comic Sans MS. Children preferred the 14-point fonts, as they were perceived to be easier and faster to read and more attractive. Comic Sans MS was the preferred choice in all three measures (easy to read, fast to read, and attractiveness), with Arial as the second choice. When surveying children, 14-point Comic Sans MS is the preferred choice.

For electronic surveys targeting older adults, a 14-point font is likewise a good idea, but opt for something like Arial. Twenty-seven participants ranging from 62 to 83 years of age were tested by Bernard, Liao, and Mills (2001). Four fonts were assessed in the study: Times New Roman, Georgia,

Arial, and Verdana. Font sizes of 12 and 14 points were used in the study. In terms of readability, the 14-point font size had significantly greater reading efficiency than the 12-point font. The 14-point font also had faster reading time and a greater perception of legibility. The preferred fonts were the 14-point Arial and Georgia.

Overall, Arial, Times New Roman, and Verdana are the best choices for adults, and 14-point fonts are preferred by children and older adults. It is best to use different fonts in your pilot tests to determine the best choice for your target audience.

## Images, Graphs, and Charts

Images, graphs, and charts should be used sparingly when creating online surveys. They can greatly increase the download time, and depending on your target audience, the respondents may not know how to interpret them. On the other hand, judicious use of images can provide a context for questionnaire items and potentially increase the validity of answers. Figure 5.17 shows the same question presented with two different photos. Without having to read extra text, respondents are given an important clue about the context of the question and immediately understand that in the first question, they should include visits to fast-food restaurants, whereas the second refers to fine dining. Similarly, providing a map and asking respondents to click on their location may result in a faster response than presenting the same information in a drop-down menu (see Figure 5.18). Finally, if you wish to have participants use a highlighter tool on a newsletter page to indicate preference for stories, the image of the page is necessary. The key is not to overuse click maps, highlighters, and other question formats requiring images.

**Figure 5.17   Questions With Images**

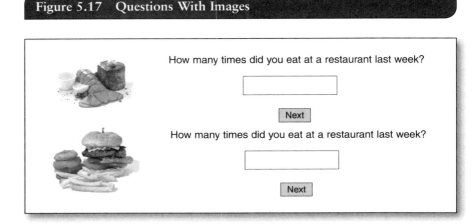

**Figure 5.18   Clickable U.S. Map**

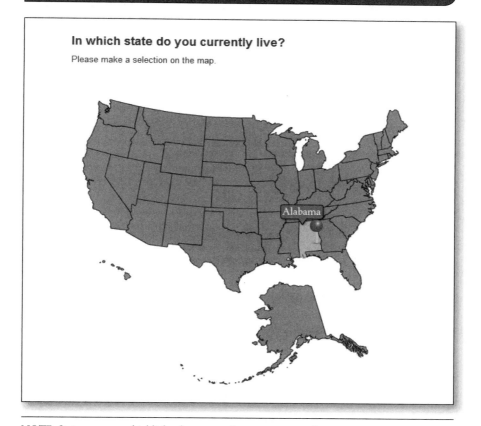

**In which state do you currently live?**

Please make a selection on the map.

NOTE: State names are highlighted as respondents mouse over the state.

## Motion, Sound, and Links

Technology enables survey designers to add motion, sound, links, graphics, and **Java applets**. All these features can make the survey more attractive, enticing, interesting, and entertaining, but these same features also can increase the time to download the survey and even make the potential respondent's computer crash. Such experiences can cause a lower response rate or frustration with the organization that hosts or disseminated the survey. While these high-tech features are compelling, the rule of thumb when it comes to online survey design is to keep it simple. To estimate the download time of your survey, you can use a download time calculator. One such calculator is available at http://download.stormloader.com/.

## Online Survey Appearance on Multiple Devices

Devices used to access the Internet include desktop and laptop computers, netbooks, tablet computers, ebook readers, videogame consoles, and mobile phones. Online questionnaires designed for desktop and laptop computer screens will not look the same on mobile and other devices. In the previous edition of this text, we cautioned survey developers to be attentive to differences in the visual appearance of questionnaires that result from different browsers (e.g., Netscape, Internet Explorer, Safari, or Firefox), operating systems (e.g., Windows XP, Windows Vista, or Mac OS), and screen resolutions. As browsers have become more compatible with one another and screen resolutions of $1024 \times 768$ have become the norm, these concerns have given way to a new set of issues brought on by the wide variety of devices now in use to access online content.

Callegaro (2010) pointed out that online surveys not optimized for mobile devices can result in several undesirable effects, including respondent confusion because the complete questionnaire page is not visible; data-entry errors, particularly with grid-type questions; and high rates of survey abandonment. He offers some potential approaches for addressing the problems that can arise when respondents use mobile devices to participate in an online survey.

1.  Don't change the survey, but analyze how many questionnaires were completed using a mobile device; this can be done by embedding some JavaScript in the online survey. The researcher would then take different actions depending on how many responses were in this category.

2.  Block responses from mobile devices. When attempting to access the survey from a mobile device, respondents will see an error message. They can be invited to complete the survey from a desktop or laptop computer. This option will clearly lead to increased drop-off rates because it involves extra steps for the participants.

3.  Optimize the survey so it will display correctly on the most common mobile devices. This requires some research to determine which devices are most common in your target market. It also calls on completely different design principles than those we've outlined in this chapter. At present, there are few standardized guidelines for designing mobile surveys. Common sense suggests that mobile surveys should be brief, rely on check-box and radio-button questions with a limited number of options, and offer direct input of numeric responses, such as age. On the other hand, matrix questions, images and sound, and open-ended text boxes are best avoided.

4. Make the survey fully compatible with any device. A growing number of vendors are providing survey platforms that can create surveys for desktop computers and optimize them for mobile devices. These may be add-ons to existing software packages or stand-alone solutions for mobile devices. As mobile survey applications continue to develop and begin to take advantage of the devices' features, such as cameras and GPS capabilities, design guidelines for mobile surveys will evolve.

## Making Your Survey Accessible to Everyone

To reduce coverage bias as much as possible, making online surveys accessible to everyone in the target population is important. Ensuring that individuals with visual or learning disabilities or who speak a different language can complete the questionnaire is methodologically sound, ethically responsible, and sometimes legally required.

### Language

If your target audience is international or includes people who may have limited English skills, you may want to consider translating your survey into multiple languages. Some software programs will allow the developer to convert a survey written in English into another language. A better option is to engage the translation services of a native speaker of the language you wish to use so features such as syntax and colloquialisms are correctly interpreted. Surveys offered in a variety of languages should provide respondents with the choice of their preferred language on the first screen they see. Figure 5.19 shows how the Inquisite survey software system presents language options for respondents.

### Visual Impairments

For people with visual disabilities, assistive software programs called screen readers are available. These screen readers enable the person to listen to the information on the webpage as the software reads the content aloud. Some web-based hosts, such as WebSurveyor, are accessible to people using screen readers.

When using screen readers, one factor that can contribute to poor web access relates to graphic images. Screen readers read the code, so surveys need to be created so that the labels are read out loud. Because screen readers read basic text, graphics that do not contain an ALT tag will not be read.

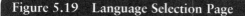
Figure 5.19    Language Selection Page

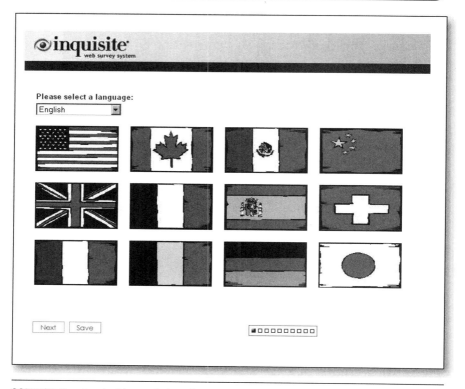

SOURCE: Reprinted with permission of Inquisite, Inc.

The ALT tag provides the reader with textual information about the graphic image. This is essential if the graphic contains a link. If an ALT tag does not exist, then the person using the screen reader will not know that the information exists. It is not difficult to create an ALT tag. For example, if you have an image that displays the words "Log In," the HTML code may be written as follows:

<IMG SRC="loginphoto.jpg" ALT="login">

When creating tables, organize the information from left to right instead of from top to bottom to help ensure greater understanding of the information.

Color deficits are another type of visual disability. About 8% of men and 0.5% of women have some form of colorblindness (Newman, 2000). That could translate into 1 in 12 visitors for some websites. According to Newman, 99% of people who are colorblind have trouble distinguishing between red and green.

Bright and distinct colors are the easiest to distinguish. Using different shades of one color can make text difficult to decipher. Exaggerate differences between foreground and background colors by using background colors that make the other image stand out—for example, red against white. Avoid using colors of similar lightness near one another. Use more than one color to design your web survey. If a link is in blue, then the reader may not be able to determine it is a link. Therefore, making the link a different color and also underlining it is helpful.

## Learning Disabilities

Dyslexia is a reading disability that affects about 15% of the U.S. population. As many as 80% of all people with learning disabilities have dyslexia. A way to help dyslexic individuals read your online survey is to use the font called Read Regular. Read Regular is designed with an individual approach for each of the characters, creating difference in the actual characters and not mirroring letters. For example, to create a large character differentiation, the letter *b* is not mirrored to make the letter *d*. The character shapes are simple and clear, creating consistency, and they are stripped of all unnecessary details.

## Legal Requirements

In 1998, Congress amended the Rehabilitation Act to require federal agencies to make their electronic and information technology accessible to people with disabilities. The law applies to all federal agencies when they develop, procure, maintain, or use electronic and information technology. Agencies must give disabled employees and members of the public access to information that is comparable to the access available to others. You can view the government site that outlines the requirements and provides other helpful information at http://www.section508.gov/index.cfm?FuseAction=Content&ID=3. The site also contains training resources.

Even if your organization is not covered by the Rehabilitation Act, designing your electronic survey to comply with the Act's requirements will ensure that your survey is available to the broadest possible audience.

# Ensuring That Participants Respond Only Once

Researchers need to be cautious of receiving completed questionnaires from the same respondent multiple times. The ethical norm of respondent anonymity and the practical goal of eliciting only one response per person are at odds with each other; however, there are some techniques for preventing or identifying duplicate responses. Using a unique identifier, such as e-mail address, is the most effective way to prevent people from submitting multiple questionnaires. Uploading an e-mail address list to a web-based survey host and deploying the survey from the host's server will effectively prevent multiple submissions from the same invitee. By using the response-checking feature of the software, you will see from which e-mail addresses responses have been received. This is applicable only to e-mail surveys, however.

In the case of surveys placed on a website, there are two options for controlling the submissions: taking note of the survey takers' Internet Protocol (IP) addresses or placing cookies on the respondents' machines. When enabled, "duplicate protection" using IP addresses prohibits more than one response from a particular IP address. This is a good option if you believe your participants will be responding from individual IP addresses. If IP addresses may be shared, such as in some business and computer labs, for example, this will not be practical.

A cookie placed on a respondent's computer when the first response is received is another method for avoiding "ballot-box stuffing." The cookie contains information that identifies the survey and the respondent and will prevent the retaking of a particular survey. Of course, respondents can clear their cookies, so this will not guarantee one response per person; it only discourages multiple submissions.

## Summary

Although some of the design principles applicable to paper questionnaires can be instructive for creating online questionnaires, web-based surveys are unique and require careful consideration when it comes to layout, user-friendliness, and technical requirements. In this chapter, we discussed general guidelines for the design of online surveys, much of which was informed by research evidence and usability testing focused on how participants interact with online surveys. We suggested that simplicity and consistency are often best when it comes to designing questionnaires and emphasized the need for clear directions and navigational aids.

We covered the most common question types, such as radio-button, check-box, matrix, and open-ended questions, and pointed out when it would be appropriate to use each one. With customized questionnaire programming, online survey researchers are unlimited in the types of questions they can use; the standard question types can be altered in a variety of ways to suit just about any need.

Many design decisions, such as questionnaire appearance, colors, response options, and the amount and level of instructions to include, will be guided by a clear understanding of the demographic and technological profiles of the target audience. Knowing that your potential respondents are likely to access a survey on a mobile device, for example, influences the number and types of questions you include, the form of the response options, as well as the appearance of the questions.

Survey software and the devices used to access online content are developing at a breakneck pace, and the diffusion of technology in society is advancing just as rapidly. As some members of target populations become increasingly tech savvy and others alter their technology preferences, guidelines for designing online questionnaires will require updating. It is incumbent on researchers using online data collection tools to keep track of the research literature in the field and adjust their techniques for developing online survey instruments accordingly.

## Exercises

The director of Human Resources for your organization notices an alarmingly high number of employees leaving the organization for comparable positions elsewhere. She wants to conduct an online survey of current and recently separated employees to determine what's causing this trend and what can be done to reverse it. You are given the assignment of designing the questionnaire for this survey project.

1. What questions would you ask the director during your initial meeting about the project?

2. The director has some ideas about the questions that should be included on the questionnaire. For each question, recommend the optimal question format and explain your choices.

   a. For current employees:
      i. What do you enjoy most about your job?
      ii. What do you like least about your job?
      iii. Are there enough resources (people and funds) to do your work?
      iv. Are the organization's priorities clear to you?
      v. Are the opportunities for advancement clear to you?
      vi. Are you aware of the training opportunities available?
      vii. How long have you been with the organization?

      viii. Do you supervise other employees? If so, how many?

      ix. Do you feel free to make decisions that affect your work?

      x. Do you feel comfortable filing complaints without fear of reprisal?

b. For former employees:

    i. Why did you leave the organization?

    ii. Did you experience health-related issues as a result of balancing your work and personal life?

    iii. How satisfied were you with your relationship with your immediate supervisor?

    iv. Are you currently employed elsewhere? If so, what attracted you to your new position?

    v. What factors are most important to you when evaluating job opportunities?

1. Salary
2. Health and dental benefits
3. Distance from home
4. Parking
5. Access to public transit
6. The work
7. Coworkers
8. Management
9. Training
10. The presence of a union

    vi. Please suggest any specific areas for improvement that may benefit employee morale at our organization.

3. Using one set of questions, either for current or former employees, lay out a questionnaire. Be sure to include all necessary elements, such as instructions, progress indicator, navigation guides, and so on.

4. Make an assumption about how the target respondents will access the survey. Based on this assumption, how do your recommendations about question types and questionnaire format change, if at all?

# CHAPTER 6

# Conducting the Survey

Research related to conducting online surveys continues to emerge as technological advances continue to occur. These events have altered the online survey world. The research has revealed some best practices for administering electronic surveys, including ways to maximize response rate, and changes in technology have resulted in new options for deploying online surveys. In this chapter, we discuss the most popular recruitment methods currently available as well as some of the newer techniques for delivering online surveys to potential respondents. The rich methodological literature surrounding the use of e-mail invitations and the placement of survey links on webpages provides a basis for our discussion of the use of these techniques. Research focused on survey deployment using mobile devices and social media is less mature but, nevertheless, offers some direction for researchers who wish to employ these channels.

## Recruitment Methods

Several methods can be used to recruit survey participants. Each approach should be evaluated with the target audience in mind. When possible, consider combining methods of participant recruitment to minimize coverage bias if you have determined this is an issue in your study. Common recruitment methods include

1. e-mail invitations,

2. a link to the survey on a website,

3. an interstitial (pop-up) window,

4. a mobile device,

5. social media, and

6. offline methods.

## E-Mail Invitations

E-mail invitations require that you have the e-mail addresses of your target respondents. For example, if you want to survey attendees of a conference, members or employees of an organization, or people who signed up to receive an online newsletter, a list of e-mail addresses for these individuals will exist; your task will be to procure this list. If, however, your goal is to measure public opinion on a topic, this approach will not work, and you should select another deployment method. (See Table 6.1 for the advantages and disadvantages of using e-mail invitations.)

To employ this method, you will need to obtain an e-mail address list for potential respondents and select a sample. Although the only essential piece

**Table 6.1    Advantages and Disadvantages of E-Mail Invitations**

| Advantages | Disadvantages |
|---|---|
| • They enable fast response time. | • Constructing an e-mail list is sometimes not possible. |
| • They are inexpensive. | • Sampling limited to e-mail addresses available to the researcher, resulting in coverage bias. |
| • Responses can be tracked and reminders sent. | • Many hurdles involved: spam filters, e-mail clutter, too many e-mail surveys. |
| • Response rate relatively high, as participants are likely to have common characteristics or interests. | • Some target audiences don't use e-mail communication channel. |
| • Branding of the invitation and personalization to respondents can create credibility for the survey and increase response. | |
| • Ideal for closed populations where lists exist and participation can be encouraged. | |

of information is respondents' e-mail addresses, if names (first and last) and other identifying information, such as a membership number, are also available, capture that information as well. Most software programs will allow you to upload a few extra fields of data, along with e-mail addresses, so you can personalize the e-mail message. When the list is ready, you have two choices: (a) upload the list into the survey software, create the e-mail invitation in the software, and allow the program to automatically insert the survey link and send the e-mails, or (b) upload the list into your own e-mail program, write the invitation message, copy and paste the survey link from the software program into the invitation, and send the message from your e-mail server.

If you send the message from the survey software, you will easily be able to track completed responses and automatically send reminders to participants who have not started or who have started but not yet completed the questionnaire. However, you will be able to include only potential respondents' first and last names and possibly one other variable, such as an identification number or date of last visit/purchase in the message. Moreover, there is a substantial risk that respondents may not receive your invitation at all. This is a problem even with existing customers or members, as you are sending the message from an unknown server (i.e., the survey vendor's) that recipients are not likely to have deemed an "approved" sender. This issue may be mitigated somewhat by sending a prenotification e-mail alerting respondents to the coming survey invitation.

Choosing to use your own e-mail provider will allow you to personalize the message as much as you like via the mail merge feature. Additionally, if you are inviting individuals with whom you have an existing relationship (e.g., students who signed up for a class or customers), they will have received messages from your organization in the past and will have identified you as an approved sender. On the other hand, tracking completed responses will be a time-consuming, manual process involving downloading the list of completed responses, looking up those individuals on the original invitation list, deleting them, and sending reminders to the remaining invitees in the sample. This manual process of mailing reminders will almost always result in inclusion of a few respondents who have completed the survey. This is because, during the time when you are downloading, scrubbing, and preparing the reminder list, some respondents will be submitting the survey, so your list will not be completely accurate. The considerations surrounding the two methods of sending e-mail invitations are summarized in Table 6.2.

**Table 6.2    Sending E-Mail Invitations From Survey Software Versus E-Mail Clients**

| E-Mail Invitations From Survey Software | E-Mail Invitations From Your E-Mail Account |
|---|---|
| • Everything is in one place.<br>• Includes automatic tracking of completed responses and sending of reminders.<br>• Personalization of invitations is limited to a few fields.<br>• Limited design options available for e-mail invitation.<br>• The recipient is unlikely to recognize the sender, thus increasing bounce-back of invitations.<br>• Confusion of your survey with others coming from the same software vendor is possible. | • Unlimited personalization of invitations is available.<br>• Increased potential for invitees' e-mail providers to recognize you as an approved sender, resulting in decreased bounced invitations.<br>• Increased response rate is likely, due to personalization and recognition.<br>• E-mail invitation can be customized and branded.<br>• Tracking of completed responses is time-consuming and error prone. |

## Writing the E-Mail Invitation

Invitations to participate in an e-mail survey may be the first point of contact with the potential respondent. This is an opportunity to sell the survey. You need to persuade the recipient that the survey is a valuable way to spend his or her time. The invitation should be as short and simple as possible while still conveying all the necessary information about the survey.

### Subject Line

The e-mail subject line is the first opportunity to gain or lose survey respondents. Ideally, the subject line should be a summary of what the recipient will see in the body of the message. It should be short enough so that recipients can see the entire subject line when viewing their e-mail list. Keeping the subject line to fewer than 50 characters will usually accomplish this, but as with all aspects of online surveys, the appearance of e-mail subject lines should be tested using a variety of e-mail providers and on the devices most likely to be used by the respondents. Other subject-line factors that will increase the chance of respondents opening the invitation include

- adding the name of your organization if it will be recognizable to recipients;
- avoiding all capital letters and symbols, such as $, !, %, and ?;

- personalizing the subject line, with past purchase activity or website visit data, for example; and
- using a call to action.

Table 6.3 provides examples of good and poor e-mail subject lines. Notice that although most of the "poor" examples include a call to action and some personalization, they also contain exclamation points, all capital letters, or promises of money and prizes for completing the survey.

**Table 6.3   Subject Line Examples**

| Poor Subject Lines | Good Subject Lines |
|---|---|
| • ENTER TO WIN $10,000<br>• FREE products with every entry!<br>• Students, your chance to win big, hurry!<br>• A chance to win an all-expenses paid vacation!<br>• Get paid to fill out surveys today!!! | • Feedback about your doctor's office visit requested<br>• Share your opinion about our website<br>• Tell us how we're doing<br>• Voice your opinion about the executive committee<br>• Invitation to provide feedback about our store |

Message Body

The body of the message should be intriguing, simple, and short. Elements such as tone, length, readability, respect for the respondent, and credibility of the researcher are important. The invitation needs to be friendly, respectful, motivating, and trustworthy; emphasize the importance and ease of responding; and provide clear instructions as to how to proceed. The following are our recommendations:

- Encourage recipients to add you to their address books. This will be particularly helpful if you plan to survey the same participants in the future.
- Include the organization's logo in the top header. However, be sure that the header image is not so large that it pushes the content of the message down on the page.
- Personalize the salutation. For example, "Dear <First Name>," "Dear Mr./Ms./Mrs./Dr. <Last Name>," or "Dear <First Name> <Last Name>."
- Explain why the individual is getting the message.
  - o "You are receiving this message after enrolling in our rewards program."
  - o "As a valued customer, we would like to hear your thoughts about some new products."
  - o "You were randomly selected from all registered students at Sun State University."

- Describe the purpose of the survey.
  - "We are working to improve the service we offer you."
  - "We would like your feedback about Dr. Johnson."
  - "Your opinions are important to us and will help us improve the products we offer to customers like you."
- Inform the reader of the approximate time needed to complete the survey.
  - "The survey will take about 10 minutes to complete."
  - "The survey takes between 5 and 10 minutes to complete."
  - "Most respondents will be able to complete the survey in less than 2 minutes."
- Address issues of confidentiality and anonymity. If participants will be entered into a sweepstakes drawing or offered some other incentive, explain how the incentive will be delivered while maintaining participant anonymity.
- Highlight the survey link. Respondents who are motivated to complete the survey will often skim the message body looking for the survey link. Separate the survey URL from the message body, and use color and/or bold text to make it easy to find.
  - Don't: "To begin the survey, click here."
  - Do: "To begin the survey click on the link below:
    Member Survey 2011."

  Including the full URL to the survey is also advisable for those respondents who wish to copy and paste it into a new browser window rather than clicking on the link from the survey invitation. For example, http://www.survey.com/membersurvey2010.
- Include an opt-out link. At the bottom of the message body, you will need to provide a way for recipients to opt out of receiving reminders and further invitations from you. If you have uploaded your e-mail address list into the survey software, the program will include an option to insert an opt-out link in the invitation. If you are using your own e-mail program to send the invitations, you will need to do one of two things: (a) instruct recipients to reply to your message with the word *unsubscribe* in the subject line, or (b) create an opt-out survey containing two items, a radio-button question indicating the respondents' opt-out preference and a text box where they can enter the e-mail address that should be removed from the list. The link to this opt-out survey can then be inserted at the bottom of the message body.
- Personalize the signature line. An invitation that comes from an individual is preferable to one that comes from a group. In any event, the invitation should come from someone; that is, do not omit the signature line. The best option is to use the name of an individual who will be recognizable to the potential respondents and whose position in the organization makes sense in the context of the survey—for example, the president of the organization, the director of research, or the principal investigator of a funded research project. If you are unable to gain permission to use an individual's name, a group name will be the second-best option—for example, "The Process Improvement Committee" or "The Research and Evaluation Team."

Message Design

Having carefully written and edited your e-mail subject line and body text, you will next need to turn your attention to the design and layout of the message. It is important to know how the message will display to respondents. Message appearance can vary widely depending on the recipients' Internet service provider (ISP) and e-mail service, as well as personal settings. Although creating a message that will look the same when viewed by all recipients is impossible, we offer some suggestions to optimize message design for most potential respondents.

- *Limit the dimensions.* To ensure that your message renders correctly in most web mail programs, such as Gmail and Yahoo, and e-mail clients, such as Outlook and Lotus Notes, limit the width of the message to 650 **pixels**.
- *Include all relevant information in the top of the message.* The top of the message is what recipients will read before they must use the vertical scroll. If you feel you cannot convey all necessary information in the top half of the message, consider using a "frequently asked questions" link at the bottom of the page, or list the questions below the signature line.
- *Limit images.* Aside from the organization's logo, include only images that are absolutely necessary to convince the potential participant to click on the survey link. Omit branded imagery, photographs of company executives, and animations. All key information, including the survey link, should be viewable with images turned off.
- *View the message as plain text.* Some e-mail clients read messages only in plain text. Check to see that the invitation viewed as plain text contains all the same information as the HTML version.

Table 6.4 summarizes the items relevant to deploying an online survey with an e-mail invitation, and Example 6.1 presents a sample e-mail invitation.

**Table 6.4 E-Mail Invitation Checklist**

*Mailbox*

- Does the "From" display correctly?
- Does the message render clearly with images turned off and on?
- Have you tested your message with several ISPs, such as Gmail, Yahoo, Hotmail, EarthLink, and AOL? How does it display in Outlook and other e-mail programs?

*(Continued)*

**Table 6.4  (Continued)**

*Subject Line*

- Is the subject text 50 characters or fewer?
- Does the subject line accurately reflect the nature of the invitation?
- Have you used all capitals or any special characters?

*Message Body*

- Have you asked respondents to add you to their address books?
- Is your logo a reasonable size?
- Is the message personalized?
- Did you include key elements such as explanations of why the recipient is being contacted, what the survey is about, why it is important, and how long it will take to complete?
- Are the benefits of participation (monetary or nonmonetary) clearly described?
- Is the survey link clearly visible?
- Are all links working properly? Check the survey link and the opt-out link.
- Did you avoid words or characters that may be flagged by spam filters?
- Does the message contain unnecessary images?

*Message Bottom*

- Have you included a way for recipients to opt out of your survey?
- Have you personalized the signature line with a well-known person's name?

*Example 6.1: Sample E-Mail Survey Invitation*

Acme Corporation is committed to ensuring you receive the best-quality service possible. We are writing to ask you to complete a short online survey about your experiences with our company. Completion of this survey is voluntary, and the information you provide will be kept completely private and confidential.

This survey should take 2 to 3 minutes to complete. To take the survey, please click on the link below or copy and paste it into your web browser:

[%Link%]

This survey will be available until May 1.

If you have any problems accessing the survey, please e-mail support@acmesurvey.com or reply to this e-mail.

Thank you in advance for your help!

Sincerely,

John Smith
Vice President of Online Survey Research

Message Deliverability

Spam blockers can prevent your invitation message from getting to potential recipients. Spam blockers defend Internet users from unwanted e-mails. **Graylisting** or **blacklisting** of your organization or e-mail domain may result if you consistently violate anti-spam regulations. Graylisting is so named because it is a cross between black- and whitelisting. A key feature of the graylisting method is automatic maintenance. The underlying assumption is that spammers will try to send the e-mail only once. Graylisting denies the spammer's first attempt to send the e-mail; the second time, the message is accepted. If it continues to be accepted, then it is added to the **whitelist** (a list of "from" e-mail addresses that a mail server is configured to accept as incoming mail) and never has to pass the graylist test again. E-mail servers that are considered off-limits or dangerous can be placed on a blacklist. A sender may be placed on a blacklist if it is known to send e-mail messages from fraudulent operations or because the sender exploits browser vulnerabilities to send spyware and other unwanted software to users. It is difficult to bypass the gray- and blacklists. You can run your invitation through a spam checker and see if it is flagged. It is important to note that ISPs are constantly updating their spam filters to protect their customers, so surveyors must continually evaluate their bounce rate by ISP to see if mail delivery problems occur. Some techniques may help increase the deliverability of your invitation. Table 6.5 lists some words and phrases to avoid. This is a sample, not a definitive list, and some messages with this content will be delivered. If possible, however, choose alternatives to these words and phrases. It also may be beneficial to run your invitation through a spam-checker program, such as MailingCheck. Programs such as this scan content looking for key words that may be flagged as spam and return a deliverability score. Many also provide suggested alternatives for problematic content.

## A Link on a Website

Banners and icons asking people to complete a survey can be placed on webpages. The user clicks on the icon, and the invitation asks him or her to complete the survey. This method of recruiting respondents is for researchers who are seeking data from the general population or a specific target audience. Links can be present for a short time for quick polling or for an extended period or permanently. The permanent links are often placed in the left- or right-side navigation bar or in the footer and are used to collect information about the website or organization.

**Table 6.5    Content Vulnerable to Spam Filters**

| | |
|---|---|
| • Act now! | • Opportunity |
| • Amazing | • Income |
| • Bonus | • Join now |
| • Cash | • Super deals |
| • Click to win | • Limited time only |
| • Earn $ | • This isn't spam |
| • Free | • Vote |
| • Get paid | • Win |
| • Money | • You have won |
| • No cost | • Winner |

After you have sufficiently tested your questionnaire and are confident it is functioning correctly, you will copy and paste onto the website the HTML code generated by the survey software. Alternately, provide this code to the owner of the website where your survey will appear. Persistent feedback links, such as those that appear in the footer of many webpages, do not require invitations. They are always available for any visitor to provide comments.

Website surveys that appear for a short period of time or are presented at the conclusion of a transaction, such as a sale, will need to include a brief introduction. This type of survey may be triggered every time a visitor clicks on a page (or every $n$th time if you are sampling page visitors) or when the user clicks a "submit" button, for example. Unlike the e-mail invitation discussed earlier, these invitations are limited to one paragraph (see Example 6.2).

---

*Example 6.2: Sample Website Survey Invitation*

Thank you for your purchase. We are working to improve our ordering process and would like your feedback about the shopping experience you just completed. To share your opinion, please click on the link below. As a thank-you gift, you will receive a $10 Amazon.com gift certificate.

---

Recall from our earlier discussion of sampling that to gather information from the general public, you can advertise your survey on a variety of popular websites. If you are targeting a more specific audience, then you will need to advertise your survey on related sites. For example, if you want to survey healthcare professionals, then you may choose to advertise your survey on several health-related sites. To use this method, you do not need the e-mail addresses of potential respondents; however, it takes longer than e-mail surveys to get an adequate sample size. The advantages and disadvantages of this method are listed in Table 6.6.

Regardless of your audience, you will want to entice respondents to complete your survey. The researcher can attract the reader by briefly describing the incentive (if there is one) in the banner. Also, research shows that non-static banners lead to higher response and completion rates. Animated banners and ones that flash or move are beneficial, but be sure that the download time is short. Involving your audience has been shown to be helpful. People like to play games, so incorporating a short quiz or game is encouraged. Location, size, and color also are important. Just like your survey, gear the banner to your target audience.

**Table 6.6    Advantages and Disadvantages of Invitations on Websites**

| Advantages | Disadvantages |
|---|---|
| • E-mail addresses are not needed. | • Passive approach; visitors may not notice or be intrigued by the banner. |
| • The visitor may be more motivated to complete the survey, as he or she has an interest in the topic, which is why the visitor is viewing the site—for example, a health-related website. | • Cooperation from other organizations is required if the researcher wants to post the survey on other websites. |
| • The survey can be placed on multiple websites. | • Takes longer than other methods to obtain the desired sample size. |
| • Allows the respondent to be proactive and is nonintrusive. | • Banners and icons need to attract the attention of the visitor and be visually appealing. |
| • Respondent may trust the organization, and thus, the survey carries more credibility. | • Software may be installed on potential respondents' computers to block banners; if this type of software is installed, then the viewer may not see your request for participation. |

## Interstitial (Pop-Up) Window Invitations

An interstitial (i.e., something "in between") is a page inserted in the normal flow of editorial content structure on a website for the purpose of advertising or promotion. A separate window pops up while every visitor, or every *n*th visitor, is viewing a webpage. A variety of pop-up styles are available. You can purchase software with customizable pop-up templates. These pop-ups can include videos, audio, be delayed, fade in or out, or move. They come in a variety of shapes and sizes, and unblockable pop-ups also are available.

This method is intrusive, and the reaction of viewers usually depends on how welcome or entertaining the message is. An interstitial is usually designed to move automatically to the page where the survey is located if the user clicks on the pop-up window. It is best to offer an incentive to motivate visitors to complete the survey. It also is a good idea to place the client's logo on the pop-up window, which adds credibility and ensures that the pop-up is not perceived as coming from a third party. The advantages and disadvantages of this method are outlined in Table 6.7.

**Table 6.7    Advantages and Disadvantages of Interstitial Windows**

| Advantages | Disadvantages |
|---|---|
| • They get the attention of the viewer. | • Viewer may not perceive the survey to be credible depending on what sites the pop-up windows appear on. |
| • E-mail addresses are not needed. | • They are intrusive; the viewer may be annoyed by the interruption. |
| • Force a response from visitors—they either have to complete the survey or close the window. | • Can irritate site visitors and cause them to leave the site. |
| • Surveyor can select a simple random or systematic (every *n*th) sample of visitors to a particular website. | • Software may be installed on the potential respondent's computer to block the pop-up window; if this type of software is installed, then the viewer may not see your request for participation. |
| • Draw the visitor's attention to the survey at the time of his or her viewing of the site—good for webpage evaluations. | |
| • Can get a high response rate if the site is frequently visited. | |

Presently, hundreds of software programs on the market are designed to block pop-ups, banner ads, spyware, and spam. Many of the programs will block basic pop-up and pop-under messages and play a sound, such as a beep (or whatever the user chooses), every time an ad is blocked. More sophisticated software allows users to block all forms of advertising, including Flash ads, messenger ads, and sponsored ads on websites such as Google and Yahoo. Many programs also include automatic updates to keep the spam blocker software current. Some ad blockers even include detailed statistics so that the user can view the number and types of ads blocked. This type of software is generally inexpensive or available for free downloading.

The proliferation of such programs is a clear indication that web users are seeking ways to eliminate what they perceive to be annoying interruptions. As web surfers increasingly adopt pop-up–blocking software and switch to web browsers and ISPs that claim to eliminate pop-up ads entirely, it will be incumbent on digital survey researchers to supplement this method of recruiting respondents with additional techniques.

## Mobile Devices

Many survey vendors such as Zoomerang, Confirmit, and SurveyGizmo provide the option of deploying surveys to mobile phones and other mobile devices, such as iPads. Surveys using Short Message Service (SMS) are brief interactive surveys accessible on any SMS-capable mobile phone. Of course, you must have access to a database of cell phone numbers to employ this method. Examples of potential audiences include students, employees, conference attendees, or patients who have signed up for appointment reminders. SMS surveys are well suited for in-the-moment research, when you wish to collect information while it is still fresh in the respondents' minds. For example, you might send an SMS survey to audience members asking them to evaluate a presentation they recently attended. Other applications include customer satisfaction surveys, opinion polls, and point-of-sale feedback.

The surveys are created using the same online survey software you would use to create an e-mail or website survey. If you are interested in this option, you will need to ensure that deployment to mobile devices is available before you sign up with the software vendor. Surveys can be deployed in two ways: inbound and outbound. Inbound surveys are administered by asking your target audience to enter a short string of numbers on their cell phones along with a response. Television shows such as *American Idol* use this technique so that audience members can vote for their favorite contestant. The other mobile SMS technique, outbound, involves sending a mobile survey invitation with questions to potential respondents. The questions can be sent all at once or as a string of text messages, each appearing after the previous one is answered. Sending a series of short text messages rather than all at once enables the use of skip logic. Software will allow you to program many question types for an SMS survey, including open-ended questions; however, consider the user experience when creating the questionnaire. Participants are unlikely to endure long surveys and will not be able to process a lengthy list of response options efficiently. Best practices for deployment to mobile devices are to keep to a few questions of the multiple-choice variety, such as yes/no, agree/disagree, rating scale responses (e.g., 1-to-5-point scale), or ranking a short list of options. The advantages and disadvantages of using text messages for recruitment are listed in Table 6.8.

## Social Media

Surveys also can be deployed to Facebook and Twitter to solicit participants. Facebook is a social networking website operated and privately owned by Facebook, Inc. Users of Facebook may create a personal profile, add other users as friends, and exchange messages, including automatic notifications when they update their profiles. Additionally, users may join common-interest user groups organized by workplace, school, college, or other characteristics. Survey software deploys to Facebook by providing the

**Table 6.8    Advantages and Disadvantages of SMS Surveys**

| Advantages | Disadvantages |
|---|---|
| • Response times are faster than with web or e-mail surveys. | • You need the cell numbers of potential respondents. |
| • They're a good choice for targeting younger populations. | • Not a good choice for some populations. |
| • Can contact the potential participant immediately after an interaction—for example, satisfaction questionnaires sent to customers right after the service date. | • Coverage bias exists, as you can survey only those whose cell phone numbers you have. |
| • Can contact target audience during an activity or event—for example, you can collect feedback from the audience during a presentation. | • Can be viewed as intrusive. |
| • May be the only way to reach certain populations. | • Limited type and number of questions possible. |

survey administrator with a direct link to the survey. The survey administrator can then create a post on his or her wall, inviting other friends to
take the survey. A Facebook wall is a personal homepage within Facebook
that friends, friends of friends, or everyone can see and access (each user
can set and update/edit privacy settings). Deploying a survey to Facebook
requires nothing more than following the instructions provided by the
survey software.

Twitter is a real-time information network that connects users to the latest
information about anything they find interesting. Simply find the public
streams you find most compelling and follow the conversations. At the heart
of Twitter are small bursts of information called *tweets*. Each tweet can be
140 characters in length. Connected to each tweet is a rich details pane that
provides additional information and embedded media. Deploying surveys to
Twitter is like sending an instant message to all your followers, as well as
to anyone and everyone who can see your Twitter homepage. The survey
administrator chooses to deploy via Twitter, and the survey software provides
a unique link to the survey. Zoomerang, for example, also provides text for a
customized message to accompany the tweeted survey link (e.g., "Please take
my survey: How much do you spend on healthcare each month?").
Zoomerang also allows the survey administrator to customize some settings,
such as "prevent respondents from taking this survey multiple times."

The advent of social media websites such as Facebook and Twitter has
altered the paradigm of online content consumption. Users are no longer
satisfied to read content; people now expect to engage in dialogue and offer
opinions on any and all active issues. Although Facebook claims more than
600 million active users worldwide and an estimated 135 million daily
visitors and Twitter has 175 million registered users and hosts 95 million
tweets a day, it is important to remember that many people are not engaged
in social media. Even among registered users, many are lurkers or specta-
tors rather than regular contributors.

Individuals who are active social media participants are likely to be opinion leaders, early adopters of new technologies, and brand advocates. These
individuals are seldom representative of the broad range of a company's
customers or an organization's membership. Also, this method of data collection relies on volunteers to opt in to the research process. Participants
cannot be randomly selected; therefore, the results obtained from these
surveys will have limited external validity and suffer from the same short-
comings as any other survey relying on a nonprobability sample.

Deploying a survey via a social media website is a simple process. Facebook
and Twitter surveys collect fast and inexpensive responses, but you get what
you pay for. Before taking advantage of this method of collecting survey

data, researchers should consider the implications: Facebook and Twitter power users tend to be under age 40, controlling who takes a tweeted survey is virtually impossible, and unpredictable respondents will receive survey invitations via retweets. It is important to weigh the ease of data collection using social media with its inherent sampling biases when determining the value of the resulting information. This method of online survey deployment is appropriate for exploratory research, entertainment polls, and querying your friends about their meal preferences for your birthday party.

## Offline Methods

If you do not have an e-mail list for your target audience, you may have a membership or customer list containing home addresses. In this case, you could recruit respondents using a letter or postcard sent by postal mail. Additionally, researchers aiming to survey open populations may put ads in newsletters or newspapers, print invitations on sales receipts, or insert flyers in mailings.

The invitation typically includes the purpose of the survey, identifies the sponsor of the survey, describes how the potential respondent benefits, and offers incentives, if applicable. The invitation also contains the survey link. It is best to keep the survey link short and simple and avoid numbers and symbols, such as ? and $; this will reduce errors when respondents type the survey URL into a web browser. The following is an example of a survey invitation:

> To serve you better, we would like feedback about your recent purchase at our store. In appreciation for your time, you will receive 10% off your next purchase at the store. The online survey takes about 5 minutes to complete, and you will receive your purchase discount coupon immediately after you finish the survey. Please go to www.CustomerSurvey@survey.com to complete the survey. Thank you. Your opinion is important to us.

An advantage of using this approach is that you can recruit respondents without having their e-mail addresses. This process is often used in conjunction with e-mail list samples when coverage bias may pose a threat to the representativeness of the responses. The major disadvantage is that it is inconvenient to potential respondents, as they must open a web browser and log on to participate in the survey.

# Additional Survey Data Collection Devices

Technological innovations have resulted in a host of devices that are increasingly used to collect survey data. These are typically multipurpose devices, originally designed for uses other than survey data collection.

However, their ability to run survey software applications has made them attractive to software developers and useful for online survey researchers. It would be impractical to list and describe all the options; in this section, we focus on three common devices used to collect online survey data: PDAs (**personal digital assistants**), kiosk terminals, and tablet PCs.

## PDAs

PDAs are often confused with smartphones. This is understandable, as the line distinguishing one from the other is not clear. Smartphones began with a focus on initiating and receiving phone calls. Additional features, such as games, digital cameras, video capabilities, Internet connectivity, and a calendar enhanced the appeal of smartphones. PDAs were microcomputers that focused on data manipulation and could be carried in a pocket or briefcase. The devices were designed to run applications with limited processor requirements. The ability to make and receive phone calls was added later, but the focus of the PDA was still on data. Functionally, the two devices are equivalent, and historic distinctions are no longer relevant.

A related device, the **Pocket PC**, is a computer that fits in the palm of the hand. It is a type of PDA that uses the Microsoft Windows mobile operating system. Pocket PC features are focused on computing and data tasks, with other features such as cellular phone capabilities being secondary to the PDA functions. To carry the Pocket PC label, the device must meet specific criteria, such as using Microsoft's Windows Mobile for Pocket PCs. Features include complete integration with a desktop personal computer, a touch screen, a touchpad, software such as Word and Excel, and voice-recording capability.

Researchers have used PDAs to collect data for several years. As prices of PDAs have declined, usage has increased. PDA data collection is the process of using a handheld or mobile computer (such as a Palm Pilot) to record data (see Figure 6.1). The user can enter data directly into the device. The information is saved in the device and then downloaded to another computer for analysis. PDAs can be useful and efficient data collection tools in a variety of industries. Typically, PDAs are utilized in field research (i.e., research conducted away from an office or central location, limiting access to a main system or database). Some examples are

- conducting field surveys about recreational fishing;
- collecting patient data in mobile medical clinics;
- gathering critical disaster management information from an organization;
- conducting interview surveys in remote locations; and
- conducting in-person interviews at malls, amusement parks, movie theaters, and other locations.

**Figure 6.1    PDA**

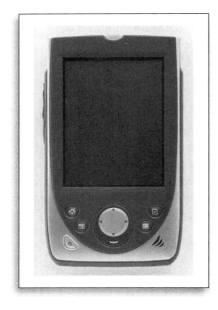

*Downloading the Survey on a PDA*

PDA software consists of two components: one part is installed on a desktop personal computer and the other on the PDA. Surveys are developed using the software installed on the desktop and then downloaded into the PDA. The desktop also is where the data is processed and exported. The desktop software manages the synchronization with the PDA component of the software. The synchronization process includes two vital tasks: (a) after the survey is created, it is downloaded onto the PDA, and (b) after the data have been entered into the PDA, they are uploaded to the desktop computer. The PDA software component has different roles than the desktop software. The PDA software is installed on each handheld device, and it runs the survey on the device. The survey can be programmed to keep track of the number of surveys taken and start and end time of the survey.

As stated, PDA surveys run on handheld PDA devices, but the survey is created on the desktop computer. This introduces the problem of determining how the survey will look on the PDA device. Because of this common concern, most PDA survey software packages include a preview of how the survey will appear on the PDA device. While the preview is a good way to get a sense of how the survey will look, when you design a mobile survey, you also need to test how the features, such as skip-logic questions, will work. One obvious solution is to deploy the survey to the PDA and view it there. While this method will show the developer how the survey looks and functions on the PDA, the process of toggling between the PDA and desktop computer, identifying and correcting problems, and redeploying the survey after each change is time-consuming. If a change is needed, then the developer will have to make the change on the desktop, deploy the survey, and view it again on the PDA.

Another concern is device orientation. Are you running the survey on a square screen or landscape device? The solution is to select software that allows you to run your PDA survey on a desktop PDA emulator. An emulator duplicates the functions of one system using a different system so that the second system behaves like (and appears to be) the first system. Using a desktop PDA emulator enables the developer to understand how the survey will look and operate on a PDA while still using the desktop computer. When the survey is altered, the emulator will automatically make the change and reload the survey. This makes the process of survey development much faster. Surveytogo offers this feature.

The survey questions and response options are individually programmed. The responses may be in the form of multiple-choice questions that use radio buttons or check boxes, drop-down menus, or other available options. Responses to open-ended questions are entered using the touch-screen keyboard or through other forms of written character recognition. If needed, inexpensive portable keyboards can be attached to the handheld device to make entering text easier.

All who use the device need training. The training should include how to back up the data, problem solve, care for the device, manage the power, install (or reinstall) software, upload data to a desktop computer, download surveys, enter data, and attach external devices. Users should learn how to create a password to prevent unauthorized access and ensure that confidentiality is not compromised. Role plays are recommended to enhance the learners' skills before going into the field. Field testing is recommended as well. Supervisors should check each interviewer's work, especially early on, to identify any problems in the data collection process.

After the data are collected, they are uploaded to a desktop computer or e-mailed to the desired location. To upload the data to a desktop or laptop, a cable (USB) is connected to the PDA on one end and the desktop/laptop on the other. The advantages and disadvantages of using a PDA are listed in Table 6.9.

**Table 6.9 Advantages and Disadvantages of Deploying a Survey Using a PDA**

| Advantages | Disadvantages |
|---|---|
| • More organized when collecting data in the field. The need for clipboards, pens, paper, and other burdensome or difficult items to carry and organize when working in the field is eliminated; these tools are all contained within the small portable device. | • Initial expense of purchasing the devices and, if used, the ongoing expense of a wireless service. There also are costs related to training data collectors how to use the device. |

*(Continued)*

**Table 6.9 (Continued)**

| Advantages | Disadvantages |
|---|---|
| • Data can be quickly entered with a few taps or clicks, reducing the time needed to reenter handwritten information collected in the field to a desktop computer. A PDA user can download all the results directly to a computer or e-mail the results to the desired location. Also, the date and time of data entry are automatically identified. | • Potential of data loss in malfunctioning devices or the user misplacing the PDA. |
| • Reduces errors and wasted time caused by illegible handwriting, misplaced papers, and extra data entry. Also, interview times may be reduced due to ease of using skip patterns and faster recording of responses. | • It takes time to learn how to use the device. |
| • Improves data quality, as the software prevents researchers from unintentionally skipping interview questions. | • Respondents may not be familiar with how to use a PDA or be comfortable using one. |
| • Reduction in data entry time can lead to sooner data analysis and more timely decision making. | • Converting the survey from a Word document to run on a PDA can be time-consuming. |
| • The data collected from some survey design systems is captured as standard **comma-separated values** (also known as comma delimited) files that can easily be read by other spreadsheets, such as Excel, and database systems, such as Microsoft Access and a **structured query language** server. | • Not appropriate for collecting private or confidential information because data is stored on a portable end device that is easily lost or stolen. |

## Kiosk Terminals

Interactive kiosk terminals are free-standing, self-service devices used to collect information, provide a service, or sell merchandise. The devices can store data, conduct transactions, exchange information, and/or distribute items to users. Kiosks have a physical structure that can be stationary or portable and consists of hardware and software. The hardware may include a touch-screen monitor, stereo speakers, a printer, and a central processing unit. The software can be programmed for a variety of transactions. Some kiosks have Internet connectivity; those that do not require that the survey be stored locally on the kiosk's computer.

Kiosks can be interactive and engage respondents. The survey kiosk can be used in virtually any location to collect data from customers and passers-by and provide an easy and accessible outlet for customers to provide immediate feedback. They are located in public areas such as retail stores, medical clinics, airports, visitor attraction sites, banks, and restaurants.

The process of creating surveys for deployment to kiosks is the same as creating one for any personal computer. The invitation process differs, as respondents are not solicited via e-mail or website pop-up advertisements. They are either directed to the kiosk—for example, a workshop leader might ask attendees to stop by a kiosk at the end of the seminar to complete an evaluation—or they happen upon the kiosk on their own and decide to participate in the survey. Researchers can download data anytime and as frequently as they wish. This makes customer survey kiosks an ideal solution for events and tradeshows, where event planners can improve attendee experiences in real time by applying satisfaction data as it becomes available. Advantages and disadvantages of using survey kiosks are listed in Table 6.10.

**Table 6.10  Advantages and Disadvantages of Deploying a Survey Using a Kiosk Terminal**

| Advantages | Disadvantages |
|---|---|
| • Offers the ability to provide the information in multiple languages. | • This is a passive approach to data collection. |
| • Appearance can be customized. | • The cost of purchasing, installing, and maintaining the terminal can be high. |
| • No limit to the number of survey questions. | • Surveys need to be short, as respondents are usually in transit, moving from one location to another. |

*(Continued)*

**Table 6.10 (Continued)**

| Advantages | Disadvantages |
|---|---|
| • Questions can be deleted, added, and modified while the survey is live. | • Coverage bias exists; kiosks are available only to individuals in the vicinity. |
| • Various question types, including open-ended questions and contingency questions, can be used. | • Difficult to control multiple responses from the same individuals. |
| • Can be placed in locations where potential respondents are likely to be found. | • Requires effort on the part of the potential respondent to go to the kiosk, log on, and participate in the survey. |
| • Can retrieve data anytime. | • Can be problematic if personal information is collected, as respondents often forget to log off and close the survey window, leaving their responses available for the next respondent to see if he/she hits the back button. |

## Tablet PCs

A tablet PC is a complete computer equipped with a stylus (pen) or a touch screen. The stylus can be used for drawing and writing or as a mouse. Depending on how your survey is constructed, it can simulate a paper survey, as one can hold the stylus the same as any writing utensil and mark check boxes, fill in radio buttons, or write a response to an open-ended question. In addition to all the standard online survey question types, questions containing photographs, sound, or multimedia content can be effectively presented.

Most tablets have Internet connectivity, are highly portable, allow for assisted as well nonassisted survey taking in a controlled environment, and can be used for recording the results of interview surveys. For example, a tablet PC might be used in a medical office for a satisfaction survey at the conclusion of a visit. A member of the office staff could present patients with the tablet, offer instructions about logging in to the survey, and be available to assist with survey completion if necessary. Used in this way, surveys on tablet PCs resemble paper surveys presented on clipboards, but with the significant benefits of direct data entry and inclusion of a wide variety of question types.

The most common tablet PC, the Apple iPad, has the added advantages of widespread familiarity, outstanding usability, long battery life, and thousands of software developers currently creating applications specifically for data collection. Surveys may be created for iPads using the same software used for other online surveys; many vendors now offer optimization for iPads (and iPhones, too). Deployed as a standard online survey, responses are captured and stored on the vendor's server, but this requires that the tablet be connected to the Internet while respondents enter their answers. Alternatively, specialized software, such as iSurvey, can be used to create surveys for the iPad, iPhone, or iPod Touch. In this case, the survey can be completed anytime and data are stored locally on the tablet until the device is connected to the Internet. Clearly, data stored on a portable device is vulnerable to loss and theft. When collecting sensitive medical or financial information, local data storage will not be an option. Other advantages and disadvantages of using tablets are listed in Table 6.11.

**Table 6.11    Advantages and Disadvantages of Using a Tablet PC**

| Advantages | Disadvantages |
|---|---|
| • One can use audio as part of the survey or use a microphone to record an interview. | • They are expensive if used only for conducting surveys. |
| • The full range of question types is available, including contingency questions. | • Introduce possible problems with illegible handwriting. |
| • Tablet PCs offer expanded data collection options such as drawing and highlighting. | • Not as durable as a laptop computer for high-use situations. |
| • They are mobile and lightweight (lighter than a laptop). | • Prone to theft. |
| • Participants can type or write responses. | • Heightened data security issues arise if the same device is passed around for multiple respondents to complete a survey. |

# Deploying the Survey

The process of deploying an online survey involves several steps. The elapsed time to complete these steps can range from a few days to several weeks depending on the scope of the project and the number of researchers involved.

## Pretesting the End-to-End Survey Process

When the questionnaire, notifications, invitations, and other survey materials have been finalized, you should conduct an end-to-end test of the survey process. You will need a sample of test respondents; between 5 and 10 individuals should be adequate. These are people who will not receive the survey. They may be colleagues, friends, or paid testers; they should not have had previous exposure to the survey. Testers go through the process from start to finish and provide comments and critique so that you may revise your materials before deploying to actual respondents. They will also provide information regarding how long it took to complete the survey so you may accurately inform the respondents, and they will report any technical difficulties they encountered. Be sure to delete test data before continuing to the next step.

## Soft Launch of the Survey

After you have made revisions based on the feedback from your testers, the next step is to send the survey to a small sample of real respondents, perhaps 1% or 2% of your sample. This soft launch will give you an opportunity to check for patterns of e-mail invitations that have bounced back, items that may not be functioning properly on the questionnaire, and the way in which the data are being recorded. These are actual data and cannot be deleted from your results; however, if you find errors at this stage, there is time to make corrections before sending the survey to the remaining sample.

## Full Launch of the Survey

Assuming you uncovered no errors (or that you made necessary corrections), you may send or make the survey available to the remaining sample. This can be done at once if the sample is relatively small (a few hundred) or in batches if the sample is large (many thousands). Monitor this launch carefully, as you did the soft launch. In most situations, you will not be able to make substantive changes to the questionnaire (such as adding a response option) once live responses have been recorded, but you will be able to correct typos and make other minor text edits. Monitoring responses will also help you decide on the exact timing of reminders and if the survey needs to remain in the field longer than anticipated or be closed before the scheduled date.

# Increasing Response Rate

Obtaining high response rates can be challenging when conducting online survey research. Multiple factors can impact response rate, such as the survey invitation, appearance of the survey, the topic, perceived security and privacy, survey design (including length, quality of the questions, and level of engagement), timing of dissemination, trust and relationship with the sender, incentives, and follow-up reminders. These topics are discussed here, as well as in other areas of this text (e.g., survey design is discussed in Chapter 5).

## Prenotify

If time allows, prenotifying audience members that a survey is coming will help increase response rate. This can be done with an e-mail message, a notice on a website, an article in an eNewsletter, or an offline communication vehicle such as a postcard or letter. In the prenotification message, outline the purpose of the survey, emphasize its importance and the value of each respondent's participation, and inform potential respondents when to expect the survey. Alerting recipients to the survey helps prime them for its arrival and aids in establishing the legitimacy of the project—spammers do not prenotify.

## Scrub Your List

A sample list that has not been scrubbed can exacerbate response rate problems. To scrub your list, verify that you are targeting the correct audience. Confirm that the individuals on your list are still active participants and have not opted out of receiving surveys from your organization. In the case of an employee satisfaction survey, for example, validate that all potential participants are still employed at the company and no deceased or retired employees remain on the list. Be sure to eliminate duplicates; some lists will include the same individual with multiple e-mail addresses. Search for domain typos, such as *yajoo.com* instead of *yahoo.com*; obviously invalid addresses, such as *nothankyou@no.com*; addresses missing the @ symbol or *.com*, *.net*, *.edu*, or *.org*; and role accounts, such as *help@*, *support@*, or *info@*.

## Use Best Practices for Writing Invitations

Use the survey invitation to build trust by following the best practices of including your logo, indicating how you got the recipients' contact information, and providing an opportunity to opt out of the survey and contact you if necessary. The invitation also should be used to manage expectations regarding the length of the survey and the deadline for completion. Explain what you will do with the data and disclose whether participation is anonymous.

## Time Delivery of Messages Thoughtfully

Consider your audience when scheduling the delivery of your invitations and reminders. When sending e-mail invitations to a professional audience, for example, Friday through Monday are days best avoided. Likewise, avoid holidays and other off days when potential respondents will not be checking their e-mail accounts. Tuesday or Wednesday mornings are optimal for professional audiences. You might also consider the academic calendar, if appropriate to your audience, and other factors such as summer holidays. Essentially, think about where your target individuals are likely to be and what they're likely to be doing when you schedule your contacts with them. If other members of your organization regularly contact the same individuals you wish to survey, it is wise to coordinate contacts so that recipients are not inundated with messages from the same sender.

## Schedule Reminders

Sending follow-up invitations can help increase the response rate substantially. If you sent out the questionnaires via e-mail, then you most likely have created a distribution list containing the e-mail addresses of the potential respondents. The actual sending of the follow-up invitations is a straightforward task, but the timing of follow-ups should be carefully considered, as it has been shown to make a difference in recipients' behavior.

One follow-up message sent about a week after the initial e-mail invitation is optimal; a second reminder will increase response rate marginally; three or more reminders borders on harassment. One week after the initial contact is a guideline; individual researchers should monitor responses daily to determine the best time to send reminders. Depending on the nature of the survey, an effective reminder may be sent two days after the first invitation.

# Offer Incentives

Social exchange theory asserts that decisions to take action are evaluated in terms of costs and benefits—that is, people want to minimize costs and maximize benefits. When offered incentives, potential respondents will weigh the value of the incentive against their perceived cost in time and effort. Incentives come in two forms, material and nonmaterial.

## Material Incentives

Research evidence consistently shows that incentives are effective in increasing response rates for online surveys. Material incentives include such things as electronic gift certificates, gift cards, entries in prize drawings, and checks sent via postal mail. The incentives given for each respondent who participates are usually of a lower monetary value than incentives for drawings, and incentives for shorter surveys usually have a lower monetary value than incentives for longer surveys. Of course, do not offer anything that you cannot deliver.

Other options for incentives include loyalty points or discount coupons, which can be given to each respondent. Alternatively, respondents can be entered into a drawing for a highly desirable prize, such as a reserved parking space in a crowded parking lot. If the incentive is offered to each respondent, then whoever completes the survey will receive a gift. In the case of the drawing, only one respondent receives the prize, but the prize is of greater value than the individual gifts.

The choice of the incentive used needs to be considered thoughtfully. There are a few special considerations when selecting your incentive for an online survey. Be sure that the incentive is one that will be relevant for all participants. For example, if your target audience is men, then offering a coupon for a free manicure and pedicure may not be a good choice. If your target audience is students at a particular college or university, then a gift certificate for the bookstore is appropriate and valuable to the target audience. You also need to consider if your respondents will be international. Gift certificates for sites such as Amazon.com, iTunes, or a donation to a charity are good choices if your target audience is dispersed geographically. You also could offer the respondent a choice from a specified list of incentives of equal value.

You will need to think about the timeliness of your incentive. If you are going to raffle off school supplies but the drawing will be held in May, then you may want to reconsider your selection. If the survey is related to breast cancer, for example, then for each person who completes the survey, the company may donate a specified amount of money to a cancer nonprofit or research center. Using the same example, you may want to conduct the survey during breast cancer awareness month.

A meta-analysis of incentive experiments conducted by Göritz (2005) revealed that incentives do motivate people to start a web survey. Incentives increase the likelihood of a person responding to a survey by 19% relative to the odds without incentives. Incentives also increase the chance that the respondent will complete the survey rather than drop out by 27% relative to the odds without incentives. Göritz also found that promised nonmonetary incentives seem to be more effective in online than offline surveys. In a stand-alone study, Göritz (2004) found that the response rate when the incentive was loyalty points was slightly higher (82.4%) than if money (78%) or trinkets (78.6%) were raffled. If more loyalty points were offered, the dropout rate was lower.

### Nonmaterial Incentives

Nonmaterial incentives also can affect the response rates. Offering to send the research results to the participant is one example. Göritz (2005) conducted three online experiments and noted that when a summary of the survey results was offered, the response rates were slightly higher than if the summary was not offered. Dropout rates were also lower when a data summary was offered. Convincing potential respondents that participation in the survey will be fun is another way to maximize their reward for taking part in the survey. It will then be incumbent on you to ensure that the survey really is fun.

## Use Behavioral Theory to Encourage Participation

Three behavioral theories are relevant to increasing participation in a digital survey: cognitive dissonance, self-perception theory, and level of involvement.

### Cognitive Dissonance

Cognitive dissonance can occur when our behaviors do not match our cognitions. This is an uncomfortable state, and individuals experiencing cognitive dissonance will take steps to reduce it. In the survey research setting, cognitive dissonance may arise if a respondent sees himself or herself as a helpful person but then refuses to participate in a survey. To reduce the dissonance (or inconsistency between self-perception and behavior), the potential respondent can take part in the survey. Survey invitations that mention that respondents will be "helping" the researcher or that "every response is essential to the accuracy of the data" can trigger cognitive dissonance in some individuals. Individuals who do not see themselves as helpful people will not be moved to participate by cognitive dissonance.

## Self-Perception Theory

The application of self-perception theory to online survey response relies on individuals' desire to view themselves as kind, helpful, and generous. By inviting people to participate in a survey, you are offering them an opportunity to manifest these qualities. Researchers can label the act of participation as "generous," thereby helping prospective respondents classify themselves. The theory predicts that potential respondents who identify with the label will choose to participate.

## Level of Involvement and Engagement

Involvement or commitment to a particular system, process, or organization can affect one's likelihood of participating in an online survey. The more involved one is, the more likely one is to participate. Once the person has opened the survey, the goal is to prevent dropouts. Because of the increasing demands on people's time and the increasing competition from social networking and other Internet sites, it is essential that researchers grasp and maintain the respondent's attention and interest in the survey. To take advantage of involvement as a motivator for participating in an online survey, researchers can point out the following, when appropriate, in the survey invitation:

- The respondent is being contacted because of his or her prior action (such as attending a conference, purchasing a product, or using a service).
- The respondent's participation has implications for the maintenance of or changes in a system or process—for example, "Your responses will help the marketing team decide on the new logo."
- The respondent will benefit tangibly from participation—for example, "We will be purchasing new inventory control software for your division and need your feedback."

Lightspeed Research (2009b) analyzed the results of seven survey satisfaction questions. These data included more than 182,000 cases and more than 240 surveys. Using that information, they constructed a factor analysis with the seven variables and created an "Engagement Index." The variables were weighted, and all variables were positively correlated. The variable that contributed most to the overall variance was "enjoyment" of the survey experience (47.2%), followed by how interesting the survey was (15.7%) and how easy the survey was thought to be (10.1%). Perceived length of the survey contributed only 6.3% of overall variance. Kantar Operations, a division of Lightspeed, then analyzed 3 million online surveys and found that length was the cause of dropouts in only one-fifth of the cases. This suggests that respondents may tolerate longer surveys if they find them engaging. A key question remains—what constitutes an "enjoyable" and interesting survey from a respondent point of view?

Lightspeed Research also studied how engagement and completion times and demographics are related. They found that women tend to be engaged more than men and that the youngest (16- to 24-year-olds) and oldest (65+) respondents tended to exhibit the lowest level of engagement (Lightspeed Research, 2009a). In this study, Lightspeed also looked at level of engagement and survey length. They did find that respondents who completed the shorter surveys reported higher levels of engagement (see Table 6.12). In their first study, Lightspeed noted that survey length is a factor but not the primary contributor to survey engagement. After conducting this second study, they concluded that researchers do need to be mindful of survey length, particularly if a survey scores low on other engagement metrics.

**Table 6.12   Levels of Engagement and Survey Length**

| Survey Length | Level of Engagement ($n = 15,031$) |
|---|---|
| Short (under 20 minutes) | Medium and low: 15%<br>High: 46%<br>Very high 40% |
| Longer (between 20 and 60 minutes) | Medium and low: 20%<br>High: 47%<br>Very high: 33% |
| Very long (more than 60 minutes) | Medium and low: 20%<br>High: 49%<br>Very high: 32% |

SOURCE: Lightspeed Research (2009a).

# Thank-You Messages

There are three ways to thank respondents for completing an online survey. The first is to add a thank-you page to the end of the survey, typically following the "submit" page. The thank you should express gratitude for completing the survey and offer instructions about redeeming incentives, if applicable. A second technique is to send a separate e-mail (or text message) to the respondents. Finally, a thank you could be delivered as a follow-up message after the project is completed. This method permits the researcher to share results with the respondents and possibly illustrate how their feedback impacted change in a process or organization.

# Summary

After laboring over the creation of measurable survey objectives, writing valid and reliable survey questions, selecting a sample, and creatively designing an online questionnaire, the final challenge in the online survey data collection process is getting participants to respond to your survey. Online survey researchers can avail themselves of a wide variety of recruitment options, including e-mail invitations, links on websites, pop-up invitations, invitations sent to mobile devices, social media websites, and many different offline venues. Each of these mechanisms has benefits and limitations that should be considered in light of research objectives, the research timeline, and audience characteristics. Social media, for example, is inexpensive, convenient, and fast but relies on volunteers to opt in to the survey, rendering the results of limited usefulness.

Informed by the survey research literature and the knowledge base of the professional online survey research community, we offered a set of best practices for writing e-mail invitations that are likely to avoid spam filters and arrive successfully in recipients' e-mail inboxes. Creating short subject lines, writing compelling invitations that contain a clear link to the survey, and avoiding certain words and phrases are some of the techniques to encourage survey participation.

We presented survey deployment as a multistage process involving pretesting, then a small or soft launch, followed by the full launch of the survey. Each stage is designed to minimize error and maximize the chances of collecting valid and useful data. Moving through the stages of survey deployment may take days or weeks depending on the nature and scope of the project.

As in any type of survey research, obtaining high response rates from online surveys is a challenge. Some of the techniques we discussed for improving survey response are not unique to online surveys. For example, prenotifying respondents, writing persuasive invitations, sending reminders, and offering incentives are common in many survey settings, even if the delivery system is different. These time-tested methods for increasing response rate, combined with scrubbing invitation lists and thoughtfully timing the delivery of invitations, offer online survey researchers a good chance of collecting the number of survey responses necessary for accurate data reporting.

## Exercises

A nonprofit community health clinic wants to conduct a survey examining the healthcare needs of low-income families in the two counties served by the clinic. It has developed a questionnaire that covers topics such as health history, record of inpatient and outpatient care, participation in state-run programs, employment status, and demographic factors such as race/ethnicity, primary language preference, family size, gender and ages of all family members, and household income. The clinic has a list of names and addresses of patients who have received services in the past 2 years. The list contains very few e-mail addresses but does include mobile phone numbers for about half the patients. The proportion of patients who have Internet access at home is unknown.

1. Suggest a method to recruit participants for an online survey for the clinic. Describe the advantages and disadvantages of the method you recommend.

2. You are given further information about the survey requirements: (a) it must be completed in 2 weeks, (b) the clinic has a small budget for the project, and (c) the primary targets for the survey are mothers with children at home. Does this information change your recommendation from question 1? If so, why?

3. Given the nature of the information to be collected, what, if any, data security issues should the clinic be mindful of as they consider data collection options?

4. The clinic has virtually no budget to offer financial incentives to survey respondents; what can they do to encourage participation?

# CHAPTER 7

# Processing and Analyzing the Survey Data

When planning a survey, it is necessary to consider the analyses that will be required of the report. Do you simply want to describe your respondents? Or is the goal to make inferences about the population from which the survey sample was chosen? By considering data analysis as part of the survey planning process, you will be more likely to collect data that will adequately address your objectives.

Most web-based survey hosts permit users to conduct data analysis via the hosts' websites. Some hosts provide options for descriptive statistics only, others allow researchers to conduct more complex analyses, and almost all offer the ability to download data so that they may be imported and used in statistical software programs. In no situation will you have to compute statistics by hand. You will, however, need to decide which statistics to compute using software, and you will need to interpret the results of the analyses. This chapter outlines strategies for analysis planning and data management. We also cover some basic statistical concepts and commonly used statistical tests for the analysis of survey data. An in-depth study of statistical techniques is beyond the scope of this book.

## Planning for Data Analysis

The plan for data analysis begins with survey objectives, continues with suitable questions on the questionnaire, and ends with specification of the statistical tests, if any, to be performed. Example 7.1 shows two objectives from the same survey project, the survey questions used to measure the concepts, and the analysis plan for each objective.

---

**Example 7.1**

*Survey Objective 1:* To determine whether guilt is induced in an individual when that individual perceives he or she has acted incorrectly in an interpersonal situation

> *Measurement:* Fourteen survey questions, each addressing a unique dimension of guilt; example question—"You are taking care of your close friend Chris's dog. While Chris is on vacation, the dog runs away. How likely are you to feel guilty when Chris returns and asks what happened to the dog?" (Measured on a 0- to 10-point scale: 0 = not at all guilty, 10 = extremely guilty)
>
> *Analysis plan:* (a) Present descriptive statistics (frequencies and summary statistics) for each of the 14 guilt questions. (b) Create a guilt index by combining the 14 questions that measure guilt. Present descriptive statistics of the index.

*Survey Objective 2:* To determine whether a gender difference exists in the level of guilt induced in males and females

> *Measurement:* Index of 14 guilt-inducing situations; gender variable (male/female)
>
> *Analysis plan:* A *t* test for differences in guilt index mean between males and females

---

By thinking ahead to your analysis plan, you can adjust your survey questions to ensure that the level of measurement is appropriate for the planned statistical tests. For example, *t* tests require a dichotomous grouping variable and a continuous variable. If your questionnaire contains only nominal variables—for example, questions measured with yes/no options—you will not be able to use a *t* test. It also may be useful to sketch the summary tables, charts, and graphs you expect to use in presenting your report. Previewing the form in which you would like to present your data allows you to choose the statistical technique most appropriate for providing results in the necessary format.

You will be able to view descriptive summary statistics and perhaps simple cross-tabulations on your survey host's website. If you will need more advanced statistical analysis, it is important to investigate the features available on the host website before signing up for a service. High-end web survey applications offer embedded statistical analyses packages that permit users to conduct a wide variety of analyses. The more basic programs allow users to download data in an Excel spreadsheet, which can then be imported into a third-party statistical software package. This is not difficult (e.g., the SPSS wizard will take you step by step through importing data from Excel into SPSS) but does involve a few extra steps and introduces more opportunity for error in data handling. Because of the growing demand for advanced statistical analyses, many survey software vendors now offer data downloads in SPSS format. For example, SurveyMonkey customers can opt for a Gold account package that offers this feature.

## Tracking the Surveys

Keeping track of the questionnaires as they are completed is necessary so that you can monitor response rate, send reminders to nonrespondents, and identify problematic data early in the process.

If you have chosen to distribute an e-mail survey from your own e-mail application, such as Outlook Mail, response tracking will probably be a manual process. As the questionnaires are returned, you will need to compare the completed questionnaires against the master list from which the e-mail invitations were sent. This requires that the questionnaires contain identifying information: either a randomly assigned value that can be used to identify respondents in the master list or another unique value such as respondents' names or e-mail addresses.

Many researchers find it useful to create a return rate graph. The graph allows you to track the progress of the returns and decide when to send follow-up reminders. In the survey depicted in Figure 7.1, the initial invitations were sent on a Monday; by Thursday, responses had dropped to a third of Wednesday's total. The increase in responses on Friday was the result of a reminder e-mail. By the following Monday, only a small number of responses were being returned, and the survey was closed. These graphs are most practical when the survey will be in the field for at least a week; overnight polls and other quick surveys would not benefit from this type of graph.

Uploading an e-mail distribution list to a web-based survey host for the deployment of the survey simplifies the process, as you can track completed responses via the host's software. You will be able to view

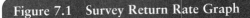

Figure 7.1    Survey Return Rate Graph

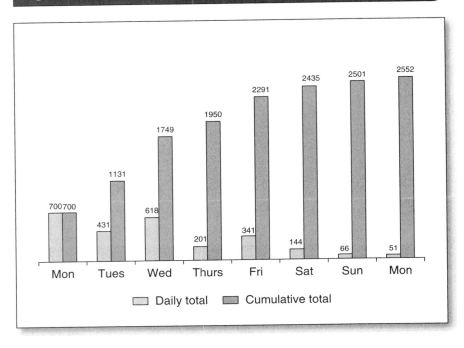

whether or not each individual recipient has responded. In this scenario, sending reminders to nonrespondents is a straightforward process of filtering out those who have completed the survey and sending the reminder e-mail to those who have not yet started or who have started but not yet completed the survey. Figure 7.2 shows an example of a survey recipient tracking screen. Of the 10 respondents to whom the survey was sent, 4 have completed the questionnaire, 3 have not, 2 have declined to participate, and 1 started but did not finish the survey. Using this list, the researcher can instruct the software to send a reminder e-mail to individuals who have not responded nor completed the survey. This is considerably faster and less error prone than the manual process of tracking and filtering completed responses. Why not always send e-mail survey invitations from the software application? Although it requires additional manual tasks, it may be desirable to send a survey invitation from an e-mail address that potential respondents may previously have saved in their e-mail address books or from a domain that is recognizable to the invitees' e-mail servers. This increases the chances of

**Figure 7.2   Tracking Report of E-Mail Recipients**

| | E-Mail List Management | | | |
|---|---|---|---|---|
| | **E-Mail Address** | **First Name** | **Last Name** | **Status** |
| 1 | asmith@aol.com | Alice | Smith | Responded |
| 2 | kthompson@yahoo.com | Kathy | Thompson | No response |
| 3 | rcahill@gmail.com | Ryan | Cahill | Declined |
| 4 | ckelley@yahoo.com | Candice | Kelley | Responded |
| 5 | mjohnson@att.com | Mary | Johnson | Responded |
| 6 | cmlee@msn.com | Cindy | Lee | No response |
| 7 | mmadison@yahoo.com | Myron | Madison | No response |
| 8 | dhashimoto@gmail.com | Darrell | Hashimoto | Declined |
| 9 | dbeckman@yahoo.com | David | Beckman | Incomplete |
| 10 | aedwards@yahoo.com | Aaron | Edwards | Responded |

the invitation making it through spam filters and arriving in the recipients' inboxes successfully.

Most survey hosts allow you to view and download responses as frequently as you like. Many offer "real-time" viewing of results—that is, every time another respondent completes the questionnaire, you can update the results to view the changes. This is a useful feature and can help uncover technical or content errors in the questionnaire. Suppose you examine the results of an employee satisfaction survey after the first 20 questionnaires have been completed and you notice there are no answers to questions about the new lunchroom policy. Maybe the employees have no opinion about the new policy and are skipping the questions, or perhaps an error in the questionnaire's skip logic is preventing respondents from seeing the questions. In this situation, you can correct the error so that the remaining respondents will be presented with all the questions. Responses from the first 20 respondents, however, will be missing from the final data file.

Real-time viewing of survey results can sometimes lead researchers to close an electronic survey prematurely, after a desired result has been achieved. This may occur when the surveyor has a vested interest in the outcome of the project. A researcher who is hoping to show support for a new proposal and sees 60% of the first 300 survey respondents have indicated strong support for the proposal may decide to close the survey before the remaining respondents possibly bring down that percentage. A survey result based on this sort of practice is useless and violates the principles of ethical data collection and reporting.

## Survey Codebooks

Codebooks, or data definition dictionaries, are guides to survey data. They contain comprehensive documentation that enables other researchers who might subsequently want to analyze the data to do so without any additional information. A codebook provides information on the structure, contents, and layout of a data file. The idea is to define all response options on the questionnaire. For example, question 1 on a survey asks, "Are you male or female?" You could assign to *male* the value of 1 and to *female* the value of 2. These codes (1 and 2) are arbitrary; they could be anything that makes sense to the research team. The codebook is the document that lets everyone know that *male* = 1 and *female* = 2.

The typical convention for most survey development tools is to assign the first response option in a list the code of 1, the second a code of 2, and so on. For example, a response list of racial/ethnic options might include *White, Black, Asian or Pacific Islander, Native American or Alaskan Native, African American, Mixed Race, Other*, and *Decline to State*. The first response option entered, *White*, would be coded 1; *Black* would be coded 2; and so on, with *Decline to State* being assigned a code of 8. Some questions are precoded. For example, if you ask respondents how many times in the past week they ate at fast-food restaurants, their zip code, or the year in which they were born, the numbers they provide do not need to be translated further; therefore, no code value would be assigned to these responses. Similarly, open-ended text questions do not have code values assigned. Figure 7.3 is an example of an e-mail questionnaire, and Figure 7.4 shows its codebook.

Although codebooks are not necessary for data-entry purposes in web-based and mobile surveys (because the data file is created automatically when respondents type in their answers), online survey programs include the option to create codebooks so that any researcher working on the survey project will be able to identify the codes associated with each response value.

**Student Learning Survey**

Thank you for taking the time to answer these questions. Your responses are important to us. All of your answers will remain confidential and results will be reported in the aggregate only.

**How many times this year have you been involved in a group learning experience?**

- ○ Never
- ○ Once
- ○ 2–3 times
- ○ 4–5 times
- ○ More than 5 times

**Overall, how would you rate your group learning experiences?**

- ○ Excellent
- ○ Very Good
- ○ Good
- ○ Fair
- ○ Poor

**When working in groups do you usually find yourself in a leadership position?**

- ○ Yes
- ○ No
- ○ Don't know

**How easy or difficult is it for you to communicate your thoughts in group settings?**

- ○ Very easy
- ○ Easy
- ○ Unsure
- ○ Difficult
- ○ Very difficult

**What size team do you prefer to work in?**

- ○ 2 person
- ○ 3 person
- ○ 4 person
- ○ 5 person
- ○ 6 or more person
- ○ I do not like to work in teams

**What do you like most about working in groups?**

Please be as specific as possible.

**What do you like least about working in groups?**

Please be as specific as possible.

**Are you male of female?**

- ○ Male
- ○ Female

**In what year were you born?**

Please enter numeric response only; format 19XX.

**Figure 7.4    Example of an E-Mail Questionnaire Codebook**

| Question | Answer | Code |
|---|---|---|
| **RespondentID** | | |
| **Q1_Group_Learning** | Never | 1 |
| | Once | 2 |
| | 2–3 times | 3 |
| | 4–5 times | 4 |
| | More than 5 times | 5 |
| **Q2_Rate_Learning** | Excellent | 1 |
| | Very Good | 2 |
| | Good | 3 |
| | Fair | 4 |
| | Poor | 5 |
| **Q3_Leadership_Position** | Yes | 1 |
| | No | 2 |
| | Don't Know | 3 |
| **Q4_Communicate_Thoughts** | Very easy | 1 |
| | Easy | 2 |
| | Unsure | 3 |
| | Difficult | 4 |
| | Very difficult | 5 |
| **Q5_Team_Size** | 2 person | 1 |
| | 3 person | 2 |
| | 4 person | 3 |
| | 5 person | 4 |
| | 6 or more person | 5 |
| | I do not like to work in teams | 6 |
| **Q6_Like_Most** | Verbatim | |
| **Q7_Like_Least** | Verbatim | |
| **Q8_Gender** | Male | 1 |
| | Female | 2 |
| **Q9_DOB** | Verbatim | |

## Codebook Contents

Codebooks vary widely in quality and the amount of information provided. A typical codebook includes

- ID numbers,
- variable name,
- variable description,
- variable format (e.g., number, text, date),
- codes used to indicate nonresponse and missing data,
- the exact questions and skip patterns used in a survey, and
- other indications of the content and characteristics of each variable.

Codebooks also may contain

- frequencies of response;
- survey objectives;
- concept definitions;
- a description of the survey design and methodology;
- a copy of the survey questionnaire (if applicable); and
- information on data collection, data processing, and data quality.

# Data Cleaning

Before data analysis can proceed, the survey data should be cleaned. Sources of "dirty" data include data-entry errors, incomplete answers, answers out of the possible range, and errors associated with questionnaire programming mistakes. Data cleaning is the process of identifying and correcting these errors. Data cleaning does *not* mean throwing out answers that do not support your research objectives. It is important not to let your goals get in the way of what the data actually say.

## Data Cleaning as a Process

Data cleaning deals with data problems once they have occurred. Error prevention strategies, such as writing clear questions, providing instructions for answering, using skip logic wisely, and programming response validation rules that check for impossible answers and present respondents with error messages, can reduce many problems. Although you may encounter data errors incidentally throughout the analysis process, performing systematic data cleaning is advisable before commencing with analysis. Van den Broeck,

Argeseanu Cunningham, Eeckels, and Herbst (2005) outlined a three-stage process for data cleaning that can be effectively applied to data from digital survey projects. The process involves screening, diagnosing, and editing suspected data abnormalities.

## Step 1: Screening Phase

Data screening formally begins when the data have been downloaded from a survey host and analysts can start to scan spreadsheets and summary tables. The screening can begin earlier, however—as soon as the first questionnaires are returned. Checking the questionnaires early sometimes allows researchers to catch problems and rectify them before the research is too far under way. As we noted earlier, a block of missing answers may be due to inaccurate questionnaire programming or perhaps an editorial issue, such as a response option inadvertently omitted from the questionnaire.

At the screening level, look for patterns of missing data, inconsistencies in the data, strange patterns in the distributions, and extreme values (outliers). In addition to scanning the data file, researchers also can create frequency distribution tables and graphs to look for odd data points.

## Step 2: Diagnostic Phase

The purpose of the diagnostic phase is to identify the cause of the strange data points. Some values may be clearly impossible—for example, a respondent reporting that she watched 25 hours of television in one day. Others will be unlikely—such as a college student reporting that he is 12 years old. Possible causes of these odd data points include the following: the data may have been entered incorrectly by the respondent (perhaps the college student respondent meant to type in *21* instead of *12* and transposed the numbers), the question may have been misunderstood, or the data may be real (the unlikely, not the impossible data). The first situation could be easily avoided by programming the survey not to accept answers in excess of 24 hours. In the second example, you could also program the questionnaire to accept only numerical answers of 18 or greater; however, this may not adequately provide for all possible responses. The researcher needs a good sense of the possible range of responses when programming the survey's data validation rules.

## Step 3: Treatment Phase

After you identify errors, missing and strange values, and true but extreme data, you will need to decide what to do about the problematic observations. Impossible values are the easiest to tackle. If the survey was not anonymous—that is, if you have information that identifies the respondents—you may be able to fix the error by using existing data sources to replace the incorrect value. If ascertaining the real value is not possible because you have conducted an anonymous survey, then you should mark the value as missing.

When it comes to possible but unlikely values, the options are less clear. Some statisticians recommend that extreme values always remain in the data file unchanged. Others suggest statistical treatments such as imputation (e.g., replacing the value with the group mean for that variable). A third school of thought permits the deletion of extreme values as long as the final report notes that some values were "excluded from the analysis." The overriding concern here is with accurate and ethical data analysis and reporting. When a researcher begins to toss out data, the integrity of the data may be compromised. It is best to evaluate extreme data points on a case-by-case basis and reserve the option of deleting unlikely cases as a last resort.

## Data Transformation

Once the data have been downloaded and cleaned, it is almost always necessary to transform some of the raw data into values that are usable in the analyses. For example, if you collected information about respondents' ages by asking for date of birth, you will have to do some arithmetic to transform the data into age in years. Other issues such as missing values on some questions and the need to recode some scales must be addressed before data analysis can begin.

### Missing Values

Many analysis programs automatically treat questions without a response in the data file as missing values. In others, you need to define specific codes to represent missing values. For instance, you might use a value of 99 to indicate that the respondent did not enter an answer for that question. Checking the specifications of the analysis program you are using is important to determine how missing values are handled.

### Recoding Data

Before analyzing the data, you may need to recode some scale items so that all the response options are consistent. For instance, let's say you had a 5-point response scale for a self-esteem measure, where 1 meant "strongly disagree" and 5 meant "strongly agree." One item is "I generally feel good about myself." If the respondent strongly agrees with this item, he or she will enter a 5, and this value will be indicative of higher self-esteem. Alternatively, consider an item such as "Sometimes I feel like I'm not worth much as a person." Here, if a respondent strongly agrees by rating this 5, it will indicate low self-esteem. To compare these two items, we would reverse the scores for one of them (we would probably reverse the latter item so that high values always indicate higher self-esteem). If the original value was 1, it changes to 5; 2 changes to 4; 3 remains the same; 4 changes to 2; and 5 changes to 1. While you could program these changes as separate statements in most data analysis programs, it is easier to accomplish this with a simple formula—for example,

New Value = (High Value + 1) − Original Value.

In our example, the high value for the scale is 5; so to get the new (transformed) scale value, we simply subtract each original value from 6 (i.e., 5 + 1). Many data analysis programs can perform the same data transformation on several variables at once.

The other common recoding situation we mentioned earlier requires you to compute respondents' ages from their dates of birth. Recent versions of SPSS contain a "Date and Time Wizard" (found under the "Transform" menu), which will take you through the steps of this process. In Excel, a simple formula will do the trick:

=INT((TODAY()-A1)/365.25).

In this formula, "TODAY" inserts the current date and "A1" references the cell containing the date of birth.

Finally, attend to values that have been assigned to response options such as "not applicable" or "don't know." A question with a 1- to 5-point response scale, where 1 = "not at all" and 5 = "extremely," may have included a sixth, "not applicable" option. If you entered "not applicable" as the sixth item in a list of response options, the default behavior of most survey programs will be to code it as 6. This value will need to be coded as missing data or flagged in some other way so it does not factor into the computation of summary statistics and is not used in statistical tests.

## Descriptive Statistics

Descriptive statistics are used to describe the basic features of the data in a study. They provide summaries about the sample characteristics and responses to individual survey questions. Together with tables and charts, descriptive statistics form the basis for quantitative data analysis.

Descriptive statistics are typically distinguished from inferential statistics. Whereas descriptive statistics are used to describe what is going on in a data set, inferential statistics are used to make statements beyond the sample data. For example, we might use inferential statistics to try to make inferences about public opinion in a large population of voters based on data from a random sample.

The first step in any data analysis strategy is usually to look at each questionnaire item individually. There are two convenient ways to do this: (a) create frequency distributions for each question or (b) compute summary statistics for each question.

## Frequency Distributions

The frequency distribution of a particular questionnaire item shows the numbers (and/or percentages) of respondents who selected each response option. Almost all web-based survey software includes the option of creating frequency distributions and presenting them as either tables or charts. These basic frequency distributions are usually the default mode in which survey software hosts present results. The function can be found in the host's "analysis" or "analyze" menu. Figure 7.5 shows a frequency distribution of responses to one question on a student survey. Students were asked what grade they expected to earn in an online class. The students were confident: all believed they would earn at least a C grade, and 45.2% expected to earn an A.

Another useful way to quickly view the results of a particular question is to construct a chart, such as the one in Figure 7.6. This horizontal bar chart shows responses to an employee job satisfaction question. Viewed this way, readers can see at a glance that the majority of the respondents agreed that their work was enjoyable. Figure 7.7 is a pie chart of the race/ethnicity of

**Figure 7.5   Frequency Distribution Display**

### What grade do you expect to earn in this class?

|  |  | Response count | Response percent |
|---|---|---|---|
| A |  | 14 | 45.2% |
| B |  | 13 | 41.9% |
| C |  | 4 | 12.9% |
| D |  | 0 | 0.0% |
| F |  | 0 | 0.0% |
| **Answered question** |  | 31 | 100% |
| **Skipped question** |  | 1 |  |

Figure 7.6    Bar Graph of Responses to an Individual Survey Question

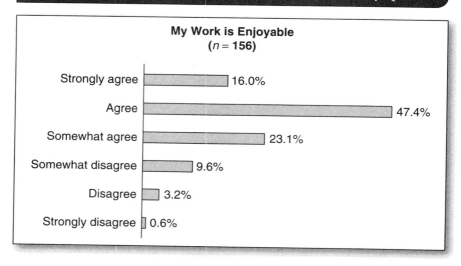

Figure 7.7    Pie Chart of Survey Respondents' Race/Ethnicity

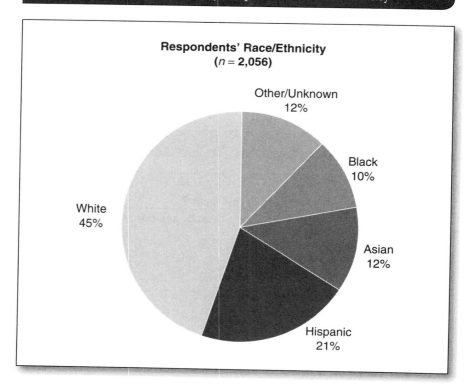

the same survey participants; it is easy to see that almost half (45%) of the respondents to this survey were White. We will have more to say in Chapter 8 about representing data in charts.

## Summary Statistics

Summary statistics provide concise descriptions of the distributions of answers to survey questions. Distributions are often described using five statistics: three measures of central tendency (mean, median, and mode) and two measures of dispersion (range and standard deviation). The measures of central tendency summarize data by describing what is "typical" or "average" in a set of values. Measures of central tendency are useful but provide incomplete, and sometimes misleading, information. The range and standard deviation add important context for interpreting typical values by describing how data are dispersed.

### Mean

The sample **mean** (denoted by $\bar{x}$) is the arithmetical average of a set of observations in sample data and is the most commonly used statistic for describing what is typical in a distribution. The mean is computed by summing the values and dividing by the number of values in the set. Here are the ages of six students who participated in a class evaluation survey:

22          25          18          20          19          22

The sum of these six values is 126, so the mean equals 126/6 = 21.

One problem with the mean is that it is susceptible to the influence of **outliers**. Outliers are scores that lie an extreme distance away from the other scores in a distribution. What constitutes "extreme" is largely up to the data analyst. Some take the view that any data point more than three standard deviations away from the mean is an outlier; others apply a more subjective approach, looking at individual questionnaire items and applying different criteria to each one depending on the overall look of the distribution. As an illustration, let's revisit the ages of the six students mentioned above and add a seventh:

22          25          18          20          19          22          95

By adding the seventh (95-year-old) student, the mean of ages becomes 31.6. While the mean is correct, it may not accurately reflect the "typical" situation. Strategies for dealing with outliers include the following:

- *Ignoring*—act as if the outlier isn't there, and proceed with analysis as planned. (bad solution)

- *Investigating*—find out the cause of the outlier. Is there really a 95-year-old college student? If there is, maybe you should leave him or her in the data. If not and this score is due to a recording error, delete it. (good solution)
- *Deleting without investigating*—remove the data point from the distribution without investigating why it's there. (bad solution)
- *Accommodating*—leave the outlier in the data description and explain. (good solution if the outlier is a legitimate part of the data)

In addition to investigating and acting appropriately, as described above, it is always a good idea to use the median in addition to the mean as a measure of central tendency, as it isn't as sensitive to outliers. (We discuss the median in the next section.)

The mean is a logical choice for summarizing interval data such as age, test scores, money, and time. The majority of opinion survey data, however, is ordinal in nature (e.g., Likert-type scales). Recall from our earlier discussion that attitude scales are ordinal because the distance between "strongly disagree" and "disagree" is not necessarily the same as the distance between "disagree" and "somewhat disagree." In these situations, the median, rather than the mean, may be the appropriate measure of central tendency. Although it technically requires that we assume the distances on the scale are equal and respondents share a common understanding of each response category, using the mean to summarize attitude measurements is common practice among survey researchers. We will return to this discussion shortly.

## Median

The **median** is the middle value in a distribution; half the observations are above the median, and half are below it. To determine the median, first list the values in order from smallest to largest, then count to the middle. If you have an odd number of values, the median is the number in the middle; if you have an even number of observations, the median is the average of the middle two values. Say you collected salary data for six midlevel managers at a corporation. These are the salaries in thousands of dollars:

$114      $65      $80      $78      $72      $55

First, order the data from lowest to highest:

$55      $65      $72      $78      $80      $114

Then, find the midpoint; in this case, because the group contains an even number of data points, we will need to average the two middle values. The

median salary is (72 + 78)/2 = 75. The median can often be located on a frequency distribution, as it is the data point that represents the 50th percentile.

If repeated values appear in the data (e.g., with Likert-scale data), the
median is still the middle value, as follows:

1, 1, 1, 2, 2, 2, 2, 3, 3, 3, 3, 3, 3, 3, 3, 4, 4, 4, 5, 5 median = 3

The median is an appropriate summary statistic when reporting the
results of ranking questions. For example, say you asked respondents to
rank seven problems facing their community by giving a rank of 1 to the
most important problem, a rank of 2 to the next most important one, and
so on. You could compute the median for each problem that was ranked.
Example 7.2 presents the ranks that were assigned to the problem of
"crime" by nine respondents. Because the data are already in order, it is
easy to see that the median rank is 3.

---

*Example 7.2*

1, 2, 2, 2, 3, 4, 5, 5, 7

---

Earlier, we noted that the median is the appropriate summary statistic for
reporting the results of attitude questions but that survey researchers more
often use the mean. Now, let's consider how we can use these two statistics
together to more fully understand survey responses. Table 7.1 shows the
means and medians for a selection of items from an employee satisfaction
survey. The response scale was as follows: 1 = Strongly disagree, 2 = Disagree,
3 = Somewhat disagree, 4 = Somewhat agree, 5 = Agree, 6 = Strongly agree.

**Table 7.1    Mean and Median Ratings on Employee Satisfaction
Survey (1 = Strongly disagree, 6 = Strongly agree)**

| Questionnaire Item | Mean | Median |
|---|---|---|
| 1. I make a difference. | 5.23 | 5.00 |
| 2. My work is enjoyable. | 4.62 | 5.00 |
| 3. I am able to utilize my strengths. | 4.58 | 5.00 |
| 4. My responsibilities are clear. | 4.29 | 5.00 |
| 5. I trust my manager. | 4.29 | 4.00 |

Described only with the medians, we would conclude that the employees *agreed* with the first four statements and *somewhat agreed* with the last. Looking at the means, however, we are able to discern more detailed information about each set of responses. We can see, for example, that the employees felt better about their ability to make a difference than they did about the clarity of their job responsibilities.

## Mode

The **mode** is the most frequently occurring value in the set of scores. To determine the mode, you might again order the values as shown above and then count the number of times each value appears. In the age data above, two 22-year-old students are listed; therefore, the mode is 22. The salary data has no mode (no value occurred more than once). The frequency distribution of survey participants' department in Table 7.2 reveals that the mode is "Accounting." The mode is the summary statistic most often used when reporting nominal data such as gender, major in college, music genre, and so on. A data set can have two or more modes (i.e., bimodal, multimodal).

## Range

The **range** is the difference between the largest and the smallest values in a distribution. It tells us about the spread, or dispersion, in the data. The range is a limited statistic, because it depends on only two numbers for its

**Table 7.2    Distribution of Survey Participants' Department**

| Department | Frequency | Percentage |
|---|---|---|
| Accounting | 35 | 28.2 |
| Customer Service | 18 | 14.5 |
| Human Resources | 19 | 15.3 |
| Sales | 10 | 8.1 |
| Shipping | 29 | 23.4 |
| Telecommunications | 13 | 10.5 |
| Total | 124 | 100.0 |

value—the largest and the smallest—and, like the mean, can be greatly exaggerated by outliers. Recall the example of the ages of seven students:

| 22 | 25 | 18 | 20 | 19 | 22 | 95 |

The range of these values is 95 − 18 = 77; that's a wide range of student ages. Removing the outlier (95) reduces the range to 7 (25 − 18 = 7). The range is often reported so that readers have a context for interpreting other summary statistics, such as the mean, median, or mode.

## Standard Deviation

Like the range, **standard deviation** is a measure of variability. Unlike the range, however, standard deviation takes into account all the data points in a distribution. Standard deviation indicates how close to the mean the observations are, on average. If all the observations are the same, the standard deviation equals zero. The more spread out the observations are, the larger the standard deviation. Put another way, the larger the standard deviation, the more variation is evident in the data. The scores in Example 7.3 are from three groups of respondents. Each group has the same mean, but the standard deviations are different.

---

*Example 7.3: Means and Standard Deviations for Three Groups of Scores*

Group A:   15   15   15   15   15   15   15   (Mean = 15, SD = 0)

Group B:   14   14   14   15   16   16   16   (Mean = 15, SD = 0.93)

Group C:   0   5   10   15   20   25   30   (Mean = 15, SD = 10)

---

As you can see, Group A has no variability (standard deviation = 0) and Group C has the most variability (standard deviation = 10). The distance of the individual scores from the mean determines the size of the standard deviation. Group C's scores vary greatly from the mean of 15, hence the large standard deviation of 10.

Although it would be easy to compute the standard deviation, and the other summary statistics, for seven scores by hand, your survey data is unlikely to contain only seven values. When you are dealing with hundreds or thousands of data points, a software program to compute these values for you is necessary. Every statistical software package is capable of doing this; your task will be to determine the proper commands and, of course, to interpret the results.

The basic-level online survey software packages do not routinely provide summary statistics but sometimes offer users the ability to upgrade their service so they can compute these statistics. An alternative is to export the raw data as a spreadsheet and compute summary statistics in Excel.

## Inferential Statistics

The distribution of individual variables depicted by frequency distributions and summary statistics provides an important and necessary first view of the survey data. For some research purposes, these descriptions may be the only way in which the data need be reported. In other situations, however, examining how two or more variables interact with one another will be necessary. For example, you may want to know whether males and females differ on an opinion question. Or you may want to make a statement about the population from which the sample was selected. When we use data to test hypotheses or draw conclusions about populations, we are no longer simply describing the data; we are making inferences.

The statistical method you choose to compare respondents is determined by the number and type of variables you are comparing. When comparing two nominal (categorical) variables, you can usually use the chi-square test. When comparing the means of two random samples, a $t$ test is often appropriate. And when evaluating the relationship between two interval variables, you could conduct a **correlation** analysis. You will be able to conduct these analyses by exporting your raw data into a statistical analysis software package such as **SPSS**, **SAS**, or **Minitab**. Off-the-shelf web survey software solutions usually are not capable of performing these tests. If you determine that you will need to conduct $t$ tests, correlation analysis, or something more advanced, such as analysis of variance or regression, it may be worthwhile to invest in software that allows direct export of raw data into the statistical analysis package of your choice or to consider an inclusive package that provides a web survey development application and advanced data analysis software.

### A Note About Alpha and $p$ Values

When researchers write, "The results of the test were statistically significant at a significance level of .05 ($p < .05$)," they are saying that the relationship described by the observed test statistic is not likely due to chance. More specifically, the likelihood that the relationship is due to chance, given that there is no real relationship, is less than 5%. The .05 is referred to as alpha. There is nothing sacred about the .05. It is one frequently used alpha level; .01 is another commonly used alpha level.

A **p value** represents the probability of seeing results as extreme as or more extreme than those actually observed if, in fact, the variables you are testing have no relationship. Statistical software routinely provides $p$ values associated with statistical tests—for example, $p = .027$. Traditionally, the $p$ values of a test are compared with a predetermined alpha level. If the $p$ value is greater than alpha, then you can conclude that the results of the test are "not significant" at level alpha; if the $p$ value is less than or equal to the predetermined alpha level, then you can conclude that a "statistically significant" relationship exists between the variables at level alpha (see Example 7.4).

---

**Example 7.4**

$p = .003, < .05$: The $p$ value is less than alpha; the variables have a statistically significant relationship.

$p = .214, > .05$: The $p$ value is greater than alpha; the variables do not have a statistically significant relationship.

---

This type of analysis is called fixed-level testing because the researcher determines the acceptable level of alpha before analysis begins. Many contemporary statisticians have moved away from fixed-level testing and the language of "statistical significance." One reason is that reporting the significance of a test using a predetermined alpha without citing the $p$ value limits the reader's ability to fully interpret the results. For example, if a report claims that the results of a test show a statistically significant relationship using alpha .05, the $p$ value could have been .049 or .001 (or anything in between). In the first case, the results are just barely significant; in the second, they are more extreme.

A second concern regarding fixed-level testing is about the use of the term *significant*. Some researchers worry that readers will confuse the concepts of statistical significance and practical significance. As we have seen, statistical significance means that we are certain (to a specified degree) that our results are not due to chance. Practical significance, on the other hand, is a subjective judgment about the importance or usefulness of a finding.

Although there are good reasons to report $p$ values associated with statistical tests, it is still common practice in many social scientific disciplines and applied research settings to predetermine alpha levels and state conclusions about statistical significance.

## Cross-Tabulated Tables and Chi-Square

Multivariate data analyses often begin with cross-tabulated, or contingency, tables. These are tables that show the responses to one question in the rows and the responses to another question in the columns. Many web-based survey software programs allow researchers to create cross-tabulation tables.

Nominal data were described earlier in this text as data that fall into unordered categories, such as the response options for gender, occupation, or city. To compare two questions, each measured with nominal response options, you can create a contingency table that shows the categories to which each respondent belongs. Table 7.3 is a contingency table showing respondents' gender and their opinions on a ballot proposition. The cell contents show response frequency (and percentage) for each category column.

Looking at Table 7.3, we can see that a relationship seems to exist between gender and opinion. More women than men favor the proposition, and more men than women said they had "no opinion." Because the primary purpose of creating the cross-tabulation is to determine if a relationship exists between the two variables, it is necessary to apply a statistical test to verify whether the apparent pattern is real or due to chance. The chi-square test is the suitable choice because both variables are measured on a nominal scale.

A chi-square test will examine the observed frequencies in a category and compare them with the expected frequencies in the same categories. The observed frequencies are the data collected by the survey. The expected frequencies are the values that would occur if chance alone were operating or if no relationship existed between the variables. If the questions are independent of one another, then the results of the chi-square

**Table 7.3    Contingency Table of Gender by Opinion**

|  | Favor | Oppose | No Opinion | Total |
|---|---|---|---|---|
| Male | 10 (43.5%) | 17 (65.4%) | 26 (83.9%) | 53 (66.3%) |
| Female | 13 (56.5%) | 9 (34.6%) | 5 (16.1%) | 27 (33.7%) |
| Total | 23 (100%) | 26 (100%) | 31 (100%) | 80 (100%) |

NOTE: Chi-square = 11.0, $p < .005$.

test will be nonsignificant—meaning we believe no relationship exists between the variables. If the questions are found to be related, then the results of the test will be significant, suggesting a relationship does exist between the variables.

The chi-square test statistic ($\chi^2$) shown below Table 7.3 and its associated significance level (noted by $p < .005$) confirms that a relationship does exist between gender and one's opinion on this proposition. Put another way, if these variables were independent, there is a very small chance that the observed results would occur.

The chi-square test is subject to certain restrictions. First, each cell of the contingency table should contain an expected frequency of at least 5. In situations where expected cell frequencies fall below 5, categories may be combined (if reasonable) to increase the frequency of responses in a given cell. If this is not possible, chi-square cannot be used and a different statistical test must be employed. It is also important to note that the results of a chi-square test tell us only if a relationship exists between two nominal variables; they do not inform us about the nature of the relationship. Thus, we cannot make statements about causation (i.e., one variable being the cause of another).

## Independent Samples *t* Test

The independent samples *t* test compares the means of two groups and determines whether those two means are different enough to be statistically significant. This is an appropriate statistical test if you are examining the means of independent samples taken from two populations and if either the sample sizes are relatively large ($n > 30$) or you can assume that the data have roughly a bell-shaped or "normal" distribution. For example, say you wanted to determine if Republicans differed from Democrats on an authoritarian personality inventory. Party identification (Republican/Democrat) would be the grouping variable, and score on the authoritarian personality inventory (from 0 to 100, 100 indicating a highly authoritarian personality) would be the test variable. The means on the personality inventory would be computed for each group and compared. If the means turned out to be significantly different (determined by the value of the *t* test statistic), then we would say that the authoritarian personality scores of the Democrats and Republicans are significantly different statistically. The direction of the difference (which group was more authoritarian on average) is determined by looking at the means of the two groups.

Example 7.5 displays a portion of the computer output showing the results of a *t* test comparing the amount of guilt men and women said they would feel in a variety of interpersonal situations.

*Example 7.5*

|  | Gender | N | Mean | Standard Deviation |
|---|---|---|---|---|
| Guilt | Male | 21 | 96.1 | 29.3 |
|  | Female | 45 | 112.0 | 17.1 |

The first step is to examine the descriptive statistics for the two groups. We see that the mean for females is higher (112.0) than the mean for males (96.1). On average, women in this sample reported that they felt more guilt than did the men. (The column labeled "N" in the table indicates the number of respondents in each category, and the last column contains the standard deviations for each group.)

*Example 7.5 (Continued):* **t *Test for Equality of Means***

|  |  |  |  |  | 95% Confidence Interval of the Difference | |
|---|---|---|---|---|---|---|
| *t* | *df* | Significance (Two-Tailed) | Mean Difference | Standard Error Difference | Lower | Upper |
| −2.32 | 26.55 | 0.028 | −15.95 | 6.88 | −30.07 | −1.83 |

We know based on the previous table that the sample means for men and women are different, but we do not know if that difference is significant. The second table in Example 7.5 shows a *t* statistic of −2.32 (see the first column of the table) and a significance level (*p* value) of .028 (third column of the table). From this, we can conclude that the mean amount of guilt reported by females in the sample was significantly higher than the mean amount of guilt reported by the male respondents. Using the fixed-level testing approach, with alpha set at .05, you could report the results as follows: "Female respondents had higher guilt scores ($M$ = 112.0, $SD$ = 17.1) than did male respondents ($M$ = 96.1, $SD$ = 29.3), $t$ (27) = −2.32, $p$ < .05." Using the $p$-value approach, most of the sentence would remain the same, but the last element would read, "$p$ = .028."

## Pearson Correlation

The Pearson product-moment correlation coefficient (or Pearson correlation, or just correlation) is used to determine the degree of the linear relationship between two interval variables. If there is a high degree of linear relationship, either positive or negative, then a "linear" equation (straight line) based on one variable can be used to accurately predict the other. When discussing sample data, the Pearson correlation coefficient is denoted with the lowercase letter $r$. The value of $r$ ranges from −1 to 1. An $r$ of −1 indicates a perfect negative relationship, 0 means that no relationship exists between the variables, and 1 indicates a perfect positive relationship. These relationships are depicted in Figures 7.8, 7.9, and 7.10.

**Figure 7.8   Perfect Positive Relationship Between $x$ and $y$**

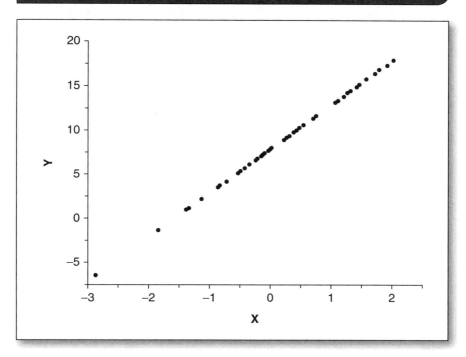

**Figure 7.9    Perfect Negative Relationship Between *x* and *y***

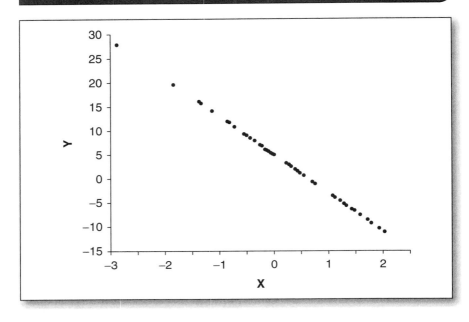

**Figure 7.10    No Relationship Between *x* and *y***

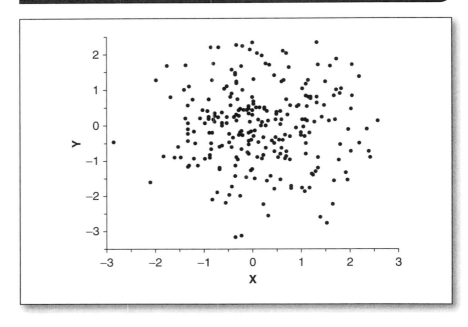

*Example 7.6*

Suppose you are interested in the relationship between age (measured in years by an open-ended question) and attitude toward technology (measured with a 20-item scale: 0 = negative attitude toward technology, 20 = positive attitude toward technology). Because age is an interval variable and attitude toward technology is an attitude scale treated as an interval variable, we can compute a correlation coefficient. The computer output looks like this:

|  | Age | Technology Attitude |
|---|---|---|
| Age | 1 | −.331** |
| Significance (two-tailed) |  | .007 |
| N |  | 68 |
| Technology Attitude | −.331** | 1 |
| Significance (two-tailed) | .007 |  |
| N | 68 |  |

The correlation coefficient, $r$, in Example 7.6 is −.331, and the $p$ value is .007. From this, we can conclude that a significant negative relationship exists between age and attitude toward technology: as age increases, attitude toward technology decreases, on average.

Earlier, we noted that responses to opinion scale items (e.g., strongly disagree to strongly agree) are commonly treated in analysis as interval data; therefore, we can compute correlation coefficients when examining opinion questions, provided a wide range of choices accompanies each question. Yes-or-no questions, for example, cannot be analyzed using this type of correlation analysis. Consider political ideology (measured on a liberal to conservative scale) and opinion on the death penalty. Example 7.7 shows the correlation matrix for these two questions. (Prior to this analysis, the scales were recoded so that higher numbers on the ideology variable indicate more liberal and higher numbers on the death penalty question indicate more strongly opposed to the death penalty.)

*Example 7.7*

|  | Ideology | Death Penalty |
|---|---|---|
| Ideology | 1 | .494** |
| Significance (two-tailed) |  | .001 |
| N |  | 195 |
| Death penalty | .494** | 1 |
| Significance (two-tailed) | .001 |  |
| N | 195 |  |

Reading the results from the table in Example 7.7, we can see that a positive and statistically significant relationship ($r = .494$, $p < .01$) exists between being liberal and opposing the death penalty: as liberalness increases, so does opposition to the death penalty, on average. In this example and in Example 7.6, both correlation coefficients were significant (at the .01 level) but also relatively small (not very close to −1 or 1). This may leave you wondering about the proper way to interpret the size of correlation coefficients. In fact, the value of the correlation coefficient necessary for statistical significance depends on the sample size (i.e., the larger the sample size, the less extreme the correlation coefficient needs to be to imply a significant correlation). Some authors (Babbie, 2004; Fink, 2003) provide the following general guidelines:

$r = 0$ to .25 (or −.25), means little or no relationship.

$r = .26$ to .50 (or −.26 to −.50), means a fair degree of relationship.

$r = .51$ to .75 (or −.51 to −.75), means a moderate to good relationship.

$r =$ more than .75 (or −.75), means a very good to excellent relationship.

Although having rules to guide the interpretation of correlation coefficients may be comforting, they are not useful in practical applications. As we saw in the previous two examples, both coefficients were in the "fair-degree-of-relationship" range, not very impressive by some standards. If, however, we take note of the $p$ value associated with each correlation coefficient (.007 in Example 7.6 and .001 in Example 7.7), the picture is different; both correlations are significant because they are based on large ($n > 30$) samples. Interpreting correlation coefficients is largely situational; the reader must consider the value of $r$ and the size of the sample from which $r$ was computed.

## Summary

We began this chapter by discussing the importance of thinking ahead to data analysis as you are writing your survey objectives and developing the questionnaire. The need for this sort of planning cannot be overstated. It would be disappointing to have invested the time and effort collecting survey data only to realize that the analyses required to address your research questions or hypotheses cannot be conducted because the data have been measured inappropriately. Carefully mapping individual survey questions to the project's objectives and aligning questionnaire items with analysis strategies can help avoid this frustration.

Once in the field, a survey needs to be monitored. The material about tracking survey responses is best reviewed before fielding the survey, as the process for sending reminders differs depending on how invitations are sent. E-mail survey invitations sent from your own e-mail software typically require manual tracking of completed questionnaires, whereas invitations sent from the survey software usually permit automatic reminders to participants who have not yet responded. The method should be considered in light of the researcher's relationship (or lack thereof) with the potential respondents.

The process of data cleaning and preparation for analysis is often overlooked, particularly by novice researchers who are anxious to dive into data analysis. While the activities of searching for impossible or improbable values, defining missing data, and transforming variables may seem less exciting than performing statistical tests, they are essential parts of the process. One way or another, data must be cleaned—if not automatically by the survey software or at the outset of the analysis, then later when you discover corrupted results.

If you are familiar with basic statistics, much of what we covered in the latter part of this chapter will have been a review for you; if you are new to data analysis, this material may have been less accessible. It is important to underscore the point that this chapter does not provide enough detail for the survey researcher who wishes to conduct complex data analysis. For that, we recommend additional study and perhaps a consultation with a survey statistician before beginning your project.

Our aim has been to provide you with enough information so you will be able to communicate your needs clearly should you choose to consult with a data analyst and so you can effectively interpret data output if it is provided by your web survey host or survey software program.

## Recommended Reading

Freedman, D., Pisani, R., & Purves, R. (2007). *Statistics* (4th ed.). Scranton, PA: Norton.
Lowry, R. (2011). *Concepts and applications of inferential statistics*. Retrieved from http://faculty.vassar.edu/lowry/webtext.html
Stark, P. B. (2011). *SticiGui*. Retrieved from http://statistics.berkeley.edu/~stark/SticiGui/index.htm

## Exercises

1. A healthcare provider is planning to conduct an e-mail survey to examine individuals who care for elderly parents. The study's objectives are

   - to explore the issues and challenges of adults who care for elderly parents,
   - to identify the information and support resources individuals caring for elderly parents turn to and where gaps exist,
   - to inform the development of a set of information resources and tools for individuals caring for elderly parents, and
   - to determine how best to communicate with these individuals about the tools and resources available to them.

     a. Write at least two questionnaire items for each of the survey objectives listed above. Be sure to specify the response scales for each of the survey questions you write.
     b. Outline the analysis plan associated with each objective.

2. Although many illogical data patterns can be effectively avoided with appropriate use of skip logic in electronic surveys, questionable response patterns nevertheless persist. In a recent workshop evaluation survey, a respondent indicated that the content was valuable, the instructor was effective, the materials were appropriate, and she was overall extremely *dissatisfied* with the workshop. Assume that you noticed this pattern while you were cleaning the data and suspected that the respondent clicked on the wrong response option and really meant to indicate that she was extremely *satisfied*. What would you do?

3. Here are some data from 20 respondents who participated in a customer satisfaction survey after making a purchase at an online toy store:

| | Birth Date | Gender | Occupation | Checkout Satisfaction | Price Satisfaction | Would Recommend |
|---|---|---|---|---|---|---|
| 1 | 7/10/1971 | Male | Ferris wheel operator | 3 | 4 | 1 |
| 2 | 8/14/1970 | Female | Real estate | 3 | 4 | 1 |
| 3 | 8/2/1986 | Female | Transportation | 3 | 4 | 1 |
| 4 | 8/12/1962 | Male | Education | 4 | 4 | 1 |
| 5 | 10/21/1952 | Male | Graphic design | 2 | 3 | 2 |
| 6 | 12/15/1980 | Male | Retired | 3 | 4 | 1 |
| 7 | 11/11/1961 | Male | Office manager | 2 | 3 | 2 |
| 8 | 1/16/1935 | Female | Manufacturer | 2 | 3 | 2 |
| 9 | 6/13/1956 | Female | Law enforcement | 4 | 4 | 1 |
| 10 | 7/1/1947 | Female | Sales | 5 | 5 | 1 |
| 11 | 4/9/1954 | Female | Security | 3 | 4 | 1 |
| 12 | 10/10/1952 | Male | Tattooist | 2 | 3 | 2 |
| 13 | 5/5/1951 | Female | Opera singer | 3 | 2 | 2 |
| 14 | 1/1/1986 | Male | Education | 3 | 4 | 1 |
| 15 | 11/23/1959 | Male | Simultaneous translator | 4 | 4 | 1 |
| 16 | 11/3/1956 | Male | Educator | 3 | 3 | 2 |
| 17 | 2/17/1988 | Male | Retail sales | 4 | 4 | 1 |
| 18 | 5/10/1956 | Male | Healthcare | 3 | 4 | 1 |
| 19 | 5/6/1946 | Female | Librarian | 4 | 5 | 1 |
| 20 | 7/5/1967 | Female | Professor | 4 | 3 | 1 |

The satisfaction questions are measured on a 1- to 5-point scale: 1 = Totally dissatisfied, 2 = Dissatisfied, 3 = Neither satisfied nor dissatisfied, 4 = Satisfied, 5 = Totally satisfied. For the "would recommend" question, 1 = Yes, 2 = No.

a. Use Excel or SPSS to compute the ages for these participants.
b. Calculate the mean, median, mode, range, and standard deviation of the distribution of ages.
c. What is the modal occupation of these participants?
d. How satisfied were these customers with the checkout process? Which summary statistic(s) would you use to describe the respondents' satisfaction?
e. Do men and women differ in their likelihood to recommend the online store? Which statistical test would you conduct to find the answer?
f. Do men and women differ in their satisfaction with the price of the products? Which statistical test would you employ to find the answer?

# CHAPTER 8

# Reporting the Survey Results

Y ou can present survey results in writing, orally, or both, and can incorporate pictures, graphs, tables, and diagrams to present the findings visually. Although venues for research presentation in the academic and commercial worlds are greatly varied, some basic principles will help researchers present the results of their online surveys clearly and accurately. In this chapter, we discuss the essential components of written reports, oral presentations, and poster presentations and how to effectively present data using graphs and charts.

## Preliminary Considerations

Before beginning to write, consider your audience—that is, think of who will read your report. If the survey report is to be prepared for an academic audience, such as conference participants or journal editors, strict guidelines will govern length, citation style, and data presentation. Be certain to have these guidelines handy as you prepare your report. Additionally, you will need to use language appropriate for the intended audience. For example, discipline-specific jargon, which might be inappropriate for a lay audience, very well may be expected in an academic or technical venue.

On the other hand, if your readers will not have the requisite background to comprehend jargon, you should avoid the use of technical terms. Similarly, complex graphic illustrations of data and/or research methods should be avoided if the audience is not expert in your field or in survey research methods. We begin this chapter by outlining the components of a formal research report, such as the type you might create for a thesis or dissertation committee or as a journal submission.

# Format of a Survey Report

Although a formal research report is typically disseminated at the end of a survey research project, you likely will be working on the report throughout the project. This type of report is comprehensive and has many required elements. The genesis of this report is often the project proposal. In the proposal, you will find the justification for the project, the goals and objectives, and frequently, a literature review. This material can be used as the basis for starting the report. Careful organization of the report will allow people to read your work selectively. When people read a survey report, they may have different interests—that is, one person may be interested in just the methods, whereas another reader may want to see a summary of the paper to determine if it is relevant to his or her study. The following is a list of the typical components of formal survey reports:

- Title page
- Acknowledgments
- Abstract or executive summary
- Table of contents
- List of tables
- List of figures
- Glossary or list of operational definitions
- Introduction
- Methods
- Results
- Discussion
- Conclusion
- References
- Appendix

The same format is generally used for journal articles, with the exception of tables of contents and lists of tables and figures. Executive summaries are usually included in technical and commercial reports; abstracts are the norm for academic papers. Either an abstract or an executive summary is included, not both.

Many publishers have a specific format in which they want the work to be submitted, such as in the American Psychological Association (APA) or the Modern Language Association (MLA) style. APA style is used in many social science and related fields, such as anthropology, communication, education, linguistics, political science, psychology, and sociology. MLA publication guidelines are used in the humanities: philosophy, history, literature, and rhetoric. Determining the publisher's preferred style is usually simply a matter of consulting the publisher's website.

## Title Page

Include the title of your study, your name, the organization with which you are affiliated or that sponsored the study, and the date of the report. Good titles are short and contain the key words that will allow potential readers to easily find your study when conducting an online search. The title is the first clue audience members will have about the content of your paper. It is, therefore, essential that the title accurately describes the content of your paper.

## Acknowledgments

This is your opportunity to acknowledge the people who have contributed to the study and supported you in both professional and personal aspects of your life. If the research was funded, the sponsoring agency should be mentioned here. Sample language for acknowledgement statements is provided in Example 8.1.

---

**Example 8.1**

"The authors are grateful to their colleagues Monette Gordon and Suzi Meng for their advice and insights during the preparation of this report."

"The Primary Care Survey Project was made possible in part by Grant No. CD00516 from the California Center for Excellent Surveys."

---

## Abstract

An abstract is a concise one- or two-paragraph summary of the completed work. Abstracts are usually limited to 100 or 200 words. In a minute or less, a reader can learn about the sample who participated in the study, the rationale behind the study, the general approach to the problem, pertinent results, and important conclusions or new questions. Write your abstract after the rest of the paper has been written. After all, how can you summarize something that is not yet written? Being clear and concise is important throughout any paper but especially in an abstract. Include the following elements in the abstract:

- The purpose of the study—hypothesis, overall research question, or objective(s)
- A brief description of the characteristics of the sample
- A brief description of the type of survey conducted
- Results, including limited but specific data
- Important conclusions or questions that follow from the study

The abstract should be written in the past tense. The focus should be on summarizing the results, and background information should be limited. The information in the abstract must be consistent with what is contained in the paper.

### Executive Summary

The executive summary highlights the purpose and rationale of the study, the methodology, and key findings. The executive summary contains more detailed information than the abstract, and it is longer than the abstract, usually about one page in length. It is not necessary to include an abstract and an executive summary; academic reports typically require abstracts, while executive summaries are more appropriate for corporate or commissioned survey projects.

### Table of Contents

A table of contents lists all the major sections in the report and their associated page numbers. First- and second-level headings are the norm for most tables of contents. If the report is long, third-level headings are included to help the reader easily find particular elements in the paper. Tables of contents normally do not exceed three pages long. If they do, it may be necessary to create two tables: a "contents in brief" and a "detailed table of contents."

### List of Tables and List of Figures

There should be two lists: one showing the title of each table in the report, with its associated page number, and a similar one for showing the title of each figure, with its associated page number. Figures include graphs, photographs, illustrations, diagrams, and so on. Tables have a row-and-column structure—that is, tables contain cells.

### Introduction

The introduction is the beginning of the paper, and it should entice your audience to continue reading. The purpose of an introduction is to acquaint the reader with the rationale behind the study and explain why your study is important. Try to keep your introduction brief. Your readers will want to quickly get to the body of the paper. The introduction places your work in a theoretical context and enables the reader to understand and appreciate your objectives. The introduction should

- describe the purpose of your study,
- describe the importance of the study—why it was worth doing in the first place (provide a broad context),
- explain why you used a particular theory or model and what its advantages are (you might comment on its suitability from a theoretical point of view as well as indicate the practical reasons for using it),
- provide a rationale—state your specific hypothesis(es) or objective(s) and describe the reasoning that led you to select them,
- briefly describe the research design and how it accomplished the stated objectives, and
- provide a brief overview of the literature specifically related to your project.

## Glossary or Operational Definitions

Define all technical terms or terms open to misinterpretation—for example, *e-health*, *job aid*, *networks*. You also should indicate what the abbreviations used in the paper stand for and explain their meanings. This information is usually included in the paper with the introduction.

## Methods

The methods section describes what was done, who was involved, and how it was done. The procedure by which you conducted the study should be explained so that another individual can reproduce the study or judge the scientific merit of your work. It should not be a step-by-step description of everything you did or a set of instructions. In this section, you should describe

- the type of survey used;
- the survey questions (give examples and include a copy of the questionnaire in the appendix if you cannot include all the questions in the paper);
- the types of response categories—that is, drop-down menus, checklists, open-ended;
- the distribution methods—how the survey was distributed, how the participants were recruited, how the nonrespondents were handled (i.e., were follow-up e-mails sent and, if so, how many and when? How long was the online survey posted?);
- information about incentives, if any were offered;
- how the survey was pilot tested;

- how reliability and validity were addressed;
- how the survey was constructed (i.e., what languages was it available in, what software program was used, what was the reading level, were graphs incorporated?);
- how many people were e-mailed the survey, where you obtained their e-mail addresses, and what the eligibility criteria were;
- if the survey was anonymous;
- how you handled incomplete surveys; and
- how informed consent was handled.

## Results

The purpose of a results section is to present and illustrate your findings. Make this section a straightforward report of the results, and save all interpretation for the discussion section of the report. Most survey results can be presented effectively using figures and tables. The content of this section should include

- the number of respondents;
- a summary of your findings, illustrated, if appropriate, with figures and tables;
- a description of each of your results, noting the observations that are most relevant;
- a context, such as describing the research hypothesis addressed by a particular analysis; and
- an analysis of your data, followed by presentation of the analyzed data in a figure (graph), in a table, or in text.

When writing the results section of your research report, do not attempt to interpret or explain the results. Also, be mindful of presenting the same data more than once—for example, in a table and in a graph, or in a graph and again in the text.

## Discussion

The objective of this section is to provide an interpretation of your results and support for your conclusions, using evidence from your survey results and generally accepted knowledge, if appropriate. The significance of findings should be clearly described.

Interpret your data in the discussion *in appropriate depth*. When you explain a phenomenon, you must describe mechanisms that may account for the observation. If your results differ from your expectations, explain why that may have happened. If your results agree, then describe the theory the evidence supported. Simply stating that the data agreed with expectations and letting it drop at that is never appropriate. Additionally, consider the following when writing the discussion section of your paper:

- Decide if each hypothesis is supported or rejected, or if you cannot make a decision with confidence. Do not simply dismiss a study or a part of a study as "inconclusive."
- Research papers are not accepted if the work is incomplete. Draw what conclusions you can based on the results you have, and identify the questions that remain unanswered and explain why.
- You may suggest future directions, such as how the survey might be modified to accomplish another objective.
- Explain all your observations as much as possible.
- Decide if the research design adequately addressed the hypothesis and whether or not it was properly controlled.
- Try to offer alternative explanations if reasonable alternatives exist.

## Conclusion

While the discussion section addresses the survey's results in light of the research questions or hypotheses, the conclusion positions the study within a body of work. In the conclusion, you might discuss the contribution of your study to the theoretical or methodological literature. Have you extended the work of another researcher? Or perhaps you developed a new framework for examining a problem or issue. You also could discuss next steps: What questions remain to be addressed? What recommendations can you offer based on your study's results? And, finally, what message should readers take away from your report?

## References

List all the literature cited in your paper using the format dictated by the preferred style manual of the organization for which you are writing. References should include *only* work included in the paper, and all work cited in the paper should be included in the reference section.

## Appendix

Include any pertinent information or copies of documents that do not fit within the body of the report. You may include materials such as a printed copy of the questionnaire; the e-mail invitation; the consent form, if applicable; or detailed participant demographic data.

# Dashboard Reports

An alternative to a formal research report that may be appropriate in corporate, nonprofit, or other institutional settings where detailed reporting is not required is the dashboard report. As the name implies, a dashboard contains primarily visual images presented in a colorful and easy-to-read manner (see Figure 8.1).

**Figure 8.1    Survey Dashboard Report**

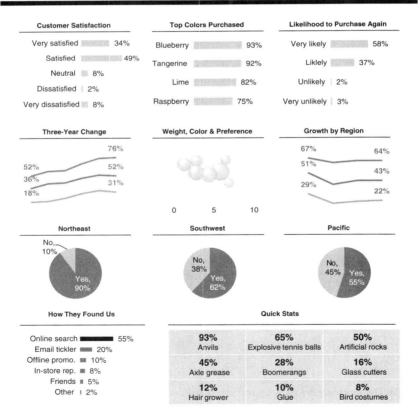

## ACME Customer Survey
### Fourth Quarter 2010

**Customer Satisfaction**

| | |
|---|---|
| Very satisfied | 34% |
| Satisfied | 49% |
| Neutral | 8% |
| Dissatisfied | 2% |
| Very dissatisfied | 8% |

**Top Colors Purchased**

| | |
|---|---|
| Blueberry | 93% |
| Tangerine | 92% |
| Lime | 82% |
| Raspberry | 75% |

**Likelihood to Purchase Again**

| | |
|---|---|
| Very likely | 58% |
| Liklely | 37% |
| Unlikely | 2% |
| Very unlikely | 3% |

**Three-Year Change**

76%
52%   52%
36%   31%
18%

**Weight, Color & Preference**

0    5    10

**Growth by Region**

67%   64%
51%   43%
29%   22%

**Northeast**

No, 10%
Yes, 90%

**Southwest**

No, 38%
Yes, 62%

**Pacific**

No, 45%
Yes, 55%

**How They Found Us**

| | |
|---|---|
| Online search | 55% |
| Email tickler | 20% |
| Offline promo. | 10% |
| In-store rep. | 8% |
| Friends | 5% |
| Other | 2% |

**Quick Stats**

| | | |
|---|---|---|
| **93%** Anvils | **65%** Explosive tennis balls | **50%** Artificial rocks |
| **45%** Axle grease | **28%** Boomerangs | **16%** Glass cutters |
| **12%** Hair grower | **10%** Glue | **8%** Bird costumes |

**About the Survey**
  A random sample of 20,000 customers was invited to participate in this online survey. E-mail invitations containing a link to the survey were sent to the participants. The survey was available for one week in December 2010; 2,681 customers participated in the survey. The average age of the respondents was 59 and 60% were women.

It is a way to provider readers with a summary of the project's results at a glance, similar to how one would look at a car's dashboard to determine how much fuel is remaining. Dashboard reports facilitate discussion of the survey results and are effective tools for generating interest in research projects. Although a dashboard report may be the only report required, they are best used in conjunction with a complete report and/or oral presentation.

The content of a dashboard report should be built around the most important findings from the survey or those that were surprising or might be especially influential. When selecting the results to be included in the dashboard, researchers normally consider the potential for a particular finding to be presented effectively in a graph, such as a pie, column, or line chart. This consideration embodies one of the dangers of dashboard reporting: the content is sometimes determined by the ability to present the result in a chart rather than solely on the importance of the finding. Although good visuals are essential, decisions about what to include in the report should be guided by the data's relevance for the audience.

The charts in a dashboard report frequently lack the level of detail of the charts in a full report. To facilitate the placement of many charts on a page, chart sizes are often reduced, making the inclusion of rich detail or complex legends prohibitive. Line graphs, for example, may include data labels for the end points of the line and not all the points in between. This feature contributes to another danger of relying on a dashboard alone to understand survey results: readers may feel that they know the complete story when, in fact, they have only a superficial view of the results. When delivering a dashboard report, it is important to emphasize this point and offer the opportunity to view further detail, either in a full report or in an oral presentation.

## Oral Presentations

Oral presentations are another way of disseminating your survey results. Before you consider giving your presentation, you need to decide who your target audience is and be sure that the attendees will be interested in the topic of your survey. When you have a match between your topic and the audience, you can begin the preparation. It is useful to research specific information about the audience, such as their level of education and knowledge about the topic, so you can make thoughtful decisions about how much context to include and the level of detail that will be necessary to present.

Oral presentations are often given at meetings, conferences, and summits. There are two main types of oral presentations: those that take place in person and those that are delivered via **webinars** or **web conferences**.

A webinar, short for web seminar, is a type of web conference where people participate remotely. Typically, the presenter speaks to the audience using a conference call phone number while showing a PowerPoint presentation. The audience members view the presentation by going to the webinar URL and listen to the audio portion via the call-in phone number or Internet audio. They may communicate with the presenter and other participants by typing questions and comments in a chat window. Many conferences now include some web-based sessions, and a few have moved to web-only or virtual conferences. We will first review the materials that accompany oral presentations and then discuss some techniques for delivering presentations in person and via webinars.

## Preparing for Your Presentation

Regardless of the delivery method (in person or via a web conference), the presentation consists of three parts: the introduction, the main message, and the conclusion. Only 25% of your presentation should be dedicated to the introduction and the conclusion. The introduction defines the purpose of the presentation and the topics to be covered and captures the audience's interest. The main message section includes information about why the survey was conducted, how it was conducted, and the results. The conclusion influences the audience's ability to retain information and is, therefore, a crucial component of the presentation. The conclusion should not add new information but should serve as a review of the major points of the presentation.

Consider your allotted time carefully. If you are given 10 minutes to present, you may not have time to present all the survey results. In this case, you will need to select the most interesting findings for the particular audience. Even if you're afforded an hour or more for the presentation, being selective in the information you present is still prudent. Information overload will adversely affect audience members' ability to recall details of your presentation. For greatest effectiveness, opt to focus on a few key messages and invite the audience to read the full research report to learn more.

## Designing Visual Aids

Visual aids can greatly enhance an oral presentation if used correctly. Use visual aids to simplify complex ideas or concepts, share numeric data, help the audience organize ideas and understand abstractions, control the listeners' attention, and assist them with retaining the information. You can use visual aids to present a problem; show solutions and benefits; and illustrate processes, procedures, and steps in a sequence.

PowerPoint shows are the norm for most presentations. Sometimes, hard or soft copies of the slides are distributed beforehand so that audience members can follow along and take notes. Obviously, this limits speakers' ability to make last-minute changes and increases the challenge of maintaining audience attention on the oral portion of the presentation. It is important to note that a PowerPoint show created to accompany an oral presentation includes different material than one designed to be sent to readers who will view it without the benefit of live narration. The discussion that follows applies to PowerPoint shows used in oral presentations, not the stand-alone variety meant to be read independently.

## Preparing PowerPoint Slides

PowerPoint slides serve as an outline for the speaker while helping the listeners follow the presentation. An increasing number of web survey hosts offer the ability to save as PowerPoint files figures and tables created on the site. This "save as" feature can usually be found as an option located in the download menu of the survey software program. You also may wish to insert on one of the PowerPoint slides a hyperlink to the webpage containing your survey. This is an effective addition, as the audience can view the questionnaire the same way the respondents did. Before doing this, however, it is imperative that you inquire about the Internet connectivity in the room where the presentation will be given. If the Internet connection in the facility is unreliable or unavailable, it is advisable to insert pictures of the questionnaire pages (as .jpg or .pdf files) into your PowerPoint presentation rather than risk stalling the presentation while the computer searches for the Internet connection.

There are many divergent points of view regarding the preparation of PowerPoint slide shows. For every expert who says always to use sans serif fonts, there will be another who says always to use serif fonts; likewise, some recommend using light text on dark backgrounds and others suggest dark text on light backgrounds. The goal is to create slides that augment the oral presentation and engage the audience by illustrating key elements of the message. Below, we offer some guidelines for creating effective PowerPoint slides. These are not rules, merely suggestions. After creating your first draft of the PowerPoint slides, you should evaluate them for clarity of message, ease of reading, and effectiveness in supporting the oral portion of the presentation, and then revise, revise, revise.

- *Minimize text.* When it comes to text, less is more. One common rule of thumb is the six-by-six rule: no more than six lines of text on one slide and no more than six words per line. This is a bit proscriptive. There are some situations when more text is needed and others when far less is desirable. The rationale behind the rule is that less text is easier to read, which will keep the audience focused on the speaker rather than on the screen. Instead of counting words, try eliminating all nonessential words and reducing complete sentences to phrases that express your main points. Better still, look for opportunities to replace text with images, such as charts, photographs, diagrams, and other illustrations that will support your main message.

- *Choose simple fonts.* As we noted previously, some PowerPoint experts swear by sans serif fonts. The idea is that the serifs can cause the letters to appear run together. Fonts without serifs (such as Helvetica) are thought to be easier to read because they are cleaner. Other experts claim the opposite, that the serifs make the letters easier to distinguish, which is why books are typeset using fonts such as Times New Roman. Text style should be chosen to maximize readability. In most situations, that means using a maximum of two or three fonts, with sans serif fonts (e.g., Arial, Helvetica, or Verdana) used for headings and serif fonts (e.g., Times New Roman or Palatino) used for the body text. In any event, avoid fancy or specialty fonts. Finally, consider making the font size as large as possible, within reason. Audiences rarely complain about the text on a PowerPoint slide being too large; we have, however, seen many audiences squinting in frustration as they try to read text printed in a 10- or 12-point font. We won't suggest specific font sizes; there are too many variables, such as the particular font chosen, the size of the room, and the distance between the audience and the screen. As you create your presentation, consider whether audience members at the back of the room will be able to see comfortably everything on your slides; if they can, then the font is large enough.

- *Do not shout at the audience.* The best option for capitalization is to use standard title capitalization rules for titles and upper- and lowercase characters for body text. If you must use all capital letters, try to limit it to one or two key words that need special emphasis, such as the word *NOT*, for example. Alternatively, consider bolding or using a contrasting color to add emphasis to particular words (italics are not a good choice, as italicized characters can be difficult to read, and underlining is likewise a poor option because it is used to indicate a URL).

- *Do not fade into the background.* Whether you decide to opt for light text on a dark background or dark text on a light background, the guiding principle is the same: ensure that the background and the text sufficiently contrast. Light text won't show up well on a light background, and dark text will blend into a dark background. Also, remember that the colors you've chosen will look different when projected on a screen than they do on your computer monitor.

- *Transition smoothly.* PowerPoint offers nearly 60 slide-transition options and hundreds of animation choices (even more if you count custom animations). A simple transition from one slide to another, such as a smooth fade, can enhance the overall look of a PowerPoint show. Similarly, a subtle animation, such as a wipe or a fade-in, used to introduce bullet points can help keep the audience's attention on a relevant point until you're ready to move on. When using slide transitions and text or image animations, choose subtle effects and apply them consistently throughout the presentation. The audience should not notice transitions and animations that are used effectively; they will simply remember that the presentation was well done. (See Figures 8.2 and 8.3 for examples of PowerPoint slides.)

## Delivering Your Presentation in Person

Delivering the presentation will call into action your basic public-speaking skills. An extensive discussion of the principles of public speaking is not appropriate here; however, we do provide a review of some of the factors worth noting as you contemplate delivering your presentation.

### Dress Appropriately

Professional face-to-face presentations require professional dress; usually, this means dressing in a fashion appropriate to the setting and consistent with the other presenters (if there are other presenters). Err on the side of overdressing if you have any doubt about what is suitable.

### Be Aware of Nonverbal Communication

It is estimated that 55% of what the audience "hears" is gathered from nonverbal communication. This includes facial expressions, gestures, posture,

**Figure 8.2   Example of a PowerPoint Slide**

**Respondents' Demographic Characteristics**

- The gender distribution of the sample approximates that of the population where 59% is female and 41% is male. The average age of all adult customers who used the product was 48.7; the population median age is 49 and the modal age is 61. There is an age disparity between the survey sample and population; this is most likely an artifact of the survey process as older adults are generally more apt to respond to surveys than are younger individuals.
- Exploratory analyses verified that age was not significantly related to factors such as satisfaction and evaluations; younger customers were just as likely to be satisfied (or dissatisfied) with the process as were older customers.
- More than half of the sample reported having a college or post graduate degree.
- About 80% of the survey sample opted to report their income; half said they earned $75,000 or more a year.

Figure 8.3 Improved PowerPoint Examples

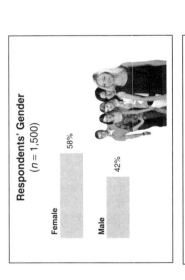

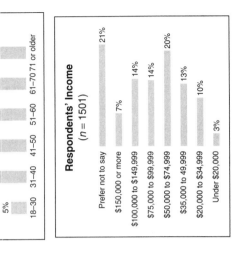

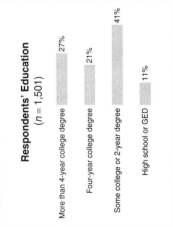

and use of space. Strive to project a confident but natural style. Overuse of hand gestures to emphasize a point, for example, can be distracting and can lead to misunderstanding of the message.

### Manage Eye Contact

Eye contact with members of the audience is one of the most important aspects of effective message delivery. Speakers who are able to make appropriate eye contact with individual audience members are usually regarded as confident and trustworthy. Depending on the size of your audience, you will need to adjust the amount of eye contact you make with particular individuals. Maintaining eye contact is generally easier when audiences are large (at least, giving the appearance of maintaining eye contact is easier) than when they are small. In settings with small audiences, guard against gazing too long or too intently at individual audience members, as this might be misinterpreted as hostility or a sexual overture.

### Rehearse

Some experts recommend three rehearsals for formal presentations: one in front of your computer, especially important if you'll be demonstrating technical aspects of your online survey; another in front of a group of colleagues; and the third in the room where the presentation will take place (if possible). If extensive rehearsals are not feasible, try to go through your presentation at least once, timing yourself so that you make sure to stay within the allotted time frame. Use pitch, volume, and rate changes, including pauses, to add variety to your speech. Remind yourself to stress important words by highlighting key words or phrases in your notes.

## Delivering Your Presentation Virtually

You need to work harder when presenting research results via a web conference than when presenting in person. Because you can't see the audience and they can't see you, the visual and oral components of the presentation require special attention. To be effective in this setting, the presentation must be more engaging than the myriad distractions (e.g., e-mail, the Internet, text messages, Angry Birds, etc.) against which you are competing. In addition to speaking slowly, loudly, and clearly and rehearsing as much as you can, a few techniques specific to webinar presentations can help with effective message delivery.

### Conduct a Prepresentation Survey

If possible, find out before the presentation what the audience expectations are and if there are particular topics of interest that you should be sure to cover. Tailoring the web conference to the specific audience will increase the chances of participants attending to your message.

### Establish Ground Rules at the Beginning of the Presentation

Some questions routinely arise in web conferences: (a) Will the presentation slides be distributed? (b) Will the presentation be recorded? (c) Will questions be taken throughout the presentation, or only at the end? (d) How long will the presentation really last? Preparing answers to these questions will expedite the start of the discussion.

### Avoid Text-Only Presentations

Presentations in this setting need to be more captivating than those delivered in person. Photos, videos, and web demonstrations can help attract and maintain attention. If your presentation is text heavy or requires lengthy explanation of complex statistical procedures, consider forgoing the web conference and opting for an in-person presentation.

### Check for Understanding Frequently

Throughout the presentation, use the features of the web conferencing software to interact with the audience. For example, ask questions and instruct participants to type their answers in the chat box. Correct answers could be awarded points toward a prize to be distributed at the end of the session. The polling feature of the web conferencing software can be used in the same way. Similarly, you could ask attendees to use the "raise hand" icon if they understand (or don't understand) a point you've illustrated.

## Poster Session Presentations

Poster exhibits are a popular way to present information about research projects at conferences. They encourage conversation and personal interaction between authors and attendees. Also, posters can be displayed without the author being present. Individuals who are uncomfortable giving oral presentations may find posters to be a comfortable way of sharing their survey results.

The typical poster exhibit is an opportunity to visually display research and to illustrate investigations and findings. Projects are generally placed in a display area, and guests come and go as their schedules permit. Exhibitors stand by their work and are prepared to discuss their research with guests from all types of backgrounds. A good poster draws attention to itself; presents information concisely, clearly, and completely; and encourages questions and interchange with the author.

## Preparing a Poster Exhibit

The content of your poster presentation is similar to that of the written report. You may include an abstract, background information, the purpose of the survey research project, information about the type of online survey conducted, results, conclusions, and implications. Although the content is similar to the complete report, the presentation is significantly different: a poster is designed to highlight the major elements of the survey project and to be viewed unaided, quickly, and usually from a distance.

Because people will be reviewing your poster and not reading a paper, you will want to break information into chunks or bite-sized pieces and use bulleted text when possible and appropriate. Do not simply paste your paper onto a poster board and call it a day. While a PowerPoint show previously created for an oral presentation may serve as a basis for a poster, it is unwise to print the pages of the PowerPoint show and paste them on the poster board. PowerPoint slides created for an oral presentation will likely contain elements that require elaboration by the researcher and are not typically suitable for this presentation format.

The poster can be supplemented with a laptop computer or tablet PC on which the researcher can demonstrate the online survey, provided that the exhibit space is adequately equipped. If wired (or wireless) Internet connections are not available, demonstrating the questionnaire on a laptop is still possible; the survey will not be "live"—that is, viewers will not be able to fill in answers—but they will be able to view static images of questionnaire pages.

## Appearance of Your Poster

Sizes of posters vary widely; you should inquire about your space allocation if the information is not readily available. Aim to create a poster that will fill the available space without being overwhelming. As a guideline, a typical display panel is about 36 inches high by 48 inches wide. We said earlier that a PowerPoint show created for an oral presentation should not be printed and used as a poster. PowerPoint, however, is a useful tool for creating a poster when used as an illustration program. Other software options for creating research posters include Quark XPress, InDesign, Adobe Illustrator, and Microsoft Publisher. Many poster templates are available online for all these programs; simply search for "poster template," followed by the name of the application program you wish to use. The templates are available in a variety of sizes and can be changed from landscape to portrait orientation. (Note: PowerPoint limits page width to no more than 56 inches. This should be sufficient for most purposes. If, however, you want to create a larger poster, you will need to design it in sections or use another program.)

Figure 8.4 provides two sample poster layouts. The following sections discuss some specific recommendations for constructing posters for the presentation of research results.

## Figure 8.4    Sample Layouts of Survey Research Posters

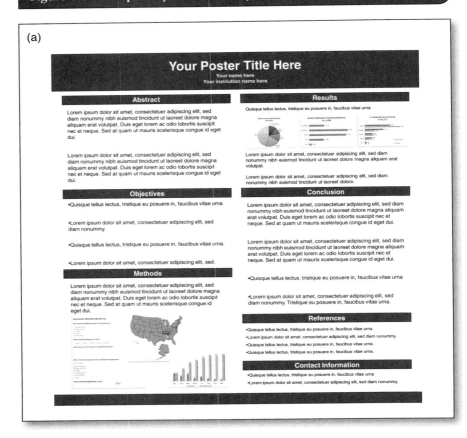

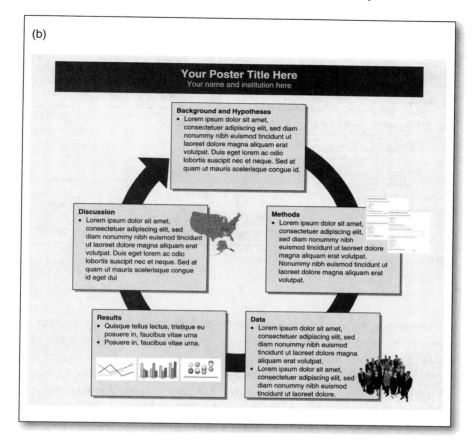

## Text

One of the biggest mistakes researchers make is including too much text on a poster. Paragraphs of text are not inviting and will force you to reduce the font size to accommodate the full text. Limit text to key concepts and avoid abbreviations, acronyms, and jargon. Bulleted lists help readers break information into digestible bits, but do not go to the extreme of presenting all text as bulleted lists. Bulleted lists are used for groups of related, nonsequential concepts; use numbered lists for sequential or ordered concepts. Each element in a list should focus on one point and be no longer than a sentence. Use sentence capitalization rather than title capitalization for text appearing in lists, and check that all text is large enough to be read from a distance of about 3 feet. (See Table 8.1 for guidelines regarding font sizes for poster exhibits.)

**Table 8.1    Typical Type Sizes for Exhibits**

| Heading | Font Size |
|---|---|
| Logo, headers | 5 ½ inches (reverse type is effective) |
| First headline (main panel) | 120 point |
| Second headline or large bullet items | 72 point |
| Smaller bullet items | 48–60 point |
| Text blocks | 30–36 point |
| Captions | 18–24 point |

SOURCE: Copyright 2006 Los Alamos National Laboratory.

### Layout

The title is the first item viewers will see because it normally appears at the top of the poster. Of course, you can be creative and place the title along the left side of the poster or in some other location, but then you will have to use a large font, contrasting color, or some other technique to reduce confusion and ensure that viewers know it is your title. Authors' names and affiliations are commonly placed below the title at the top of the poster.

Most poster templates will lay out the body of the poster in three or four columns. This is useful for novice designers, as it helps keep text and images neatly aligned. Use section headings (main headings and second-level headings) in the columns to guide viewers through the sections of the poster. If your poster should be experienced sequentially, consider using devices such as arrows or numbers to indicate the order in which the sections should be viewed. As you gain experience, you will be able to delete columns and approach the design of the poster in a more free-form fashion.

Diagrams, graphs, photos, and tables are ideal for posters. All graphic elements should be clearly labeled, should appear near the text that references them, and should be explained in a caption or legend.

Use color to emphasize titles, graphs, and photos. However, be wary of using too many different colors on one poster, as this may lend a childlike appearance to the product. A thin gray or black border or subtle shadow will help photographs stand out from the background. The guidelines for creating charts and tables (discussed later in this chapter) are applicable when creating charts and tables for posters. The bottom of the poster is generally reserved for acknowledgments, references, authors' contact information, and details—such as formulas—that do not fit well in the main sections.

### Presenting Your Poster

It is useful to prepare a one-sentence overview of your research to share with visitors who pass by your poster. After you've successfully captured their attention, you will be able to use your poster to illustrate the interesting and important elements of your research as you speak with them. As with any oral presentation, don't read material on your poster; instead, discuss how you conducted the research and what you found. Be specific about your findings and invite questions and critique. Many poster exhibitors take business cards and/or small printed versions (usually 8.5" × 11" or 11" × 17") of their posters to hand out to visitors. If the font sizes on the original poster are large enough to be read from a distance, the smaller version of the poster will be legible. Finally, thank visitors for their attention.

# Visual Aids

Each of the written and oral presentations we have discussed in this chapter requires visual presentations of data. Presenting data using tables and graphs will help your audience understand the results. Visual data presentation assists in comprehension of information and makes numbers easier to grasp and compare. Below is a list of the benefits of using graphics:

- Graphics make concepts easier to understand.
- Color, fonts, and graphics can help the reader comprehend an idea.
- Graphics support and emphasize ideas.
- Graphics generate interest and attract attention.
- Graphics are important and powerful when integrated with text.

Most web survey hosts offer the ability to create graphics (such as histograms or pie charts) in their reporting feature. These graphs are usually easy to export for use in a report or oral presentation. Many software vendors offer the option of directly exporting graphs as PowerPoint slides. If this feature is not available in the program you are using, you will be able to export your data as an Excel file and from there create the charts and graphs you need. (Note: If you will be regularly preparing PowerPoint presentations based on survey data, you may want to prioritize the software's graph export features, as this will save time and allow you to turn around data reports quickly.)

## General Guidelines for Creating Graphics

To communicate information effectively in graphs, each one should have a clear purpose, usually to illustrate a point made in the text. Verify that the data contained in your charts or figures are correct and that the format is simple and uncluttered. Remove everything that is nonessential (e.g., background photos, patterns, and prominent grid lines). Simple graphs are best; that usually means keeping them two-dimensional (unless you're preparing the graph for an oral presentation and you plan to spin it so it can be viewed from multiple angles). Graphs should be comprehensible on their own but should relate to something in the text. Title and captions describe what the graphic represents but should not be so long that they resemble paragraphs of text. If you find yourself writing long titles, reexamine the graphic to determine what's missing; perhaps the axes or data points are not well labeled.

There are many different ways to display your data in graphic format; it is important to choose the graph that is most appropriate for the type of data you are presenting and for the audience of the report or presentation. What follows is a discussion of the different types of graphs and diagrams available to you and some guidelines on how to use each tool effectively.

## Pie Charts

Pie charts show relationships among the elements that compose a whole. They should be used only when you are describing 100% of something. For example, all the responses to a particular survey question or all the age groups of the sample population are appropriate for pie charts. Pie charts make it more difficult than bar charts to compare small differences in values and are, therefore, best when you have a few categories and one or two are much larger than the others. An important consideration when creating pie charts is the scale. Each part must be in proportion to the percentage it represents. You may have as many pie "slices" as you desire; however, more than five or six will result in a cluttered graph, and labeling the sections will become a challenge. Optimally, the labels should be adjacent to, or on, the sections of the pie they reference. The next-best option is to place the labels near the appropriate pie sections using leader lines to connect the label to the referenced graph section. If these options are not possible, another labeling method is to use a legend to identify the sections on the pie chart. This is the least effective technique, as it requires readers to view the graph, scan the legend, and then look at the graph again to determine the meaning of the pie sections. If you find yourself in the position of requiring a legend for a pie chart, consider whether another type of graphical display may be more appropriate for your data. Examples of pie charts are provided in Figure 8.5.

**Figure 8.5   Examples of Pie Charts**

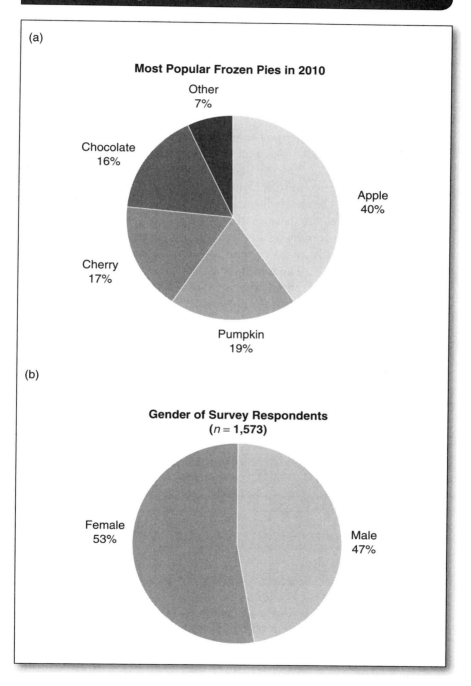

(a)

**Most Popular Frozen Pies in 2010**

Other
7%

Chocolate
16%

Apple
40%

Cherry
17%

Pumpkin
19%

(b)

**Gender of Survey Respondents**
($n = 1,573$)

Female
53%

Male
47%

A variation of a pie chart is a donut chart, a pie chart with a hole in the middle. These are sometimes used to plot multiple data series on the different rings of the donut chart. Donut charts are not commonly used to present survey data and may require more explanation (in writing and in an oral presentation) than other types of charts. If you find yourself reaching for a donut, consider a stacked bar chart as an alternative.

## Bar Charts

Bar charts are commonly used to present survey data and are easily recognized by most audiences. The wide familiarity with this type of data display is a great benefit, as readers will not need to spend time figuring out the graph. They are effective for displaying survey data because even small differences in values can be clearly illustrated. Bar charts can be used to describe one data series or to compare multiple series—for example, to compare survey participants' current health status or to compare the racial/ethnic identification of participants who were and were not enrolled in a program (see Figures 8.6 and 8.7). The bars in a bar chart are displayed horizontally; column charts show the bars vertically along the x-axis (see Figure 8.8). Technically, the column chart is the most widely used graph. Bar and column

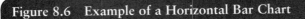

**Figure 8.6    Example of a Horizontal Bar Chart**

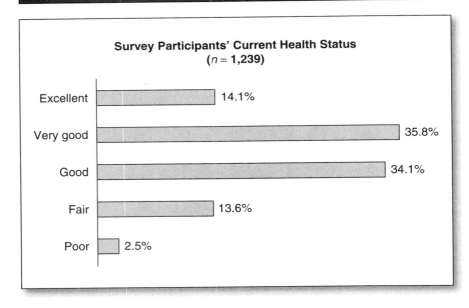

**Figure 8.7    Example of a Comparison Bar Chart**

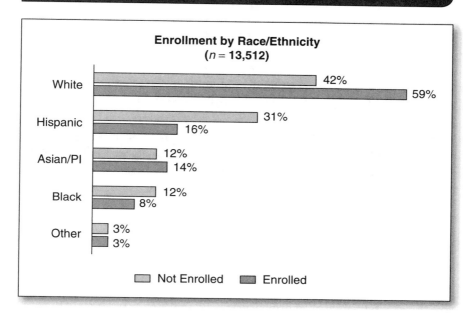

**Figure 8.8    Example of a Column Chart**

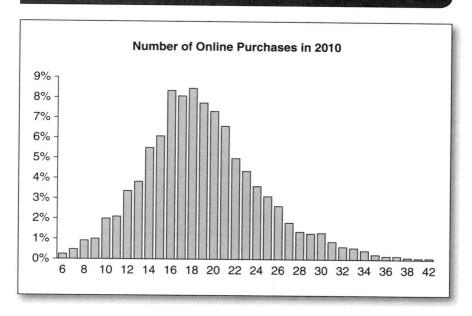

charts can be used interchangeably; the decision about which to choose is usually based on the aesthetics of the graph. Bar charts work well when the category labels are long and may not fit well on the x-axis—for example, if the labels span two or three lines (see Figure 8.9).

When displaying survey data using bar charts, attend to the scale of the axes. Programs such as Excel and PowerPoint will automatically adjust the scale of the chart's y-axis, setting the minimum and maximum values based on the data. This can be problematic when comparing two or more bar

**Figure 8.9    Example of a Bar Chart Presented Horizontally and Vertically**

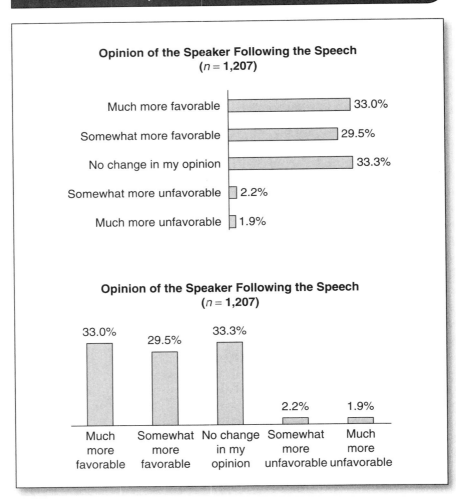

charts because each chart will be shown on a different scale. The best practice is to set the scale of the y-axis at 0% and 100%, particularly when you
will be presenting two or more charts.

For survey questions with ordered response scales—such as "strongly
disagree" to "strongly agree"—income, or number of purchases, show the
results in the order the responses were presented on the survey. For nominal
response options, such as type of mobile phone used or brand of appliance
purchased, sort the results and present them in order, typically from most
to least frequently occurring.

A histogram is a variation of the bar chart in which a number of values
of a variable fall into a set of categories—for example, participants who are
between 18 and 30 years old, 31 and 40 years old, and so on. A histogram
is an effective way to show the distribution of the data and typically provide
the option of overlaying a normal curve, which can be useful in later statistical analysis (see Figure 8.10).

Figure 8.10   Example of a Histogram

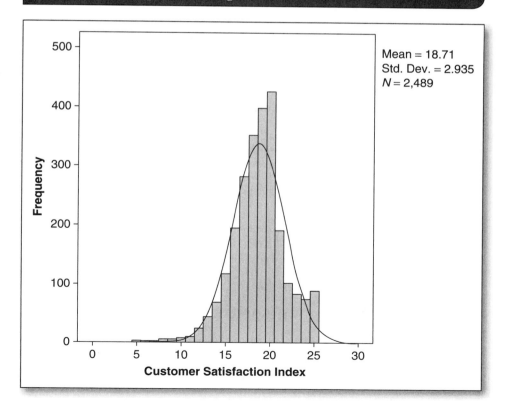

Stacked column charts show groups of data together. Stacked columns display all the values in a category as one column, with each separate value color coded on the column according to the series from which it came. This presentation emphasizes relative differences among the values and helps readers evaluate the proportion of each value to the total. A 100% stacked column chart shows each set of values arrayed by percentage over columns of the same height. Each column serves the same purpose as a pie chart, describing 100% of something, but allows you to compare one column with another more easily than one pie chart with another. Examples of stacked column charts can be found in Figures 8.11 and 8.12.

## Line Graphs

Line graphs are typically used to show change in values over time (see Figure 8.13). For example, a line graph showing time on the x-axis and mobile phone adoption on the y-axis will allow readers to examine trends, determine when adoption starts to increase, and when saturation may be reached. Line graphs also work well for showing several data elements by using multiple lines (each displayed element must be on the same scale). A multiple-series line graph could plot mobile phone adoption in several countries, for example. If you're graphing individual categories, consider using a bar or column chart instead.

**Figure 8.11    Example of a Stacked Column Chart**

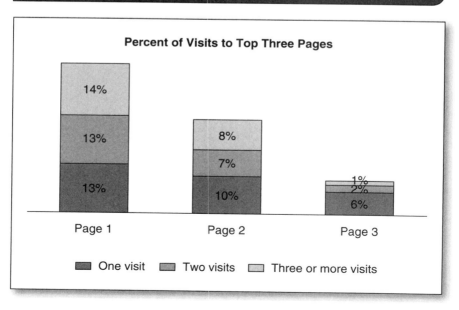

Figure 8.12   Example of a 100% Stacked Column Chart

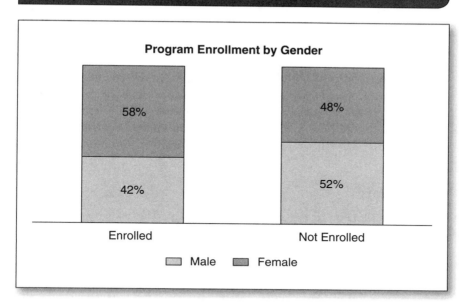

Figure 8.13   Example of a Line Graph

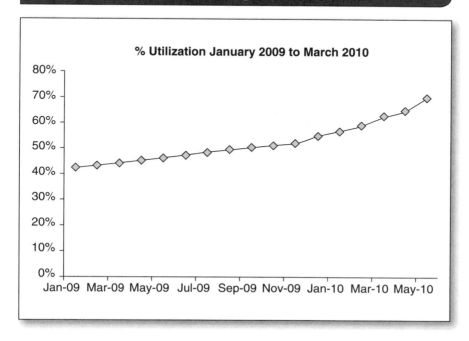

## Flowcharts

Flowcharts are diagrams that provide a visual image of a project or process. These diagrams can be helpful in explaining a process, such as how your study was conducted. Flowcharts are useful illustrations on posters and in other research reports that include information about the research methodology. Usually, the shape of the box in the flowchart is representative of a type of step in the process. For example, an arrow usually indicates movement, a diamond indicates a decision, a square may indicate a process or action, and a line often indicates the flow of the system from one process or decision to another. Figure 8.14 shows an example of a flowchart.

## Scatter Plots

A scatter plot, or scatter graph, is a graph used to visually display and compare two or more sets of related quantitative or numerical data (see Figure 8.15). The scatter plot shows relationships or clusters to illustrate the impact of one dimension on another. Each data point has a coordinate on a horizontal and a vertical axis. A dot in the body of the chart represents the intersection of the data on the x- and y-axes. For example, to illustrate the impact of age on the number of prescription medications one takes, you would plot age on one axis and number of prescription medications on the other. You might show that although there are individual variations, the points cluster notably where age and number of prescription medications are both high. Graphing data using a scatter plot is essential for determining the nature of the relationship between variables—that is, are the two variables related in a linear fashion? Is there a curvilinear pattern or no pattern at all?

If you added a third dimension to a scatter plot, you would have a bubble chart. The third dimension would be represented by the size of the point on the chart (see Figure 8.16).

## Box Plots

The box plot also is called a box-and-whiskers plot. Though it looks very different from the previous graphs, it is an effective way to show survey results. To create a box-and-whiskers plot, draw a box with ends at the quartiles $Q_1$ and $Q_3$. Draw the statistical median $M$ as a horizontal line in the box. Next, extend the "whiskers" to the farthest points that are not outliers (outliers are within 3/2 times the interquartile range of $Q_1$ and $Q_3$). Then, for every point more than 3/2 times the interquartile range from the end of the box, draw a dot. If two dots have the same value, draw them side

**Figure 8.14   Example of a Flowchart of the Research Process**

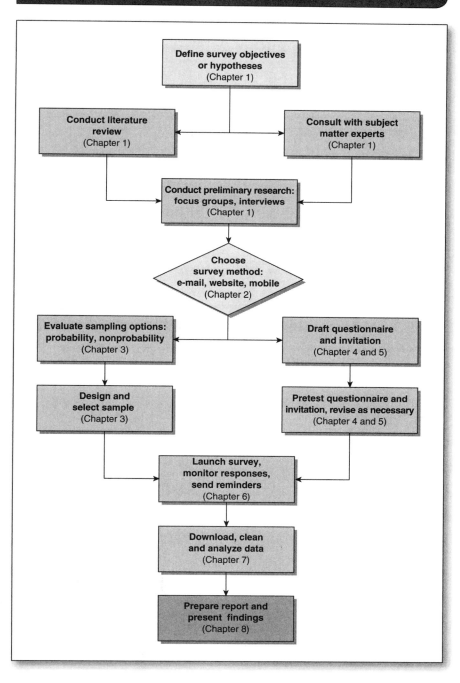

**Figure 8.15    Example of a Scatter Plot**

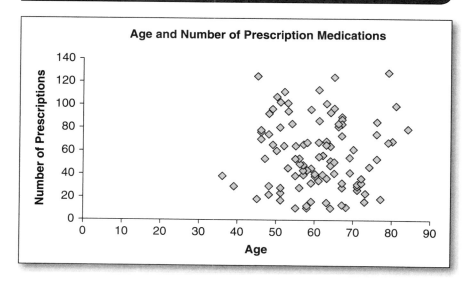

**Figure 8.16    Example of a Bubble Chart**

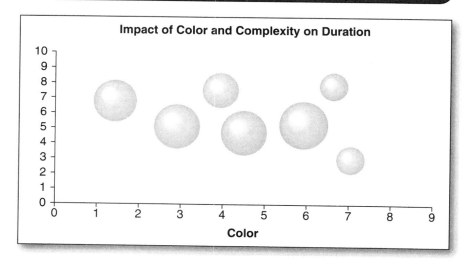

by side. The box (the rectangular portion of the graph) extends from $Q_1$ to $Q_3$, with a horizontal line segment indicating the median. Figure 8.17 shows the construction of a box plot, and Figure 8.18 is an example of a box plot.

**Figure 8.17    Example of the Construction of a Box Plot**

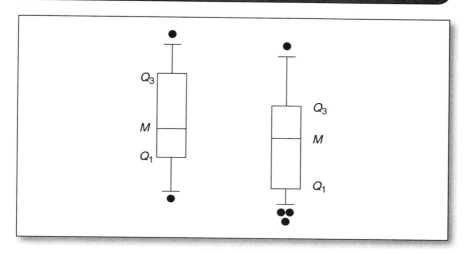

**Figure 8.18    Example of a Box Plot**

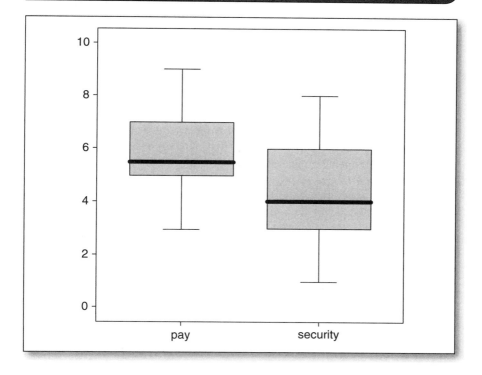

## Stem-and-Leaf Display

A stem-and-leaf display, also called a stem-and-leaf plot, is a diagram that quickly summarizes data while maintaining the individual data points. In such a diagram, the "stem" is a column of the unique elements of data after removing the last digit. The final digits ("leaves") of each column are then placed in a row next to the appropriate column and sorted in numerical order.

Table 8.2 shows the stem-and-leaf diagram for the following data set: 147, 117, 101, 149, 145, 105, 93, 94, 114, 104, 136, 140, 121, 145, 120, 142, 98, 135, 135, 132.

**Table 8.2    Example of a Stem-and-Leaf Display**

| Stems | Leaves |
|-------|--------|
| 9 | 3, 4, 8 |
| 10 | 1, 4, 5 |
| 11 | 4, 7 |
| 12 | 0, 1 |
| 13 | 2, 5, 5, 6 |
| 14 | 0, 2, 5, 5, 7, 9 |

## Maps

A map may be another useful way to illustrate survey research findings. They are used in a variety of fields, such as education, health, public safety, and agriculture. For instance, you might color code states or regions of the country to illustrate the percentage of survey respondents answering a particular way. It is important to note that this type of data presentation gives prominence to geographically bigger places.

A heat map is a type of map that shows intensity of activity or opinion. For example, you could superimpose a heat map on a webpage to illustrate the parts of the page that generated the most clicks. Or you could present a sample newsletter to survey respondents and ask them to highlight the areas that are of greatest interest to them. The resulting data could be presented in a heat map, where the areas that were most frequently highlighted would be in bright red and the areas that received little or no highlighting would be shown in blue (see Figure 8.19).

## A Note on Colors for Graphs

You have many options when it comes to choosing colors for the graphs in your paper or presentation. One option is to use a neutral color palette and show variations in saturation of color rather than using different

**Figure 8.19   Example of a Heat Map**

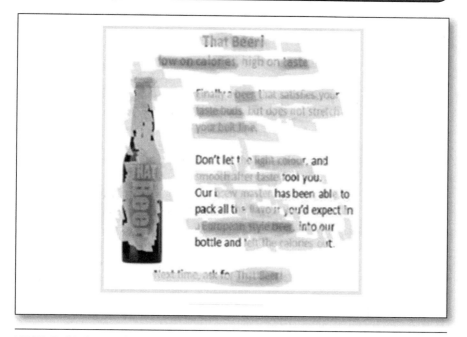

NOTE: Red indicates a high number of clicks on the area, and yellow indicates a low number of clicks.

colors. Another approach is to use rich, bright colors to help readers identify differences in categories or values. Whatever technique you choose to adopt, it is important to select colors strategically—that is, do not necessarily rely on the chart software's default color scheme to effectively convey your message.

As you create your graphs, consider maintaining the same colors throughout the presentation or poster; that is, don't change the color palette from chart to chart for the purpose of making your presentation more colorful. Data elements repeated in a presentation should generally be a consistent color throughout—for example, if you choose blue to represent female survey respondents, each graph that shows responses by gender should use blue for female responses. If your audience will likely print your presentation, it is wise to print draft copies in color and in black and white to ensure that the colors are discernable. Finally, be conscious of the meanings of colors. For instance, stop-light colors (red, yellow, and green) are often used to indicate a metric that is comfortably within the expected range (green), in danger of not meeting a target (yellow), or failing to achieve the desired target (red).

## Tables

Tables have rows and columns and enable you to show your data in an easy-to-read format. Tables work well for large amounts of data that would be too complicated to present in the text or in a chart. If you need to present a few numbers, you should do so directly in the text, not in a table.

Tables should make sense on their own. Be sure to explain all abbreviations except standard abbreviations, such as *M, SD,* and *df*. Units of measurement should be clearly defined, the cell contents labeled, and information listed in a logical order—either ascending or descending frequency, or alphabetical or rank order of the responses. In the text surrounding the table, highlight the most important pieces of information from the table that you would like readers to notice. Tables either appear within the paper or in the appendix. Every table needs a label (e.g., Table 1, Table 2, etc.) and a title (e.g., "Guests' Satisfaction With Hotel Amenities"). Good titles are brief but clearly explain the contents of the table. Table 8.3 is an example of a descriptive table in APA format.

**Table 8.3    Sample Descriptive Table in APA Format**

|  | Strongly Disagree | Disagree | Somewhat Disagree | Somewhat Agree | Agree | Strongly Agree | *n* |
|---|---|---|---|---|---|---|---|
| I enjoy my work. | 0.6% | 3.2% | 9.6% | 23.1% | 47.4% | 16.0% | 156 |
| I am valued at this company. | 1.3% | 3.2% | 10.8% | 25.9% | 39.2% | 19.6% | 158 |
| I can depend on my team. | 0.0% | 4.4% | 3.2% | 19.0% | 45.6% | 27.8% | 158 |
| My responsibilities are clear. | 1.3% | 1.9% | 15.2% | 20.9% | 43.0% | 17.7% | 158 |
| I trust my manager. | 2.6% | 6.5% | 10.3% | 29.7% | 38.1% | 12.9% | 155 |

# Matching Survey Results to Type of Display

In many situations, you will have a choice about the types of tables and graphs you use to represent your data; other circumstances will demand a particular table or chart. As mentioned previously, pie charts should be used only when describing the percentage that each part of a whole occupies, whereas line graphs are appropriate for showing changes over time. Table 8.4 provides examples of how a circumstance may be matched with a graphic or table that will best illustrate it.

# Distributing Results Using a Web-Based Survey Development Tool

Most web-based survey development tools will allow users to share survey results created by the program. This is an easy way to share simple descriptive data with colleagues or respondents. The reports can contain colorful tables

**Table 8.4   Matching Data to Display Type**

| Survey Results | Display Type |
| --- | --- |
| A comparison of voting behaviors of people in three counties | Table or map |
| How people spend their time | Pie chart |
| Changes in survey participants' reported pain levels over time | Line chart |
| Satisfaction levels of four departments at a work site | Bar chart |
| Demographic information of survey participants | Pie for gender, bar or column for others |
| Education levels of survey participants | Bar or column |
| The ages of the people who responded to the survey | Histogram |
| Comparison of males and females who reported levels of depression | Grouped bar or column |
| The relationship of reported stress levels and time spent exercising | Scatter plot |

and graphs that are automatically created by the survey program. Many survey hosts are limited to simple tables, bar graphs, and pie charts. If you would like to share more advanced results or a different variety of graphs, you will need to first export the data (either in raw form or as summary statistics) and then compute the analyses or create the graphs in another program.

There are usually a few options for sharing the results. Zoomerang, for example, allows users to share results in a "restricted" mode, where only summary statistics can be viewed by others but individual responses can be viewed by the survey owner, and a "public" mode, where summary and individual results can be viewed by others.

Dissemination options include placing the URL link to the report on a webpage or including the URL in an e-mail message. For example, the URL of the report page might be included in a thank-you e-mail message so that respondents can view the results.

## Summary

After doing the work of obtaining the survey results, you will have the opportunity to share your findings in an oral or written format or both. Reporting is an essential step in conducting any research project, because sharing what you have learned is an important part of increasing the knowledge base of your field. In this chapter, we have covered the various modes of information dissemination, from full academic research reports and poster presentations designed to be shared at conferences to live and virtual oral presentations.

Although academic research reports have a predefined structure that begins with a title and ends with a conclusion, researchers are not prohibited from being creative within this context. Clear, concise, jargon-free writing that presents data in a user-friendly and entertaining format will be welcomed by most readers. Research posters and oral presentations offer the greatest opportunities for creative expression. For researchers new to presenting survey results in these formats, many free templates are available online that will help jump-start the process.

All survey reports will contain some graphical data displays. We discussed the wide variety of graphs that can be used to illustrate survey results. Sometimes, the choice of graph is obvious; on other occasions, choosing the most effective data display technique will be at your discretion. These decisions should be guided by the goal of showing the results in the most easily comprehensible way that will minimize the chances of misinterpretation of the data.

Researchers typically use more than one method to share the information they have collected. While the information remains the same no matter how you choose to report it, it is important to tailor the form of the report to fit the particular purpose and audience.

## Exercises

1. Here are some results of an online survey designed to understand mobile phone utilization in a community.

|  |  | Respondents' Age | | | | | | |
|---|---|---|---|---|---|---|---|---|
|  |  | 18-30 | 31-40 | 41-50 | 51-60 | 61-70 | 71+ | Total |
| Mobile phone use | Yes | 31 | 83 | 85 | 179 | 153 | 84 | 615 |
|  |  | 94% | 97% | 91% | 96% | 89% | 76% | 91% |
|  | No | 2 | 3 | 8 | 7 | 18 | 26 | 64 |
|  |  | 6% | 3% | 9% | 4% | 11% | 24% | 9% |
|  | Total | 33 | 86 | 93 | 186 | 171 | 110 | 679 |
|  |  | 100% | 100% | 100% | 100% | 100% | 100% | 100% |

|  |  | Respondents' Age | | | | | | |
|---|---|---|---|---|---|---|---|---|
|  |  | 18-30 | 31-40 | 41-50 | 51-60 | 61-70 | 71+ | Total |
| Mobile phone used to send text messages | Yes | 29 | 78 | 70 | 119 | 73 | 12 | 381 |
|  |  | 94% | 94% | 82% | 66% | 48% | 14% | 62% |
|  | No | 2 | 5 | 15 | 60 | 80 | 72 | 234 |
|  |  | 6% | 6% | 18% | 34% | 52% | 86% | 38% |
|  | Total | 31 | 83 | 85 | 179 | 153 | 84 | 615 |
|  |  | 100% | 100% | 100% | 100% | 100% | 100% | 100% |

| | | Respondents' Age | | | | | | |
|---|---|---|---|---|---|---|---|---|
| | | 18-30 | 31-40 | 41-50 | 51-60 | 61-70 | 71+ | Total |
| Smart-phone use | Yes | 20 | 50 | 36 | 79 | 45 | 7 | 237 |
| | | 65% | 60% | 42% | 44% | 29% | 8% | 39% |
| | No | 11 | 33 | 48 | 100 | 104 | 74 | 370 |
| | | 35% | 40% | 56% | 56% | 68% | 88% | 60% |
| | Don't know | 0 | 0 | 1 | 0 | 4 | 3 | 8 |
| | | 0 | 0 | 1% | 0 | 3% | 4% | 1% |
| | Total | 31 | 83 | 85 | 179 | 153 | 84 | 615 |
| | | 100% | 100% | 100% | 100% | 100% | 100% | 100% |

a. Create a graph for each of the three survey questions in the table. Explain your choices.

b. Write a paragraph describing each of the graphs you created.

2. Here are some additional data from the 237 respondents who reported using a smartphone.

| Type of Smartphone | Frequency |
|---|---|
| iPhone | 83 |
| BlackBerry | 58 |
| Android | 48 |
| Windows Mobile | 9 |
| Palm | 6 |
| Don't know | 8 |
| Other (please specify) | 25 |
| Total | 237 |

a. Create a bar graph of these results.

3. Using your work from #1 and #2 above, develop a 5-minute PowerPoint presentation to present the results of this survey. Here are a few more details that will be useful in preparing your presentation: (a) 252 men and 457 women responded to the survey, (b) the respondents' median age was 48, and (c) the majority had "some college" or "a 2-year degree."

4. Prepare a dashboard of these results that you can distribute to the audience at the end of your oral presentation.

# CHAPTER 9

# Concluding Comments

The field of online survey research is still relatively young but rapidly developing. We believe that electronic surveys will continue to evolve amid the collection of methodological options as a unique response mode ideally suited to certain situations. The increased utilization and improvements in technology will enhance this increased use.

In this chapter, we recap some of the important considerations surrounding the use of online surveys; reexamine the benefits associated with their use—namely that online and mobile surveys are faster, cheaper, and sometimes more effective than other methods; and offer some concluding thoughts about the future of digital survey research.

## Opportunities and Challenges in Online Survey Research

We began this text by presenting a list of factors for researchers to consider when deciding on a survey research mode. Having discussed in detail each of the important considerations, we now offer the following summary: online surveys are an effective mode of survey administration when dealing with closed populations, when probability sampling is not essential, and when the target respondents have access to the necessary technology.

Closed populations provide the optimal situation for the use of online and mobile surveys. They typically have existing sampling frames, such as e-mail and/or mobile phone lists of employees, members, customers, or students; potential respondents will be familiar with the organization and may regard the survey as official business; and the subject matter is likely to be of interest and relevance to the respondents. For example, a global aerospace company that seeks to collect information about safety procedures from their internationally distributed group of engineers can easily send an e-mail message to the employees inviting them to link to a webpage containing the safety questionnaire. The employees will be motivated to participate in the survey because it is generated by their employer and the subject matter is pertinent to their jobs.

The current developmental state of online and mobile surveys does not allow for easy probability sampling of respondents from open populations. This significantly limits the use of electronic surveys when the research goal is to make inferences about larger populations. Presently, the most successful use of probability sampling in online surveys involves a mixed-mode design wherein respondents are first contacted by telephone or postal mail and then directed to a website to complete the questionnaire. While this marginally saves time by eliminating the data-entry chore, whether this technique increases response rate in any noticeable way is unclear. It is, therefore, best to employ online surveys of general populations when convenience sampling will suffice, such as in the case of exploratory research.

Although household penetration of Internet and mobile phone technology continues to increase, it is not yet ubiquitous; furthermore, the distribution of those who have adopted many of the newer technologies is concentrated among people under 65 years of age, the college educated, and people with higher-than-average household incomes. Technological barriers—such as spam filters, pop-up blockers, and spyware designed to protect privacy and ensure online security—also present challenges for online survey researchers. People can easily block uninvited e-mails and stop e-mail invitations from arriving in their inboxes. Lack of computer literacy and physical disabilities also prevent access to online surveys in some target populations. Technological advancements are being made to improve access for everyone, but further expansion is still needed.

## Benefits of Online Surveys

Online and mobile survey research offers the promise of speed, economy, and improved data quality. As we have discussed in the preceding chapters, and summarize here, these benefits hold only in limited circumstances. Web and mobile surveys are faster than traditional methods when respondents are contacted via e-mail or text message and directed to a web host to complete the questionnaire. In this situation, researchers can potentially create and field the survey and be ready for data analysis in a matter of days.

Online and mobile surveys are relatively inexpensive to conduct. The researcher saves on printing, mail, interviewer, and data-entry costs. Although software, web hosting, and staff time to develop the online questionnaire are necessary expenditures, a variety of low-cost software and web-hosting options on the market feature simple user interfaces and are designed for novice online survey researchers. For research projects aimed at surveying large numbers of geographically dispersed individuals, online surveys offer an affordable option.

Although significant challenges related to coverage area and response rates remain, online surveys are superior to other methods in some applications. Online and mobile surveys are well suited to situations where interviewer bias or a tendency toward providing socially desirable answers may threaten the validity of the data. Similarly, if a questionnaire contains numerous open-ended questions, emerging evidence indicates that respondents may provide longer, and often more valid, answers for web-based surveys than for paper questionnaires. Moreover, skip patterns and interactive tasks can be effectively used electronically.

## The Future of Online Survey Research

A considerable body of literature surrounding online and mobile survey research is developing. Researchers working in this area face a variety of intriguing questions about the best use of online surveys, such as, What is the optimal questionnaire design? What is the most effective use of incentives in web, mobile, and e-mail surveys? How can sampling frames of open populations be generated? How can prerecruited panels of respondents be most successfully used? How should data collected from phone or postal mail surveys be combined with data collected from online and mobile surveys? These questions, along with techniques for increasing response rates and distinguishing research surveys from the profusion of entertainment surveys on the web, will surely continue to occupy the attention of survey research scholars.

It is impossible to predict all the technological and cultural changes that will confront survey researchers in the coming years; it is safe to say, however, that online survey research is here to stay. As technology advances and computing becomes ubiquitous, new challenges and opportunities will arise for methodologists. It is our hope that this volume will serve as a useful guide for those who seek to answer research questions using electronic survey research.

# Appendix A: American Association for Public Opinion Research, Code of Ethics

W e—the members of the American Association for Public Opinion Research and its affiliated chapters—subscribe to the principles expressed in the following Code. Our goals are to support sound and ethical practice in the conduct of survey and public opinion research and in the use of such research for policy and decision making in the public and private sectors, as well as to improve public understanding of survey and public opinion research methods and the proper use of those research results.

We pledge ourselves to maintain high standards of scientific competence, integrity, and transparency in conducting, analyzing, and reporting our work; establishing and maintaining relations with survey respondents and our clients; and communicating with those who eventually use the research for decision-making purposes and the general public. We further pledge ourselves to reject all tasks or assignments that would require activities inconsistent with the principles of this Code.

The Code describes the obligations that we believe all research professionals have, regardless of their membership in this Association or any other, to uphold the credibility of survey and public opinion research.

It shall not be the purpose of this Code to pass judgment on the merits of specific research methods. From time to time, the AAPOR Executive Council may issue guidelines and recommendations on best practices with regard to the design, conduct, and reporting of surveys and other forms of public opinion research.

## I. Principles of Professional Responsibility in Our Dealings With People

A. Respondents and Prospective Respondents

1. We shall avoid practices or methods that may harm, endanger, humiliate, or seriously mislead survey respondents or prospective respondents.

2. We shall respect respondents' desires, when expressed, not to answer specific survey questions or provide other information to the researcher. We shall be responsive to their questions about how their contact information was secured.

3. Participation in surveys and other forms of public opinion research is voluntary, except for the decennial census and a few other government surveys as specified by law. We shall provide all persons selected for inclusion with a description of the research study sufficient to permit them to make an informed and free decision about their participation. We shall make no false or misleading claims as to a study's sponsorship or purpose, and we shall provide truthful answers to direct questions about the research. If disclosure could substantially bias responses or endanger interviewers, it is sufficient to indicate that some information cannot be revealed or will not be revealed until the study is concluded.

4. We shall not misrepresent our research or conduct other activities (such as sales, fundraising, or political campaigning) under the guise of conducting survey and public opinion research.

5. Unless the respondent explicitly waives confidentiality for specified uses, we shall hold as privileged and confidential all information that could be used, alone or in combination with other reasonably available information, to identify a respondent with his or her responses. We also shall not disclose or use the names of respondents or any other personally identifying information for nonresearch purposes unless the respondents grant us permission to do so.

6. We understand that the use of our research results in a legal proceeding does not relieve us of our ethical obligation to keep confidential all respondent-identifying information (unless waived explicitly by the respondent) or lessen the importance of respondent confidentiality.

B. Clients or Sponsors

1. When undertaking work for a private client, we shall hold confidential all proprietary information obtained about the client and about the conduct and findings of the research undertaken for the client, except when the dissemination of the information is expressly authorized by the client, or when disclosure becomes necessary under the terms of Section I-C or III-E of this Code. In the latter case, disclosures shall be limited to information directly bearing on the conduct and findings of the research.

2. We shall be mindful of the limitations of our techniques and capabilities and shall accept only those research assignments that we can reasonably expect to accomplish within these limitations.

C. The Public

1. We shall inform those for whom we conduct publicly released research studies that AAPOR Standards for Disclosure require the release of certain essential information about how the research was conducted, and we shall make all reasonable efforts to encourage clients to subscribe to our standards for such disclosure in their releases.

2. We shall correct any errors in our own work that come to our attention that could influence interpretation of the results, disseminating such corrections to all original recipients of our content.

3. We shall attempt, as practicable, to correct factual misrepresentations or distortions of our data or analysis, including those made by our research partners, co-investigators, sponsors, or clients. We recognize that differences of opinion in analysis are not necessarily factual misrepresentations or distortions. We shall issue corrective statements to all parties who were presented with the factual misrepresentations or distortions, and if such factual misrepresentations or distortions were made publicly, we shall correct them in as commensurate a public forum as is practicably possible.

D. The Profession

1. We recognize our responsibility to the science of survey and public opinion research to disseminate as freely as practicable the ideas and findings that emerge from our research.

2. We can point with pride to our membership in the Association and our adherence to this Code as evidence of our commitment to high standards of ethics in our relations with respondents, our clients or sponsors, the public, and the profession. However, we shall not cite our membership in the Association nor adherence to this Code as evidence of professional competence, because the Association does not so certify any persons or organizations.

# II. Principles of Professional Practice in the Conduct of Our Work

A. We shall exercise due care in developing research designs and instruments, and in collecting, processing, and analyzing data, taking all reasonable steps to assure the reliability and validity of results.

1. We shall recommend and employ only those tools and methods of analysis that, in our professional judgment, are well suited to the research problem at hand.

2. We shall not knowingly select research tools and methods of analysis that yield misleading conclusions.

3. We shall not knowingly make interpretations of research results that are inconsistent with the data available, nor shall we tacitly permit such interpretations. We shall ensure that any findings we report, either privately or for public release, are a balanced and accurate portrayal of research results.

4. We shall not knowingly imply that interpretations should be accorded greater confidence than the data actually warrant. When we use samples to make statements about populations, we shall make only claims of precision that are warranted by the sampling frames and methods employed. For example, the reporting of a margin of sampling error based on an opt-in or self-selected volunteer sample is misleading.

5. We shall not knowingly engage in fabrication or falsification.

6. We shall accurately describe survey and public opinion research from other sources that we cite in our work, in terms of its methodology, content, and comparability.

B. We shall describe our methods and findings accurately and in appropriate detail in all research reports, adhering to the standards for disclosure specified in Section III.

# III. Standards for Disclosure

Good professional practice imposes the obligation on all survey and public opinion researchers to disclose certain essential information about how the research was conducted. When conducting publicly released research studies, full and complete disclosure to the public is best made at the time results are released, although some information may not be immediately available. When undertaking work for a private client, the same essential information should be made available to the client when the client is provided with the results.

A. We shall include the following items in any report of research results or make them available immediately upon release of that report.

1. Who sponsored the research study, who conducted it, and who funded it, including, to the extent known, all original funding sources.

2. The exact wording and presentation of questions and responses whose results are reported.

3. A definition of the population under study, its geographic location, and a description of the sampling frame used to identify this population. If the sampling frame was provided by a third party, the supplier shall be named. If no frame or list was utilized, this shall be indicated.

4. A description of the sample design, giving a clear indication of the method by which the respondents were selected (or self-selected) and recruited, along with any quotas or additional sample selection criteria applied within the survey instrument or post-fielding. The description of the sampling frame and sample design should include sufficient detail to determine whether the respondents were selected using probability or non-probability methods.

5. Sample sizes and a discussion of the precision of the findings, including estimates of sampling error for probability samples and a description of the variables used in any weighting or estimating procedures. The discussion of the precision of the findings should state whether or not the reported margins of sampling error or statistical analyses have been adjusted for the design effect due to clustering and weighting, if any.

6. Which results are based on parts of the sample, rather than on the total sample, and the size of such parts.

7. Method and dates of data collection.

B. We shall make the following items available within 30 days of any request for such materials.

1. Preceding interviewer or respondent instructions and any preceding questions or instructions that might reasonably be expected to influence responses to the reported results.

2. Any relevant stimuli, such as visual or sensory exhibits or show cards.

3. A description of the sampling frame's coverage of the target population.

4. The methods used to recruit the panel, if the sample was drawn from a prerecruited panel or pool of respondents.

5. Details about the sample design, including eligibility for participation, screening procedures, the nature of any oversamples, and compensation/incentives offered (if any).

6. Summaries of the disposition of study-specific sample records so that response rates for probability samples and participation rates for nonprobability samples can be computed.

7. Sources of weighting parameters and method by which weights are applied.

8. Procedures undertaken to verify data. Where applicable, methods of interviewer training, supervision, and monitoring shall also be disclosed.

C. If response rates are reported, response rates should be computed according to AAPOR Standard Definitions.

D. If the results reported are based on multiple samples or multiple modes, the preceding items shall be disclosed for each.

E. If any of our work becomes the subject of a formal investigation of an alleged violation of this Code, undertaken with the approval of the AAPOR Executive Council, we shall provide additional information on the research study in such detail that a fellow researcher would be able to conduct a professional evaluation of the study.

---

SOURCE: American Association for Public Opinion Research.

# Appendix B: Frequently Asked Survey Questions

## Respondent Demographics

**Are you male or female?**

O   Male     O   Female

**In what year were you born?** [          ]

**What is your birth date?** MM/DD/YYY [          ]

**What is your age?**

O   18–25                          O   46–55

O   26–35                          O   56–65

O   36–45                          O   66 or older

**What is your current marital status?**

O   Married                        O   Never married

O   Widowed                        O   Domestic partner

O   Separated

**How many people live in your household?**

O 1     O 2     O 3     O 4     O 5     O 6 or more

**Do you own or rent your home?**

O   Own home                       O   Other (please specify)

O   Rent your home or apartment

**What is the highest degree or level of school you have completed? If currently enrolled, mark the previous grade or highest degree received.**

- ○ Did not complete high school
- ○ High school graduate or equivalent
- ○ Some college, no degree
- ○ Completed vocational school
- ○ Associate degree
- ○ Bachelor's degree
- ○ Master's degree
- ○ Professional degree (example: MD, DDS, DVM, LLB, JD)
- ○ Doctorate degree (example: PhD, EdD)

**What is your employment status?**

- ○ Employed for wages
- ○ Self-employed
- ○ Out of work and looking for work
- ○ Out of work but not currently looking for work
- ○ A homemaker
- ○ A student who is also employed for wages
- ○ A student who is not employed for wages
- ○ Retired
- ○ Unable to work

**Please describe your primary line of work.**

- ○ Employee of a for-profit company
- ○ Employee of a not-for-profit organization
- ○ Government employee
- ○ Self-employed
- ○ Working without pay in family business or farm
- ○ Other (please specify)

**What is your annual income? And/or: What is your total household annual income?**

- ○ Less than $10,000
- ○ $10,000 to $19,999
- ○ $20,000 to $29,999
- ○ $30,000 to $39,999
- ○ $40,000 to $49,999
- ○ $50,000 to $59,999
- ○ $60,000 to $69,999
- ○ $70,000 to $79,999
- ○ $80,000 to $89,999
- ○ $90,000 to $99,999
- ○ $100,000 to $149,999
- ○ $150,000 or more

**Are you Hispanic or Latino?**

O  Hispanic or Latino                    O  Not Hispanic or Latino

**Which of the following best describes your race?**

O  American Indian or                    O  Native Hawaiian or Other
   Alaska Native                            Pacific Islander

O  Asian                                 O  White

O  Black or African American             O  Other (please specify)

**How many children do you have?**

O None   O 1 or 2   O 3 or 4   O 5 or more

**With which political party do you identify?**

O  Democrat                              O  Other (please specify)

O  Republican                           O  None

O  Independent                          O  Don't know

# Organizational Demographics

**Which of the following best describes your company's business?**

O  Manufacturing                        O  Education

O  Service/utility/transportation       O  Technology/communications

O  Wholesaler/distributor/retailer      O  Military

O  Medical/healthcare                   O  Government

O  Finance/banking                      O  Other (please specify)

O  Insurance/real estate

**Approximately how many people are employed by your organization?**

O  1–49                                 O  500–999

O  50–99                                O  1,000 or more

O  100–499

**What is your job title?** [          ]

# Customer Satisfaction

**How satisfied were you with the selection/price/ordering process?**

O  Very satisfied                           O  Somewhat dissatisfied

O  Somewhat satisfied                        O  Very dissatisfied

**Overall, how satisfied are you with your purchase from our store?**

Extremely dissatisfied              Extremely satisfied

O 1          O 2          O 3          O 4          O 5

**Thinking about your recent experience with <company/product/service>, how would you describe the quality of the service you received?**

O  Poor                                     O  Satisfactory

O  Unsatisfactory                           O  Exceptional

O  Average

**How much do you agree or disagree with the following statements about your recent experience with us? (Strongly disagree, Disagree, Neither agree nor disagree, Agree, Strongly agree)**

- The customer services representative was courteous.
- My call was answered quickly.

- The sales representative was knowledgeable about the products.
- The ordering process was easy.

**How often do you use <product>?**

O  Daily                                    O  Every 2 to 3 months

O  Once a week                              O  A few times a year

O  Two to three times a month              O  About once a year

O  Once a month

**Have you recommended us to a friend or family member?**

O Yes   O No

**Would you recommend us to a friend or family member?**

O Yes   O No

# Event Feedback

Please rate the following elements of today's event. (Poor, Below average, Average, Above average, Excellent)

- The agenda
- Speaker #1 <name>; Speaker #2 <name>, etc.
- Networking opportunities
- Afternoon workshops
- Food served for lunch
- Venue
- Evening reception

What did you find most valuable about the event this year? ▭

What suggestions do you have for improving next year's event? ▭

# Team Evaluation

How strongly do you agree or disagree with the following statements about your team? (Strongly disagree, Disagree, Slightly disagree, Slightly agree, Agree, Strongly agree, N/A)

- Our team worked well together.
- Each individual on the team contributed to our final product.
- Team members respected one another.
- Our team worked together to solve problems.
- Team members made appropriate compromises to get the work done.
- Members of the team were sufficiently skilled to accomplish their assigned tasks.
- Team members acknowledged one another's successes.
- I felt comfortable being honest with my team members.
- Team members respected joint deadlines.
- I would work with members of this team again.

# Glossary

**ALT tag**   A command inserted in a document that specifies how the document, or a portion of the document, should be formatted

**blacklist**   A list of e-mail addresses of known spammers and other senders considered to be dangerous. An e-mail address may be placed on a blacklist because it is a fraudulent operation or because it exploits browser vulnerabilities to send spyware and other unwanted software to the user.

**census**   The set of data collected from every member of a population

**closed-ended question**   Any of a variety of survey questions that include lists of response options

**comma-separated values**   (aka comma delimited) A specially formatted plain-text file that stores spreadsheet or basic database-style information in a simple format, with one record on each line and each field within that record separated by a comma. This type of formatting enhances the ability to use the file in another application.

**cookie**   A collection of information, usually including a user name and the current date and time, stored on the local computer of a person using the Internet

**correlation**   A measure of the strength of the linear relationship between two variables

**double-barreled question**   A type of question that asks about more than one issue in a single question. This results in inaccuracies in the attitudes being measured by the question.

**downloading**   The process of copying a file from an online service to one's own computer

**dropouts**   Survey respondents who begin a questionnaire and abandon it before finishing

**eligibility criteria**   Conditions that permit or exclude certain individuals from participation in a survey

**format**   To specify the properties, particularly the visible properties, of an object. For example, word processing applications allow you to format text, which involves specifying the font, alignment, margins, and other properties.

**graylisting**   A method of protecting e-mail customers against spam. The e-mail system will temporarily reject messages from unrecognized senders. Legitimate senders will attempt to resend messages (up to a predetermined number of times); after a delay, the receiving mail server will accept the message.

**hyperlink**   An element in an electronic document that links to another place in the same document or to an entirely different document

**Java applet**   A small program that can be sent to a user along with a webpage. Applets are used to provide interactive features to web applications that cannot be provided by HTML.

**leading question**   A type of question phrased in a way that suggests to the respondent that the researcher expects a certain answer (i.e., it "leads" the respondent)

**margin of error**   Measure of how precise the data are

**mean**   The arithmetical average, obtained by adding all the values of a measurement and dividing by the total count

**median**   The middle value of a sequential group of values

**Minitab**   A computer program designed to perform basic and advanced statistical analysis

**mode**   The most frequently observed response in a set of data

**nonprobability samples**   Samples that do not rely on random selection. The likelihood of individual participants being included in the sample cannot be calculated.

**nonrespondents**   Individuals who have been invited to participate in a survey and choose not to respond

**open-ended question**   A question that does not include a list of response options

**operating system**  Every general-purpose computer must have an operating system to run other programs. Operating systems perform basic tasks, such as recognizing input from the keyboard, sending output to the display screen, keeping track of files and directories on the disk, and controlling peripheral devices such as disk drives and printers.

**outliers**  Scores that lie an extreme distance away from the other scores in a distribution

**personal digital assistant**  Technologically advanced cell phones with a wide range of communication features

**pixel**  Short for "picture element." A pixel is a single point in a graphic image.

**Pocket PC**  A hardware specification for a handheld-sized computer (personal digital assistant) that runs the Microsoft Windows Mobile Classic operating system

**population**  The total group of respondents of interest

**pretest**  An examination of the survey by a group of respondents before the survey is deployed to the full sample; used to uncover potential problems in the survey instrument or method

**probability sample**  A sample that relies on a method of random selection. The likelihood of individual elements being included in the sample can be calculated.

**$p$ value**  The probability of seeing results as extreme as or more extreme than those actually observed if the variables you're testing have no relationship.

**range**  The difference between the largest and the smallest values in a distribution

**reliability**  The extent to which a measure provides consistent results across repeated testing

**respondent**  The survey participant

**response option**  A possible answer to a closed-ended question

**sample**  A subgroup of selected respondents derived from your target population

**sampling frame**  The list of all elements in the population

**SAS**  An acronym for Statistical Analysis System, software for data management and the statistical analysis of data

**smartphone**   a device that allows the user to make and receive phone calls and contains added features that one might find on a personal digital assistant or a computer

**SPSS**   An acronym for Statistical Package for the Social Sciences, software for the statistical analysis of data

**standard deviation**   A measure of dispersion. It indicates how much values vary around the mean.

**structured query language** (SQL)   The standard language for relational database management systems; examples of common SQL commands are "Select," "Insert," "Update," "Delete," "Create," and "Drop."

**target population**   The entire group of possible respondents to your survey question. Because it is improbable that you will survey every individual in your target population, you must survey a smaller subgroup of your population, known as a sample.

**URL**   Abbreviation of uniform resource locator, the global address of documents and other resources on the Internet. The first part of the address indicates what protocol to use, and the second part specifies the Internet provider address or the name of the domain where the resource is located.

**validity**   Refers to whether the measurement tool (i.e., the survey question) accurately and appropriately measures the concept under consideration

**web conferencing**   Web conferencing is a form of real-time communication in which multiple computer users, all connected to the Internet, see the same screen at one time in their web browsers.

**web survey**   Any survey developed using software and delivered to potential respondents via e-mail, mobile phone, or a webpage

**webinar**   Web conferencing is used to conduct live meetings, training, or presentations via the Internet.

**whitelist**   A list of e-mail addresses that a mail server is configured to accept as incoming mail

**wizard**   Part of a computer program that guides users through steps in a process—for example, writing letters, creating PowerPoint slide shows, or importing data from one software program into another

# References

Alreck, P. L., & Settle, R. B. (1995). *The survey research handbook* (2nd ed.). Chicago: Irwin.

Aoki, K., & Elasmar, M. (2000). *Opportunities and challenges of a web survey: A field experiment.* Paper presented at the 55th Annual Conference of the American Association for Public Opinion Research, Portland, OR.

Babbie, E. (2004). *The practice of social research* (10th ed.). Belmont, CA: Wadsworth/ Thompson Learning.

Bernard, M., Liao, C., & Mills, M. (2001). Determining the best online font for older adults. *Usability News.* Retrieved November 14, 2005, from http://psychology .wichita.edu/surl/usabilitynews/3W/fontSR.htm

Bernard, M., Lida, B., Riley, S., Hackler, T., & Janzen, K. (2002). A comparison of the most popular online fonts: Which size and type is best? *Usability News, 4*(1). Retrieved June 5, 2011, from http://www.surl.org/usabilitynews/41/onlinetext.asp

Bernard, M., & Mills, M. (2000). So, what size and type font should I use on my website? *Usability News.* Retrieved November 14, 2005, from http://psychology .wichita.edu/surl/usabilitynews/2S/font.htm

Bernard, M., Mills, M., Peterson, M., & Storrer, K. (2001). A comparison of popular online fonts: Which is best and when? *Usability News.* Retrieved November 14, 2005, from http://psychology.wichita.edu/surl/usabilitynews/3S/font.htm

Callegaro, M. (2010). Do you know which device your respondent has used to take your online survey? *Survey Practice.* Retrieved from www.surveypractice.org

Couper, M. P. (2000). Web surveys: A review of issues and approaches. *Public Opinion Quarterly, 64,* 464–494.

Couper, M. P., Baker, P., & Mechling, J. (2011). Placement and design of navigation buttons in web surveys. *Survey Practice.* Retrieved from http://surveypractice.org

Couper, M. P., Traugott, M., & Lamias, M. (2001). Web survey design and administration. *Public Opinion Quarterly, 65,* 230–253.

Denscombe, M. (2007, Winter). The length of responses to open-ended questions: A comparison of online and paper questionnaires in terms of a mode effect. *Social Science Computer Review, 25*(4), 423–520.

Dillman, D. A. (1978). *Mail and telephone surveys: The total design method.* New York: Wiley.

Dillman, D. A. (2000). *Mail and Internet surveys: The tailored design method* (2nd ed.). New York: Wiley.

Dillman, D. A., & Bowker, D. K. (2001). *The web questionnaire challenge to survey methodologists.* Retrieved September 15, 2005, from www.sesrc.wsu/edu/dillman/papers.htm

Dillman, D. A., Smyth, J. D., & Christian, L. M. (2009). *Internet, mail, and mixed-mode surveys: The tailored design method* (3rd ed.). Hoboken: Wiley.

Dillman, D. A., Smyth, J. D., Christian, L. M., & Stern, M. J. (2002). *Multiple-answer questions in self-administered surveys: The use of check-all-that-apply and forced-choice question formats.* Retrieved October 12, 2006, from www.sesrc.wsu.edu/dillman/papers.htm

Fink, A. (2003). *How to manage, analyze, and interpret survey data* (2nd ed.). Thousand Oaks, CA: Sage.

Fowler, F. J. (2002). *Survey research methods* (3rd ed.). Thousand Oaks, CA: Sage.

Garland, P. (2009). *Alternative question designs outperform traditional grids.* Retrieved from http://www.surveysampling.com/en/news/ssi-research-finds-alternative-question-designs-outperform-traditional-grids

Göritz, A. (2004). The impact of material incentives on response quantity, response quality, sample composition, survey outcome, and cost in online access panels. *International Journal of Market Research, 46*(3), 327–345.

Göritz, A. (2005). *Incentives in web-based studies: What to consider and how to decide.* Retrieved November 29, 2005, from www.websm.org

Hill, R. (1998). What sample size is "enough" in Internet survey research? *Interpersonal Computing and Technology: An Electronic Journal for the 21st Century, 6*(3–4). Retrieved October 17, 2006, from www.emoderators.com/ipct-j/1998/n3-4/hill.html

Kish, L. (1995). *Survey sampling.* New York: Wiley.

Krosnick, J. A., & Fabrigar, L. R. (1997). Designing rating scales for effective measurement in surveys. In L. Lyberg, P. Biemer, M. Collins, L. Decker, E. DeLeeuw, C. Dippo, et al. (Eds.), *Survey measurement and process quality* (pp. 141–164). New York: Wiley-Interscience.

Krosnick, J. A., Holbrook, A. L., Berent, M. K., Carson, R. T., Hanemann, W. M., Kopp, R. J., et al. (2002). The impact of "no opinion" response options on data quality: Nonattitude reduction or an invitation to satisfice? *Public Opinion Quarterly, 66*, 371–403.

Levy, P., & Lemeshow, S. (1999). *Sampling of populations: Methods and applications* (3rd ed.). Wiley Series in Survey Methodology. New York: Wiley-Interscience.

Lightspeed Research. (2009a). What drives respondent engagement? The effects of gender, age, survey completion time, and overall cognitive burden on engagement. *LightspeedAhead Newsletter, 3*(1). Retrieved from http://lightspeedaheadnewsletter.com/?p=208/

Lightspeed Research. (2009b). Respondent engagement: How much does it matter? *LightspeedAhead Newsletter, 2*(1). Retrieved from http://images2.lightspeed panel.com/images/en-S/lightspeedahead/web/Lightspeed_Ahead_V2I1.pdf

Los Alamos National Laboratory. (2001). *Preparing a poster exhibit.* Retrieved December 28, 2005, from http://set.lanl.gov/programs/cif/Resource/Presentation/PosterS.htm

Martin, P., & Bateson, P. (1986). *Measuring behavior: An introductory guide.* Cambridge, UK: Cambridge University Press.

Morrison, S., & Noyes, J. (2003). A comparison of two computer fonts: Serif versus ornate sans serif. *Usability News.* Retrieved November 14, 2005, from http://psychology.wichita.edu/surl/usabilitynews/52/UK_font.htm

Newman, C. (2000). *Considering the colorblind.* Retrieved October 25, 2005, from http://webtechniques.com/archives/2000/08

Peytchev, A., & Hill, C. A. (2010). Experiments in mobile web survey design. *Social Science Computer Review, 28*(3), 319–335.

Reja, U., Lozar Manfreda, K., Hlebec, V., & Vehovar, V. (2003). Open-ended vs. closed-ended questions in web questionnaires: Advances in methodology and statistics. *Metodoloski zvezki, 19*, 159–177.

Scheaffer, L. R., Mendenhall, W., & Ott, R. L. (2006). *Elementary survey sampling* (6th ed.). Belmont, CA: Duxbury.

Smith, A. (2010, August 11). *Home broadband 2010.* Retrieved May 24, 2011, from http://www.pewinternet.org/Reports/2010/Home-Broadband-2010.aspx

Smyth, J. D., Dillman, D. A., Christian, L. M., & Stern, M. J. (2006). Comparing check-all and forced-choice question formats in web surveys. *Public Opinion Quarterly, 70*, 66–77.

Toepel, V., Das, M., & van Soest, A. (2009). Design of web questionnaires: The effects of the number of items per screen. *Field Methods, 21*(2), 200–213.

U.S. Department of Health and Human Services. (2006). *Research-based web design and usability guidelines.* Washington, DC: U.S. Government Printing Office.

Van den Broeck, J., Argeseanu Cunningham, S., Eeckels, R., & Herbst, K. (2005). Data cleaning: Detecting, diagnosing, and editing data abnormalities. *PLoS Med, 2*(10), e267.

Yan, T. (2005). *Gricean effects in self-administered surveys.* Unpublished doctoral dissertation, University of Maryland.

# Index

232

coverage errors and, 47
mobile surveys and, 19, 20
the survey process and, 5
*See also* Cell phone surveys
Snowball sampling, 43, 44
*See also* Sampling
Social desirability, 53–54, 55, 72
Social exchange theory, 133
Social media:
conducting surveys and, 119–122
invitations and, 137
Social networking websites:
convenience sampling and, 44
explanatory research and, 2–3
exploratory research and, 2
Social norms *See* Norms
Socioeconomic status, 18, 48
Software:
benefits of online surveys
and, 212–213
choosing, 20–27, 31
color and, 81. *See also* Color
cost of, 21–22, 31
cross-tabulated tables and, 160
data processing/analyzing
and, 139, 141
e-mail surveys and, 14, 16, 17–18
frequency distributions and, 151, 153
graphs and, 191
InstantSurvey, 14
intercept sampling and, 41
iPads and, 129
iSurvey, 129
kiosk terminals and, 127
language issues and, 101
Minitab, 158, 226
mobile devices and, 101, 119
mobile surveys and, 19
MrInterview, 59
nonresponse errors and, 48
online survey, 14, 16, 17,
22, 30, 119, 158
personal digital assistants
and, 124–125
pop-up window invitations
and, 118–119
poster exhibits and, 188
questions to ask vendors of, 26–27
SAS, 158, 227
saturation sampling and, 35
SPSS, 141, 150, 158, 228
statistical analysis, 158
STATPAC, 25, 59, 119

summary statistics and, 158
survey, 167
SurveyCrafter, 59
SurveyGizmo, 119
text-mining, 59, 60
timelines and, 8–9, 31
tracking and, 142
Verbastat, 59
Verbatim blaster, 59
WebSurveyor, 25, 101
*See also* SurveyMonkey software;
Zoomerang software
Sound *See* Audio
Spam filters, 115, 116
Split-half analysis, 46
Spreadsheets:
data processing/analyzing and, 141
data screening and, 148
simple random sampling and, 37
summary statistics and, 157
systematic sampling and, 38
*See also* Excel, Microsoft
Stacked column charts, 198, 199
Standard deviation, 157, 228
Statistical Analysis System (SAS)
software, 158, 227
Statistical Package for the Social Sciences
(SPSS) software, 141, 150, 158, 228
Statistical significance, 159, 166
Statistical theory, 45
Statistics, 139, 140, 150–151,
153, 158–159
STATPAC software, 25, 59
Stem-and-leaf display, 204
Stratified sampling, 38
*See also* Sampling
Structured Query
Language (SQL), 126, 228
Subject-matter experts, 8
Summary statistics, 2, 153–158
Survey codebooks, 144–147
SurveyCrafter software, 59
Survey error *See* Errors
SurveyGizmo software, 119
Survey methodology, xv
SurveyMonkey software, 14, 16
choosing software/web-based survey
hosts and, 21
open-ended questions and, 59
Survey process, 3, 8, 24, 26, 73, 130
Survey questionnaires *See* Questionnaires
Survey results *See* Results
Surveys, 3–5